Nadine Böhm-Schnitker, Marcus Hartner (eds.)
Comparative Practices

Culture & Theory | Volume 258

Nadine Böhm-Schnitker is a senior lecturer in English Studies: Literature and Culture at Friedrich-Alexander-Universität Erlangen-Nürnberg and serves as an interim professor of English Literature and Literary Theory at the University of Konstanz. She is a former associate member of the Collaborative Research Centre 1288 »Practices of Comparing« funded by the German Research Foundation (DFG) and particularly interested in the power imbalances entailed in practices of comparing. Her further interests include contemporary literature and culture (e.g. neo-Victorian studies, BrexLit), the literary and cultural impact on perception, as well as cultural responses to ecological concerns such as climate change.

Marcus Hartner is a senior lecturer in English Studies at Bielefeld University. He is an associate member and former principal investigator of the Collaborative Research Centre 1288 »Practices of Comparing« funded by the German Research Foundation (DFG). His main fields of research encompass the study of narrative and the intersection of race, gender, and class in early modern literature and culture. Among his further research interests are the study of migration literature, maritime humanities, and Anglo-Muslim relations in the sixteenth and seventeenth centuries.

Nadine Böhm-Schnitker, Marcus Hartner (eds.)

Comparative Practices

Literature, Language, and Culture in Britain's Long Eighteenth Century

[transcript]

This volume has been prepared within the framework of the Collaborative Research Center SFB 1288 "Practices of Comparing. Changing and Ordering the World", Bielefeld University, Germany, funded by the German Research Foundation (DFG).

SFB 1288
PRACTICES OF
COMPARING

ıpport for the publication cost
niversity.

Funded by
DFG Deutsche Forschungsgemeinschaft
German Research Foundation

Bibliographic information published by the Deutsche Nationalbibliothek
The Deutsche Nationalbibliothek lists this publication in the Deutsche Nationalbibliografie; detailed bibliographic data are available in the Internet at http://dnb.d-nb.de

First published in 2022 by transcript Verlag, Bielefeld

Cover layout: Maria Arndt, Bielefeld
Printed by Majuskel Medienproduktion GmbH, Wetzlar
Print-ISBN 978-3-8376-5799-9
PDF-ISBN 978-3-8394-5799-3
https://doi.org/10.14361/9783839457993
ISSN of series: 2702-8968
eISSN of series: 2702-8976

Printed on permanent acid-free text paper.

Contents

Comparative Practices in Britain's Long Eighteenth Century
An Introduction

Marcus Hartner & Nadine Böhm-Schnitker

1. Introduction: COVID-19 and the Study of Comparison

Comparing is one the most fundamental intellectual operations.[1] The ability to relate different objects, for example in terms of similarity and difference, is an essential part of human cognitive architecture. It is part of "the way we think" (Fauconnier/Turner 2002), and, as a result, it seems unavoidable to engage in comparative acts "when trying to cope with our everyday experience" (Eggers 2019: 33). But while the mental ability to compare may be an anthropological constant across times and cultures, the specific forms, functions, and contents of comparative acts can change in many ways. This has been painfully illustrated by the global events of the past year during which most of this book was composed. The COVID-19 pandemic (still going strong while we are writing this introduction) has served as a powerful reminder of both the omnipresence and the historical situatedness of comparative practices. It has shown, on the one hand, that we continue to live in "an age of comparison" (Nietzsche (1996 [1871] 24), i.e., in a time in which contemporary (Western) science and culture are marked by an extraordinary profusion of comparisons; and, on the other hand, that comparisons as a social practice have a historical and political dimension.

1 This book has been prepared within the framework of the Collaborative Research Centre SFB 1288 "Practices of Comparing. Changing and Ordering the World", Bielefeld University, Germany, funded by the German Research Foundation (DFG). We want to thank all contributors to this volume for their articles as well as their patience and dedication during our collaboration. We would also like to thank the SFB1288 and the Library of Bielefeld University for their support in publishing the volume.

Since the outbreak of what has become the worst pandemic in more than a century, SARS-CoV-2 has killed millions of people and severely disrupted economic and social life in countries around the globe.[2] The sudden appearance of the virus and the economic repercussions and social isolation that have affected many people as a result of the political measures attempting to contain the disease, have made it almost impossible, even for those who have not become infected themselves, to compare life during the pandemic with life before the appearance of COVID-19. In fact, there have been few times in history, as Epple (2020) suggest, in which so many people from all social strata, "the sick and the healthy, the old and the young", have been so excessively exposed to and have so intensely engaged in comparative practices as during this pandemic (25).[3]

Beyond the realm of individual, personal reflections not only scientists have embraced comparative methods in their study of the virus, for instance by comparing the effects of the disease on members from different age groups. Different types of comparison have also taken prominent positions in public discourse. Government institutions and news agencies, for example, have embraced the practice of publishing continuous live updates on the comparative numbers of COVID-19 related infections, deaths, vaccinations, (etc.); scientifically false comparisons with other (respiratory) diseases such as influenza have become a mainstay of coronavirus-sceptical discourse; and endless comparisons between political and administrative responses to the crisis in different countries, federal states, cities, and districts have fuelled heated political debates and talk show panel discussions.[4]

The political and often ideological agendas driving many comparisons in those contexts show that comparing is never an entirely neutral operation and

---

2 The WHO Coronavirus (COVID-19) Dashboard listed 4.049.372 deaths on the day we wrote this passage. ‹https://covid19.who.int› (14 July 2021).

3 "Vergleichen hat eine lange Geschichte. Aber kaum je haben sich Gesunde und Kranke, Alte und Junge mit der ubiquitären Alltagspraxis und ihren Wirkungen so intensiv beschäftigt. Wir bekommen das Verfahren *in actu* vorgeführt. Wir sind Augenzeug*innen, wie mithilfe von Vergleichen Orientierung gesucht, gefunden und begründet wird" (Epple 2020: 24).

4 For a more detailed discussion of different types of comparison related to COVID-19 in public discourse, see once more Epple (2020), who distinguishes between three major types of comparing: scientific comparisons, political-antiscientific comparisons, and conspiration-theory comparisons ("der *medizinische Typus*, der *politisch-antiscientistische Typus* und der *Typus der Verschwörungstheorien*") (24).

"always a matter of judging and choosing" (Spivak 2009: 609). Together with the crucial role of different (social) media in their dissemination to wider audiences those examples illustrate why academic investigations in this field are well advised to go beyond addressing the logical and cognitive architecture of comparing. They suggest that a better understanding of the form and function of comparisons, especially those that have consolidated into specific discursive practices, requires us to study their specific historical, technological, and ideological contexts and the agendas underlying their performance. Comparisons may be traceable in extant sources as far back classical antiquity,[5] but their specific forms and the cultural practices into which they are embedded are subject to historical change. However, while the existence of such change in general seems uncontroversial, sustained academic research into the specifics of the history of comparing is still in its infancy. Comparisons have been studied with regard to their epistemological value and methodological usage in various disciplines.[6] But as Steinmetz has recently pointed out, there is "no reasonably coherent research tradition that deals with *comparisons as practices and concepts* that have a history of their own" (2019b: 4). All in all,

> surprisingly little research has been done on the changing relationship between the comparers and the objects or persons compared, and on the different motives for and social effects of comparisons, on the variable criteria and commensurability assumptions applied, and on when and why the craze for subjecting almost everything and everyone to comparative rankings or ratings has started. (4)

While there may be no "coherent research tradition" at this point, the past years have witnessed interdisciplinary research into the history and theory of comparing becoming "something of an emerging field" in academic research (Rohland/Kramer 2021: 2).[7]

---

5 See, for example, Schulz (2020).

6 Steinmetz (2014) provides a helpful survey of debates about comparisons and comparative methodology in sociology, history, anthropology, and political science. On comparative approaches in (comparative) literature, cultural studies, and the sciences, see also the contributions in Zima (2000), Felski/Stanford Friedman (2013), and Eggers (2011).

7 See, for example, the volumes by Rohland et al. (2021); Epple/Erhart/Grave (2020); Saussy (2019); Gagné et al. (2019); Deville/Guggenheim/Hrdličková (2016), Felski/Stanford Friedman (2013), and Mauz/von Sass (2011).

Our volume is situated in the context of this emerging field. It aims to make a contribution to the larger project of studying the history of comparative practices, on the one hand, and the impact of comparative practices on the course of history, on the other.[8] Focussing on Britain's Long Eighteenth Century from the perspective of Literary and Cultural Studies, we are specifically interested in the role comparisons play in the literature, language, and culture of this period, which constitutes a crucial phase in the formation of the British Empire, the development of scientific practices, and various landmark changes in British Society and culture. Moreover, the eighteenth century is arguably of particular relevance for the study of comparing as it seems to mark in several ways the beginning of Nietzsche's "age of comparison". Thus, the period is ideally suited to investigate the connection between the development of what has been called (Western) modernity and crucial changes in the frequency, role, and function of comparisons across various discursive fields. We will attempt to outline this connection in the following, by turning to the example of one of the most famous literary texts from the period.

2. *Robinson Crusoe*, Comparative Practices and the Emergence of Western Modernity

> I now began to consider seriously my Condition, and the Circumstance I was reduc'd to, and I drew up the State of my Affairs in Writing […]; and as my Reason began now to master my Despondency, I began to comfort my self as well as I could, and to set the good against the Evil, that I might have something to distinguish my Case from worse […].
> *Robinson Crusoe, 1994 [1719]: 49*

When Daniel Defoe's Robinson Crusoe is stranded on an uninhabited island, comparison turns into a strategy for survival. Threatened to become overwhelmed by despair, he decides to "master [his] Despondency" by turning to reason. In a much-quoted passage, which has been mostly discussed with regard to the issue of Crusoe as an embodiment of the *homo oeconomicus*,[9] he attempts to evaluate his situation as objectively as possible and draws up a balance sheet on which he lists "very impartially, like Debtor and Creditor"

---

8 For an outline of this general research project, see Epple/Erhart (2015b & 2020).

9 See, for example Volkmann (2003: 554-555).

the negative and positive aspects of his life as a castaway in two opposing columns (49). This comparison of "the Comforts I enjoy'd, against the Miseries I suffer'd" has the intended effect (ibid.).

Having finished the task, he concludes that "[u]pon the whole, here was an undoubted Testimony" that no matter how miserable the circumstances, there is always "something *Positive* to be thankful for" (50). In the following years of his enforced isolation, this rather simple truism helps Crusoe to find solace in scripture and turns into a social philosophy that makes it easier for him to endure his fate.

> It put me upon reflecting, How little repining there would be among Mankind, at any Condition of Life, if People would rather compare their Condition with those that were worse, in order to be thankful, than be always comparing them with those which are better, to assist their Murmurings and Complainings. (121)

For Crusoe, as the passage illustrates, comparing has the potential to serve as a (mental) strategy for dealing with adverse circumstances. Over the course of the novel the character engages in various acts of comparing with different functions.[10] Yet, it is the deliberate and strategic way in which he draws on comparisons as a cognitive, moral, and practical resource that connects many of those individual acts. Beyond engaging in comparative reflections serving "to comfort [his] Mind with Hopes" (95), he also uses comparison, for instance, as a tool for empirical assessment. Having been thrown into a state of utmost confusion, anxiety, and agitation after encountering the famous footprint in the sand, for example, Crusoe decides to "go down to the Shore again, and [...] to measure the Mark with my own Foot" in order to test empirically by comparison whether he might have made the footprint himself (115).

The examples of the balance sheet and the footprint are of interest in this introduction because they reflect a particular usage of comparisons as conceptual and practical tools for problem-solving which not only permeates Defoe's novel, but which arguably mirrors the larger historical development of an increasing reliance on comparative practices in philosophical, scientific, and other types of discourse in the eighteenth century. Over the past decades, various scholars have suggested an intrinsic connection between the emergence of what has been called 'Western modernity' and the increasing prominence

10 See also the discussion of Defoe's *Robinson Crusoe* in Nadine Böhm-Schnitker's contribution to this volume.

and frequency of comparative practices that can be observed in a wide range of fields from the mid-seventeenth century onwards.[11] Following up the work of Michel Foucault (1966), who was among the first to point to the key role of comparative thinking in the development of Western thought, Michael Eggers (2019), for example, argues that a new "comparative *episteme* [...] asserted itself in scientific and intellectual thoughts between the Enlightenment and the Romantic period" (45). In this process, comparison joins and eventually supersedes analogy as a key "style of reasoning" (see Crombie 1994: 83-85) over the course of this period. Structurally inherent to a wide range of instruments of knowledge creation such as taxonomy, measurement, and classification, it emerges and becomes established as "one of the elementary and defining scientific methods of modernity", and, in this context, as one of the most significant methods for defining "an argument or a subject matter as scientific" (Eggers 2019: 44, 45).

But comparative thinking not only marks the development of the (natural) sciences and scientific thinking in general. Niklas Luhmann, for example, points to "the sudden appearance of an extensive and intense interest in comparisons" in the eighteenth century with regard to conceptions and questions of culture (1999: 38; my translation).[12] "Few students of eighteenth-century thought", Richter confirms this general development for the field of the humanities, "would deny the importance of comparison in that period's political and social theory, anthropology, philosophical and legal history, literature, philosophy, theology, and studies of religion" (2000: 385). Furthermore, in a different research context interested in the long-term historical development of *social* comparisons between individuals, Steinmetz (2019c) observes a nascent change in the dominant modes and forms of comparative practices over the course of the eighteenth century. In a study devoted to "the long transitional period from a society regulated by rank and inherited status to one based primarily on competition", he identifies three basic prevalent ways in which people distinguish themselves from others between 1600-1900: "above/below" comparisons, "better/worse" comparisons and "simply different" comparisons (Steinmetz 2019b: 13; 2019c: 81-82, *passim*). While all three basic types co-occur throughout and beyond the timeframe of his study, he

11 See Epple/Erhart (2015b: 14 & 2020: 25-26).

12 "Das plötzliche Auftreten eines intensiven und extensiven Vergleichsinteresses" (Luhmann 1999: 38).

suggests that up to the eighteenth century traditional, hierarchical 'above/below comparisons' relating to questions of social rank occupy centre stage. Only from the middle of the eighteenth century onwards the other two basic forms "come to the fore" (104): 'better/worse comparisons' as a type of social comparing related to a culture increasingly marked by ideas of (economic) competition, on the one hand; and 'simply different' comparisons that function as "assertions of being 'simply different'" (81) in a social context increasingly based on notions of individualism and ideas of "free and self-determining individuals" (82), on the other hand.

Beyond strategies of comparing in social discourse and its function as a theoretical instrument "in the sciences as well as in the humanities" (Eggers 2019: 45), scholars have pointed to a third field in which comparative practices appear to have played a prominent and formative role: The encounter with different cultures and foreign powers around the globe.

> [Comparisons] were crucial for coming to terms with new, sometimes challenging, or even confusing and irritating encounters with formerly little or unknown regions, cultures, geographies, people, plants, and animals—both within and outside of Europe. With comparisons, scholars, adventurers, military experts, explorers, and travelers helped—willingly or not—to naturalize or hide hierarchies by introducing allegedly neutral norms and standards for evaluations. Through comparison, they ordered the world. (Epple/Erhart 2020: 25-26)

Again, in the case of Britain, the eighteenth century constitutes a pivotal phase in the history of such encounters in the context of the development of the British Empire. While Britain's economic expansion from the late sixteenth century onwards had laid the foundation, it was not until the late seventeenth century that "an identifiable political community existed to which the term 'empire' could be fittingly applied", and not before the mid-eighteenth century that Britain emerged as one of the dominant global players in terms of political and military power (Armitage 2000: 7; see Colley 2003).

Moreover, attempts at 'ordering' and 'understanding' the world during this period were seldom 'innocent'.[13] The Western creation of knowledge about

13 The political nature of comparing and its specific relevance to the history of (post)colonialism and imperialism has been an object of intense debate in the fields of postcolonialism and comparative literary studies where it has led to a discussion of the foundational principles of comparative criticism. See, for example, Stanford Friedman

cultural and racial others in this period, as postcolonial scholars have pointed out, rather needs to be conceived as an intrinsic part of the imperialist project of "dominating, restructuring, and having authority over" the non-European world (Said 2003 [1978]: 3). As such, comparative practices in the context of intercultural encounters and conflicts, not only "ordered" the world, but they were also instrumental in changing it (Epple/Erhart 2020: 26). Western science – all ideals of objectivity notwithstanding – was deeply implicated in this process (Loomba 2015: 75-81). Ideologically tainted scientific constructions of racial, cultural, and national differences legitimised imperial conquest and informed colonial policies while economic endeavours based on colonial science "brutally altered the ecological and natural landscape of colonised societies" (76). Moreover, the relationship between European science and colonialism/imperialism was reciprocal. At the same time that science changed the colonial world, "the growth of modern Western knowledge systems and the histories of most 'disciplines' can be seen to be embedded within and shaped by colonial discourses" (78). As a result, it is not surprising that scholars have proposed the idea that intercultural encounters, conflicts, and entanglements, on the one hand, and the European evolution of a comparative methodology in science and scholarship, on the other, are causally related within the context of the emergence of modernity (Epple/Erhart 2020: 25).

Like with Western culture and literature in general, the historical development of the sciences and its comparisons in eighteenth-century Britain thus cannot be viewed in isolation from the country's overseas expansion and the effects of this expansion on British society, economy, and culture. "[T]he growth of the English economy and power", as Kaul emphasizes, "were coterminus with, and dependent upon, the expansion of trade and colonies overseas, with the result that any analysis of national culture and literature in this period must be located in an international, or more precisely, a colonial frame" (2009: 23). The question to precisely what extent comparative practices in literature, language, and culture contributed to and/or reflected the formation of this frame, in how far the comparisons found at work in (literary) works such as *Robinson Crusoe* can be integrated into or at least related to a history of comparative practices and the emergence of Western modernity are part of an ongoing research effort to which this volume hopes to contribute.

(2012), Spivak (2009), Radhakrishnan (2009), Melas (2007), Harootunian (2005), Chow (2004), Stoler (2001), and Cheah (1999).

3. From the Analysis of Comparison to the Study of Comparative Practices

The 'long' eighteenth century, as the short survey above suggests, marks an important stage in the emergence of the British empire and the development of Britain towards a modern society, in general. During this period, moral standards, habits, fashions, as well as scientific-, cultural-, and imperialist practices evolved that shaped the daily lives of individuals of all classes and their interaction in Britain, as well as the expansion of the British Empire and the structures of the modern consumerist culture we still inhabit. This volume inquires into the roles that comparisons and the (discursive) practices into which they are embedded played in these developments. As we have shown, it thus participates in a wider scholarly effort to rethink and investigate the relevance of comparative practices in our understanding of (modern) history and culture that has gained increasing momentum in the humanities over the past years.

Not primarily interested in methodological discussions of the function of comparisons as a scientific tool, this approach proceeds from an understanding of comparing as the performance of a comparative act in which "different items (*relata* [or *comparata*]) are compared in relation to one respect (*tertium comparationis*)" (von Sass 2020: 89). The comparison itself thus constitutes a logical or structural operation putting into perspective (at least) two entities with respect to a particular *tertium comparationis.*[14] The act of comparing, on the other hand, is an operation that takes place in a specific situation, often with a specific underlying purpose. It is, in other words, an activity framed and influenced by its particular situative, ideological, and historical setting. By shifting the focus of attention in this way from the structure or method of comparison to the phenomenon of comparing, "the actors and agencies that perform the comparisons and connect them with their purposes and possible outcomes" come into view (Epple/Erhart 2020: 17). As a result of this conceptual change, individual acts can and need to be situated within larger discursive patterns and historical contexts.

> As a practice—according to the insights of practice theory – comparing has to be reconsidered not as an individual singular action performed randomly

14 For a more detailed account, see also Grave (2015: 135-139) and Epple/Erhart (2020: 15-16).

> and spontaneously across space and time [...], but as part of a framework of comparative practices that have been established through repetition and routines, cultural habits, and historical patterns. As such practices, comparative acts in history are no longer contingent and arbitrary, but are clustered and organized along collective cultural schemes and models according to different framings of actors, groups, classes, nations, or other historical conditions and circumstances. (17-18)

The advantage of this approach, as Grave (2019: 55) points out, is that it is neither exclusively focussed on the acting individual and its intentions, nor on the structures into which comparative acts are embedded. The analysis of comparisons as practices rather occupies a middle ground between both approaches. It enables us to turn our attention "to a diverse bundle of factors", including "the practices, habits and routines, the corporeal executions and implicit orderings of knowledge, the material properties of the involved object, as well as the processes of representation" (56).

Adopting this approach inspired by the Practice Turn in the social sciences,[15] allows us to conceive of social practices of comparing as being entrenched in networks of circulation of bodies, artefacts, discourses and ideas. Within this conceptual framework, the contributions to this volume not only attempt to contribute to a better understanding of the history of comparing; they also aim to make a genuinely valuable contribution to the study of eighteenth-century British literature, language, and culture by investigating how comparative practices ordered and changed different aspects of British society and culture.

4. The Volume and Its Contributions

As we have seen, one of the key concerns of this volume lies in the question in how far comparisons not only prove fundamental in the epistemological foundation of modernity (Foucault; Luhmann), but to what extent they fulfil a central function in social life and the processes of intercultural encounter. In this context, the volume takes one of its starting points in the assumption that human beings tend to look towards their fellow beings in the negotiation of adequate and desirable behaviour and attitudes, and the sanctioning

15 See, for example, Schatzki (1996); Schatzki/Cetina/Savigny (2001); Reckwitz (2003).

of inadequate and undesirable ones. Similarly, comparisons between self and other play a central role in the discursive formation of national and cultural identities. In other words, comparative practices are deeply ingrained in manifold aspects of social life and their discursive negotiations. Moreover, we believe that fictional and non-fictional texts, images, and artefacts contributed to the formation and dissemination of cultural practices of comparing in the eighteenth century, either by explicitly presenting comparisons of actions and persons, or by offering more or less implicit invitations to compare how people act, think, and feel. Hence, this volume is dedicated to exploring the scope of comparative practices in the fields of language, literature, and culture.

Our volume opens with **Julia Wiedemann**'s chapter on "The Creation of the English Nation: Alfred the Great as Role Model". She explores the foundational function of comparative practices for the construction of an English, or, respectively, British national identity by analyzing both literary and political functionalizations of Alfred the Great as well as "the formation of the Alfredian myth" (29). With her cultural analysis of national identity, she not only clarifies what 'Britain' means in the long eighteenth century, for instance after such historical landmarks as the Act of Union in 1707; she also lays the foundations for many of the consecutive chapters, for example by investigating the function of Britain's Anglo-Saxon history and its discursive connection to ideologies of racialized whiteness and inherent notions of freedom or liberty, or by highlighting Daniel Defoe's contributions to this discourse as a central pamphleteer, journalist and novelist.

In "The Circulating Library, the Novel, and Implicit Practices of Comparing in 18th-Century England: Assembling 'Middle-Class' Literariness", **Ralf Schneider** analyzes the social function of circulating libraries with a view to their setting the scene for a great array of social comparisons, those of class in particular. In addition, he offers a crucial methodological reflection on the interaction between texts and contexts and combines Actor-Network-Theory with a focus on comparative practices. In his cultural analysis, he is particularly interested in performances of politeness and forms of social as well as cultural distinction. He does not as yet investigate the content or narrative strategies of particular novels but argues that the emergence of the genre is closely tied to these material, social and cultural performances in the public sphere. Ultimately, he claims "that access to the novel through the circulating library involved comparative practices of performance of class identity for the emerging middle stratum of society, and that these performances possessed a crucial comparative aspect" (50).

In the following joint contribution, "Comparing Conduct: English Novels of the Long Eighteenth Century and the Formation of Ideals of Social Behaviour", **Marcus Hartner** and **Ralf Schneider** continue to explore literary negotiations of comparative practices *in* the novel. Addressing the role practices of social comparing play in eighteenth-century fiction, they provide a survey of central novels from the period ranging from Daniel Defoe to Maria Edgeworth. In doing so, they introduce a heuristic distinction between direct and indirect comparisons with a clear emphasis on the dominance of indirect comparisons in the novel genre. This chapter thus adds a decidedly literary, or more precisely, narrative analysis of comparative practices and fills a research lacuna, as "the various ways in which comparisons are deliberately enacted in literary works of all genres, i.e., the question in how far comparative practices play a constitutive role in literary texts themselves, remains profoundly understudied" (77). By studying the social and moral comparisons on the level of characters, their analysis confirms the central social function of the eighteenth-century novel and its comparative practices as a potential means of (moral) orientation for the emerging middle classes regarding questions of behaviour and conduct.

In the following contribution, "The Complexity of Narrative Comparisons in Wollstonecraft's *Maria; Or, The Wrongs of Woman* and Lennox's *The Female Quixote*", **Anne Lappert** takes the heuristic distinction between direct and indirect comparisons introduced by Marcus Hartner and Ralf Schneider further and introduces "three basic types, namely imagery comparisons, narrative comparisons and intertextual comparisons" (106) in eighteenth-century women's writing. Interpreting the novels by Wollstonecraft and Lennox, Lappert investigates the complex overlaps of these different kinds of comparative practices and shows that only their combined analysis reveals the feminist arguments put forward in the respective novels.

The chapter by **Monika Class**, "'tis by Comparison we can Judge and Chuse [sic!]": Incomparable Oroonoko", is equally interested in women's writing. It analyzes Aphra Behn's 1688 novella *Oroonoko*, thus exploring a central text at the onset of the long eighteenth century. Taking her cue from established allegorical readings of Oroonoko as a stand-in for different Stuart monarchs, Class employs Paul Ricoeur's hermeneutic-phenomenological concepts of emplotment and configuration to highlight moments of incomparability that render Oroonoko exceptional and make him transcend such Eurocentric analogies. Class highlights the affective singularity of the character and thus illustrates how the interconnection between incomparability and affect may serve as a critique of slavery in the novella.

In "Articulating Differences: Practices of Comparing in British Travel Writing of the Long Eighteenth Century", **Nadine Böhm-Schnitker** takes her cue from Class' investigation of *Oroonoko*'s relevance for the development of the novel and analyzes the relationship between 'self' and 'other' in Behn's novella as well as in Daniel Defoe's *Robinson Crusoe*. She explores the function of comparative practices for the construction and authorization of authorship that is fundamentally associated with the newly racialized marker of skin colour as a central signifier of social hierarchies in narratives of interethnic colonial encounters. She argues "that the literary 'individual' emerges defined by a close articulation of economic/capitalist, political/colonial and social discourses that shapes and determines the viability of subjects in the long eighteenth century" and understands comparative practices as "the means by which this subject gains its contours" (150-151).

Caroline Koegler equally concentrates on self-other relations from a postcolonial vantage point in her chapter "Oceans of Non-Relation: Affect and Narcissistic Imperialism in Sea Poetry by James Thomson, Charlotte Brontë, and Hannah More". Like Nadine Böhm-Schnitker, she is interested in options of the viability and particularly the grievability of subjects modulated by skin colour and social status; like Monika Class, she emphasizes the role of affect in comparisons as well as the function of incomparability. For instance, she reads Thomson's poem "Rule, Britannia!" as a case of imperial narcissism that is characterized by the "necessity of perpetually re-inscribing incomparable superiority (also: beauty) and comparative liberty (Britons "never will be" 'like slaves')" (184); imperial narcissism thus presents a condition that bolsters ideologies of empire by way of dehumanizing others. Similar to Anne Lappert, Koegler also emphasizes how important it is to pay attention to "who compares and to what effects/affects" (199) and critiques the functionalizations of comparisons for ideologies of empire.

Our volume ends with a linguistic reflection on the scope of English that slowly develops into a global *lingua franca* over the course of the eighteenth century and thus ties in with the previous postcolonial analyses. In "Practices of Comparing in Eighteenth-Century Grammars of English", **Göran Wolf** explores the impact of comparative practices on prescriptive eighteenth-century grammars. In a similar fashion to novels, they negotiate and establish social norms and values. Complementing Ralf Schneider's argument about the performance of politeness in the public space of circulating libraries, Wolf shows that 'propriety' serves as a central value transported by a particular usage of language. Since propriety presents a social rather than a linguistic value, Wolf can illustrate the complex overlaps between cultural and linguistic analyses. Closing the frame opened up by Julia Wiedemann with her focus on national identity, Wolf concludes "that the progress of English went hand in hand with neglectful behaviour towards the neighbouring languages foreshadowing the nationalism that was to take root in England and elsewhere in the following century" (216).

In sum, the collected essays in this volume shed light on the manifold but interconnected forms and functions of comparative practices in language, literature, and culture. As a salient feature of eighteenth-century modernity, they prove crucial for constructions of national identity (British/English) and for the performativity of social conduct in the public sphere. Such performativity also codifies and delimits the scope of viable behaviours coded by gender, race, class and many other categories of difference, which is equally negotiated in the literature and culture of the period. The novel, the dominant genre of the long eighteenth century, is fundamentally structured by comparative practices that not only calibrate the interaction between characters and thus unfold corresponding subject effects; they also calibrate the interrelation between characters and the spaces they inhabit. As fundamental patterns of language, literature, and culture in the long eighteenth century, comparative practices deserve further and continued scrutiny, because they are performative practices with a clear impact on the scope of 'the human' as well as the understanding of 'the human' in/against their environments, and thus with central concerns of our 'modernity'.

Bibliography

Armitage, David. *The Ideological Origins of the British Empire*. Cambridge: Cambridge University Press, 2000.

Cheah, Pheng. "Grounds of Comparison." *Diacritics* 29.4 (1999): 523-545.

Chow, Rey. "The Old/New Question of Comparison in Literary Studies: A Post-European Perspective." *English Literary History* 71.2 (2004): 289-311.

Colley, Linda. *Captives: Britain, Empire and the World, 1600-1850*. London: Pimlico, 2003.

Crombie, Alistair C. *Styles of Scientific Thinking in the European Tradition: The History of Argument and Explanation Especially in the Mathematical and Biomedical Sciences and Arts*. London: Duckworth, 1994.

Defoe, Daniel. *Robinson Crusoe*. Ed. Michael Shinagel. New York: Norton, 1994 [1719].

Deville, Joe, Michael Guggenheim and Zuzana Hrdličková, eds. *Practising Comparison: Logics, Relations, Collaborations*. Manchester: Mattering Press, 2016.

Eggers, Michael, ed. *Von Ähnlichkeiten und Unterschieden: Vergleich, Analogie und Klassifikation in Wissenschaft und Literatur (18./19. Jahrhundert)*. Winter: Heidelberg, 2011.

Eggers, Michael. "Outlines of a Historical Epistemology of Comparison: From Descartes to the Early Nineteenth Century." *The Force of Comparison: A New Perspective on Modern European History and the Contemporary World*. Ed. Willibald Steinmetz. New York: berghahn, 2019. 33-52.

Epple, Angelika and Walter Erhart, eds. *Die Welt beobachten: Praktiken des Vergleichens*. Frankfurt: Campus, 2015a.

Epple, Angelika and Walter Erhart. "Die Welt beobachten: Praktiken des Vergleichens." *Die Welt beobachten: Praktiken des Vergleichens*. Eds. Angelika Epple and Walter Erhart. Frankfurt: Campus, 2015b. 7-31.

Epple, Angelika and Walter Erhart. "Practices of Comparing: A New Research Agenda Between Typological and Historical Approaches." *Practices of Comparing: Towards a New Understanding of a Fundamental Human Practice*. Eds. Angelika Epple, Walter Erhart and Johannes Grave. Bielefeld: Bielefeld University Press, 2020. 11-38.

Epple, Angelika, Walter Erhart and Johannes Grave. *Practices of Comparing: Towards a New Understanding of a Fundamental Human Practice*. Bielefeld: Bielefeld University Press, 2020.

Epple, Angelika. "Die Schule des Vergleichens und die Suche nach der Wahrheit wissenschaftlicher Fakten." *Die Corona-Gesellschaft: Analyse zur Lage und Perspektiven für die Zukunft*. Ed. Michael Volkmer and Karin Werner. Bielefeld: transcript, 2020. 25-36.

Fauconnier, Gilles and Mark Turner. *The Way We Think: Conceptual Blending and the Mind's Hidden Complexities*. New York: Basic Books, 2002.

Felski, Rita and Susan Stanford Friedman, eds. *Comparison: Theories, Approaches, Uses*. Baltimore: Johns Hopkins University Press, 2013.

Foucault, Michel. *The Order of Things: An Archaeology of the Human Sciences*. London: Routledge, 2005 [1966].

Friedman, Susan Stanford. "Why Not Compare?" *PMLA* 129.3 (2011): 753-762.

Gagné. Renaud et al., eds. *Regimes of Comparatism. Frameworks of Comparison in History, Religion and Anthropology*. Leiden/Boston: Brill, 2019.

Grave, Johannes. "Comparative Practices and Their Implications: The Case of Comparative Viewing." *The Force of Comparison: A New Perspective on Modern European History and the Contemporary World*. Ed. Willibald Steinmetz. New York: Berghan, 2019. 53-79.

Grave, Johannes. "Vergleichen als Praxis: Vorüberlegungen zu einer praxistheoretisch orientierten Untersuchung von Vergleichen." *Die Welt beobachten: Praktiken des Vergleichens*. Ed. Angelika Epple and Walter Erhart. Frankfurt: Campus, 2015a. 135-159.

Harootunian, Harry. "Some Thoughts on Comparability and the Space-Time Problem." *boundary 2* 32.2 (2005): 23-52.

Kaul, Suvir. *Eighteenth-Century British Literature and Postcolonial Studies*. Edinburgh: Edinburgh University Press, 2009.

Loomba, Ania. *Colonialism/Postcolonialism*. London: Routledge, 2015.

Luhmann, Niklas. *Gesellschaftsstruktur und Semantik: Studien zur Wissenssoziologie der modernen Gesellschaft*. Vol. 4. Frankfurt a. M.: Suhrkamp, 1999.

Mauz, Andreas and Hartmut von Sass, eds. *Hermeneutik des Vergleichs: Strukturen, Anwendungen und Grenzen komparativer Verfahren*. Würzburg: Könighausen Neumann, 2011.

Melas, Natalie. *All the Difference in the World: Postcoloniality and the Ends of Comparison*. Stanford: Stanford University Press, 2007.

Nietzsche, Friedrich. *Human, All Too Human*. Cambridge: Cambridge University Press, 1996 [1871].

Radhakrishnan, Rajagopalan. "Why Compare?" *New Literary History* 40.3 (2009): 453-471.

Reckwitz, Andreas. "Grundelemente einer Theorie sozialer Praktiken: Eine sozialtheoretische Perspektive." *Zeitschrift für Soziologie* 32.4 (2003): 282-301.

Richter, Melvin. "Two Eighteenth-Century Senses of 'Comparison' in Locke and Montesquieu." *Jahrbuch für Recht und Ethik [Annual Review of Law and Ethics]* 8 (2000): 385-406.

Rohland, Eleonora and Kirsten Kramer. "Introduction: On 'Doing Comparison' – Practices of Comparing." *Contact, Conquest and Colonization: How Practices of Comparing Shaped Empires and Colonialism around the World*. New York: Routledge, 2021. 1-16.

Rohland, Eleonora et al., eds. *Contact, Conquest and Colonization: How Practices of Comparing Shaped Empires and Colonialism around the World*. New York: Routledge, 2021.

Said, Edward. *Orientalism*. London: Penguin, 2003 [1978].

Sass, Hartmut von. "Incomparability: A Tentative Guide for the Perplexed." *Practices of Comparing: Towards a New Understanding of a Fundamental Human Practice*. Ed. Angelika Epple, Walter Erhart and Johannes Grave. Bielefeld: Bielefeld University Press, 2020. 87-109.

Saussy, Haun. *Are We Comparing Yet? On Standards, Justice, and Incomparability*. Bielefeld: Bielefeld University Press, 2019.

Schatzki, Theordore R. *Social Practices: A Wittgensteinian Approach to Human Activity and the Social*. Cambridge: Cambridge University Press, 1996.

Schatzki, Theodore R, Karin K. Cetina, and Eike von Savigny, eds. *The Practice Turn in Contemporary Theory*. London: Routledge, 2001.

Schulz, Raimund. *Als Odysseus staunte: Die griechische Sicht des Fremden und das ethnographische Vergleichen von Homer bis Herodot*. Göttingen: Vandenhoeck Ruprecht, 2020.

Spivak, Gayatri C. "Rethinking Comparativism." *New Literary History* 40.3 (2009): 609-626.

Steinmetz, Willibald. "Comparative History and Its Critics: A Genealogy and a Possible Solution." *A Companion to Global Historical Thought*. Ed. Prasenjit Duara, Viren Murthy and Andrew Sartori. Chichester: Wiley Blackwell, 2014. 412-436.

Steinmetz, Willibald, ed. *The Force of Comparison: A New Perspective on Modern European History and the Contemporary World*. New York: berghahn, 2019a.

Steinmetz, Willibald. "Introduction: Concepts and Practices of Comparison in Modern History." *The Force of Comparison: A New Perspective on Modern European History and the Contemporary World*. Ed. Willibald Steinmetz. New York: berghahn, 2019b. 1-32.

Steinmetz, Willibald. "Above/Below, Better Worse or Simply Different? Metamorphoses of Social Comparison, 1600-1900." *The Force of Comparison: A New Perspective on Modern European History and the Contemporary World*. Ed. Willibald Steinmetz. New York: berghahn, 2019c. 81-112.

Stoler, Ann L. "Tense and Tender Ties: The Politics of Comparison in North American History and (Post)Colonial Studies." *Journal of American History* 88.3 (2001): 829-865.

Volkmann, Laurenz. *Homo oeconomicus: Studien zur Modellierung eines neuen Menschenbilds in der englischen Literatur vom Mittelalter bis zum 18. Jahrhundert.* Heidelberg: Winter, 2003.

Zima, Peter, ed. *Vergleichende Wissenschaften: Interdisziplinarität und Interkulturalität in den Komparatistiken.* Tübingen: Narr, 2000.

The Creation of the English Nation: Alfred the Great as Role Model

Julia Wiedemann

1. Introduction

Despite the fact that comparisons "count as one of the most basic intellectual operations" (Eggers 2019: 33), practices of comparisons do also constitute a social activity. For Willibald Steinmetz, "comparisons are an important social practice that leads to changes in behaviour and creates new routines" (2019: 2). At the same time, practices of comparing help shape group identity. As Angelika Epple and Walter Erhart show, both the assumption of comparability of the *comparata* as well as the *tertia comparationis* used in comparisons depend on social and historical contexts. For them, "comparing is not neutral or innocent, but is always interwoven with the interests and perspectives of the ones who compare and is related to the situations and contexts in which comparisons are made" (2020: 16).

This becomes evident when looking at practices of comparing in the context of encounters between different cultures. Beginning with the age of European expansion, comparisons between European and non-European cultures had become an important means to grasp reality. Epple and Erhart stress that intercultural comparisons thus contributed not only to the description of non-European cultures, but at the same time helped define European cultures (2015: 10ff.; see also Erhart 2015). Due to the fact that, by the beginning of the eighteenth century, as Michael Eggers has shown, practices of comparing had become an expression of rational thought, they also served as a basis for scientific depiction and classification of non-European cultures. Eggers further demonstrates that, simultaneously, comparisons played an important role in temporalizing human experiences. Natural histories as those written by Linné used comparisons in order to establish a progressive timeline of before and after (Eggers 2019: 37-38; see Epple/Erhart 2015: 12).

With a reference to Benedict Anderson's *The Spectre of Comparison*, Epple and Erhart point out that practices of comparing were not only used in an intercultural context but also served processes of nation-building (2015: 24). For the British context, this means that, in the eighteenth century, British national history began to be conceived of as a narrative of success which started with the Anglo-Saxon period. Comparisons with Alfred the Great played a decisive role within such narratives.[1] As Alfred was soon conceived of as an epitome of 'Englishness', politicians also referred to him in order to justify their positions. In this context, comparisons with Alfred the Great were used either to foster change or to defend the *status quo*.

Referring to Epple and Erhart, the following essay assumes that comparing as a practice is a "part of a frame-work of comparative practices that have been established through repetition and routines, cultural habits, and historical patterns" (2020: 18). By means of practices of comparing, different effects may be achieved. According to Angelika Epple, comparisons help organize the world by putting two entities into a relation. This organization may be hierarchical, and in fact, in the context of European encounters with non-European cultures, this has often been the case. However, by being put into a new context or by using a different kind of *tertium*, comparisons may also provoke change or stimulate new dynamics. This is due to the fact that a third characteristic of comparisons is that, although they are socially framed, they are still individual practices. Individual actors thus may put comparisons into different contexts, a process which Epple calls 'de- and recontextualization'. As a result, whether they foster change or contribute to traditional concepts, comparisons create seemingly coherent entities. Last but not least, comparisons legitimate specific actions or practices (Epple 2015: 165-170).

By considering these aspects, the following article will focus on comparisons with Alfred within the political context of the eighteenth century. In doing so, the essay will point to the eclectic use of these practices of comparing. Finally, the article will discuss how practices of comparing were crucial in establishing a cultural memory which was then pertinent to a definition of an imagined Anglo-Saxon community.

---

1 For the eighteenth century, see Keynes (1999). However, he does not concentrate on Alfred's role in political discourses. For the nineteenth century, see Parker (2007).

2. The Creation of the 'English' Nation

As Linda Colley and others in her wake have shown, after the Act of Union in 1707, which had united the Scottish and English parliaments, the long eighteenth century was characterized by a negotiation of 'national' identity.[2] While Colley focuses on the creation of a British 'national' identity, other scholars, like Stephen Conway, point to the fact that there is evidence for a "persistence of localism and the continuing appeal of older national loyalties", such as Englishness.[3] Although the two crowns of the Scottish and English kingdoms had been united since 1603 through James VI (Scotland) / I (England), the formal union of the Scottish and English parliaments took it one step further – a step which was not welcomed by all.[4]

One of the early supporters, however, was Daniel Defoe who wrote lengthy pamphlets on the advantages of this union, showing a sympathetic understanding towards the Scottish people, as can be seen in his *Union and No Union* (1713). In this pamphlet, as in others, Defoe stresses the necessity of a real union among the people, not only on a political level, but also on an emotional one (see 1713: 3-4). For this purpose, he recurrently pointed to the fact that the Scottish and English shared many characteristics, that they were "Natives of the same Island, ally'd by Intermarriage, both in Kings, Nobility, and Common People, and live among one another, trade together, speak the same

---

2 In her pioneering study *Britons: Forging the Nation 1707-1836* (1992), Colley uses the expression 'the long eighteenth century' for the timespan between the Act of Union and the beginning of the Victorian era, Colley (2009). Following this, Evan Gottlieb concentrates on the era between the Act of Union in 1707 and the death of Walter Scott in 1832 (Gottlieb 2007: 15).

3 Conway (2001: 863). For Colley, exterior influences such as the rivalry with France are among the main reasons for an attempt to define Britishness (2009: 4 ff.). Gottlieb, on the other hand, focuses on interior forces, thereby concentrating on the contribution of Scottish Enlightenment authors. He also states that "Britishness was often in productive tension with these competitors [i.e. other forms of identification such as gender, rank, religion and region] for people's attention and loyalty" (2007: 14). In this context, the main competitor to Britishness is the notion of Englishness.

4 This was also connected to the religious conflict between Catholicism and Protestantism, which resulted in a series of upheavals, generally known under the term 'Jacobite rebellions', in the years between 1689 and 1746. As Stephen Conway demonstrates, it was the English and the Catholic Irish who strongly opposed the idea of 'Britishness' (2001: 870 ff.).

Language, profess the same Protestant Religion".[5] In his satirical poem *A True-Born Englishman* (1701), Defoe had already emphasized that the idea of a 'true Englishness' was misleading since the Englishman represented "a het'rogenous thing", a "mixture of all kinds" (1835: 7). Referring to the Anglo-Saxon times, Defoe makes clear, that it was the "Western Angles" who had 'united' the different people on the British Isle by force:

The Western Angles all the rest subdu'd,
A bloody nation, barbarous and rude,
Who, by the tenure of the sword, possest
One part of Britain, and subdu'd the rest.
And, as great things denominate the small,
The conqu'ring part gave title to the whole.
The Scot, Pict, Briton, Roman, Dane, submit,
And with the English-Saxon all unite;
And these the mixture have so close pursu'd,
The very name and memory's subdu'd;
No Roman now, no Briton does remain;
Wales strove to separate, but strove in vain.
The silent nations undistinguished fall,
And Englishman's the common name for all.
Fate jumbled them together, Gods [sic!] knows how,
Whate'er they were, they're *True-Born English* now.[6]

Unlike many of his contemporaries, Defoe did neither celebrate an assumed superiority of Englishness nor link this ideal to specific historical figures. In his *A True-Born Englishman*, Defoe thus deconstructs the idea of aetiological myths. In his *Racial Myth in English History: Trojans, Teutons, and Anglo-Saxons* (1982), American historian Hugh A. MacDougall has shown that many eighteenth-century writers, however, did refer to one of two story cycles which have served as aetiological myths for Great Britain: the Arthurian legends

5 Defoe (1706a: 11-12). Therein, Defoe furthermore mentions that a union would be of advantage for the British Isles in their dealings with other European nations (1706a: 3-4, 26-27).

6 Defoe (1835: 8) (original emphasis). As can also be seen in his *Jure Divino* (1706), Defoe attacks all kinds of 'racial' belongings. Therein, he further points out that it was not only the Normans but also the Saxons who proved to be violent conquerors. Defoe adds that all property and all government stems from violence: "The longest Sword the longest Scepter brings" (1706b: 217). See Hill (1958: 92-93).

and the Anglo-Saxon narratives (see MacDougall 1982). Although in the seventeenth and eighteenth centuries, many writers related to King Arthur, others focused on later – Saxon – figures and used them as role models for kings, politicians and common people alike. While during the Stuart reign, it had been customary to refer to the saintly king Edward the Confessor in a laudatory manner,[7] this ceased to be appropriate with the accession of the House of Hanover in 1714, represented by George I. In order to fill this void of a heroic model, Alfred the Great became increasingly popular (see Pratt 2000: 140). Thus, according to Simon Keynes, it was during the eighteenth century that Alfred developed into "the archetypal symbol of the nation's perception of itself" (1999: 225). Despite the fact that the Anglo-Saxon past could be made use of in order to justify the union and thus to serve as a basis for "Britishness", Alfred and the emerging study of Anglo-Saxonism was more closely connected to notions of "Englishness". This becomes obvious when looking at the radical discourse of the mid-eighteenth century. In the 1790s, however, when political discussions focused on an assumed French threat, Alfred and Anglo-Saxonism began to be more closely related to ideas of "Britishness". Before discussing these discourses in more detail, however, the essay will concentrate on the formation of the Alfredian myth.

3. "[O]ne of the wisest and best that has ever adorned the annals of any nation": The Alfredian Myth[8]

Alfred the Great was King of Wessex from 871 to 886, Wessex being one of the most important Anglo-Saxon kingdoms.[9] His reign was characterized by enduring battles with Danish invaders. These disputes led to a co-operation

7 Edward was the second to last Anglo-Saxon king and considered to be the last Anglo-Saxon king of the house of Wessex. He was praised, for example in John Hare's *St. Edwards* [sic!] *Ghost, or, Anti-Normanisme* (1647) (see Hill 1958: 73 and 57-58).

8 Hume (1854: 76). David Hume's *History of England* (1754), which also dedicated some space to Alfred the Great, will not be considered in this essay.

9 When the Romans left the British Isles, members of the Jutes, the Angles and the Saxons came from North Germany and Denmark to Britain where they settled and finally founded several kingdoms. The crucial kingdoms were Wessex, Sussex, Kent, East Anglia, Essex, Mercia and Northumbria (nowadays also known as the Anglo-Saxon heptarchy).

and finally a union of several Anglo-Saxon kingdoms, making Alfred king of the Anglo-Saxons from 886 until his death in 899.

According to Simon Keynes, who published a detailed study on the eighteenth-century "cult of Alfred", the creation of the Alfredian myth had already begun during Alfred's lifetime. As Keynes further demonstrates, most of the stereotypes used in the eighteenth century had already been developed by the end of the fourteenth century; however, it was only in the first half of the seventeenth century that Alfred turned into a national idol (1999: 227-237, 246). Despite the fact that Alfred had been part of the English, or British, cultural memory since the Middle Ages, it is due to de- and recontextualisations that comparisons with Alfred played an important role in eighteenth-century political discourses.

Apart from the notion that Alfred was a great warrior, who defended his home from the 'barbaric' Danish invaders, one of the most relevant stereotypes created during the Middle Ages was the idea of Alfred being the founder of the English nation, uniting the several Anglo-Saxon kingdoms against the Danes. According to Keynes, this idea spread due to *The Ecclesiastical History of Orderic Vitalis*, which was written by a Norman monk in the middle of the twelfth century (1999: 231). Together with the notion of Alfred being a law-maker, this was what would later lead to the idea that Alfred's reign represented an early version of a constitutional monarchy.[10] This was mainly propagated by the anonymously published *Historical Essay on the English Constitution* (1771), which had a great impact on writers of the radical wing (see Hill 1958: 95-96). Another feature which was mirrored in the eighteenth-century radical discourse and which had been linked to Alfred since the Middle Ages was the ideal of liberty. As can be seen when looking at radical authors, such as John Wilkes and Catherine Macaulay, this ideal and its connection to the Alfredian myth became prevalent.

It was not only the notions of constitutional monarchy and of liberty, which were of special relevance for the formation of a British or English identity in the eighteenth century, but also the navy. During this century, the navy became crucial in conflicts with other imperial powers, especially Spain and France. It was at this time that the idea spread that Alfred was the founder

10 According to Parker, this has already been suggested by John Spelman's biography of Alfred (written in the 1640s and published in 1678) (2007: 58, 118). For the image of Alfred as law-maker, see Keynes (1999: 234-235).

of the navy – an idea which was mainly inspired by John Spelman's *Life of Alfred the Great* (1678), as Joanne Parker argues (2007: 58). Spelman's biography was dedicated to the Prince of Wales, the later king Charles II, and, as Joanne Parker stresses, "the earliest serious attempt to enlist Alfred for political ends" (2007: 57).

However, Alfred was not praised for his military and political successes alone. One other important feature in the idealization of the Saxon king was his interest in learning and his support of the arts and the sciences. Closely connected to this idealization of Alfred as philosopher-king, was the assumption that he founded the University of Oxford, a legend which came up in the middle of the fourteenth century (Keynes 1999: 235ff.).

4. "Make former days in future ages live": Alfred as Ideal King[11]

One of the first to promote Alfred as the new role model was Richard Blackmore in his epic poem *Alfred*, published in 1723 and dedicated to "the Illustrious Prince Frederick of Hanover" (1723). Almost thirty years earlier, in his *Prince Arthur* (1695), Blackmore had depicted the Saxons as "fierce" and "warlike" (3, 101); at the same time, however, he had praised Alfred as a "pious Souldier" (sic!), "humble King", "*Hero*" and "*Bard*"[12] and even included him in a future vision of "Britannia"[13]. As an open supporter of the Glorious Revolution, Blackmore had celebrated the virtues of William III with this poem, presenting him as being of equal rank to both Arthur and Alfred.[14]

In the preface to *Alfred*, Blackmore stresses the fact that it is the combination of historical truth with poetical fancy, which has a special appeal for future kings in guiding them in their behaviour:

> Besides living Examples, the Histories of excellent Kings, published by celebrated Authors, have great Influence in kindling a warm Desire in young

11 This line is taken from "Britannia's Reward – A Vision", an ode written in honour of the historian Catherine Macaulay, see later in this article.

12 Blackmore (1695: 147) (original emphasis). Note that Arthur is also described as "pious" (ibid.: 281).

13 Note that, throughout the poem, Blackmore refers to the British Isles either as "Britannia" or as "Albion".

14 See Liss (1911: 11, 24). Blackmore is hardly read nowadays, and was despised by his contemporaries such as John Dryden and Alexander Pope. See also Solomon (1980: 165).

> Princes, to resemble them in their admirable Virtues and glorious Actions; And not only true Histories of applauded Monarchs transmitted to Posterity, but likewise those, that are partly real and partly extended by a copious Variety of invented Incidents, and the Embellishments of a fertile Imagination, that by conveying Instruction in a delightful Manner, facilitate its Admission to the Mind, may much conduce to the Accomplishment of young Princes, and prepare them for the Exercise of imperial Authority. (1723: Preface)

Thus, with the example of Alfred, whom he described as "one of the greatest Monarchs, that ever ruled this or any foreign Nation" (ibid.), Blackmore hoped to inspire Prince Frederick in his future government of "Great Britain".[15] As the Hanoverian House was rather unpopular among the British people (Colley 2009: 205-206), Blackmore likewise intended to enhance Frederick's esteem. In order to achieve this, he presented Frederick as a descendant of Alfred and as a representative of "Hope [for] fair *Britannia's* Land" (1723: 292; original emphasis; see Keynes 1999: 275).

Prince Frederick readily accepted this example. Frederick, grandson of George I, had remained in Hanover during his grandfather's reign and only came to England in 1728. A year later, he was granted the title Prince of Wales. He was strongly opposed to his father George II and the then Prime Minister Sir Robert Walpole, criticizing both for subjugating Britain to foreign interests and for fostering domestic disharmony. For his supporters, he became himself a symbol for constitutional kingship and the representation of a 'patriot king'.[16] Frederick, thus, was well aware of the problems the dynasty of the Hanoverians faced as British rulers. Just as Blackmore suggested in his epic poem *Alfred*, Frederick invested in the arts, planning to create a national academy of art, which could take care of "patriotic culture". However, as he died in 1751, it was up to his son, George III, to accomplish such goals (Colley 2009: 210).

In order to visualize his link with the Anglo-Saxon past, Frederick commissioned a statue of Alfred, the "Founder of the Liberties and Commonwealth of England" (qtd. after Pratt 2000: 141). This stress on the 'Englishness' of Alfred is also taken up in *Alfred – A Masque* (1740), written by David Mallet and James Thomson on behalf of Frederick (Parker 2007: 63-64). Although,

---

15 Blackmore (1723: Dedication). In this context, Blackmore also points to Frederick's descent from "the ancient *Saxon* Race" (original emphasis).

16 This becomes obvious in Bolingbroke's *The Idea of a Patriot King* (1738). For Frederick's opposition to his father and his connection to the Tories, see Glickman (2011).

throughout the masque, they only refer to 'England' and call Alfred "England's king", it is in a future vision presented at the end (when Alfred has successfully defeated the Danes) that they use the term "BRITANNIA" in order to refer to the British Isles.[17] Likewise, in the still famous patriotic song "Rule Britannia", there is only talk of "Britons" and "Britannia" (Mallet/Thomson 1751: 64-65). As both authors were Scottish, it is hardly astonishing that they would finally refer to a broader concept of nationality.[18]

5. "[T]he most sacred regard to the liberty of his people": Alfred in Eighteenth-Century Politics[19]

Although Frederick and his supporters had tried to disentangle Alfred from the Whig tenure, Alfredianism and Anglo-Saxonism still played a considerable role in what has been termed the 'Whig interpretation of history'. This version of history has regularly traced the common law, the constitutional monarchy and the ideal of liberty back to the times of the Anglo-Saxon society ruled by Alfred the Great (Hill 1958: 87-88; Keynes 1999: 246-247). While Alfred starred in the radical discourse of the 1760s,[20] in which he was often used in order to criticize parliament and king, at the end of the century, he was referred to either to combat revolutionary developments in Great Britain or to stimulate anti-French sentiments. Thus, following Linda Pratt, the essay argues that the figure of Alfred was used in order to support a wide variety of political stances.[21] The subsequent paragraphs will trace this development by

17 Mallet/Thomson (1751: 16, 63). The vision of a Hermit who serves as a spiritual guidance for Alfred in this play is meant to illustrate the future greatness of the navy serving as a "bulwark of [the] separate world [i.e., England]" (Mallet/Thomson 1751: 63). This depiction of England as a "separate world" points to the conviction that its insular character distinguishes the nation from most of the other European countries, a notion which is still expressed (see Lowenthal 1991: 214).

18 It is Stephen Conway who also points to the Scottish nationality of Thomson (2001: 869).

19 Hume (1854: 79).

20 As Amanda Goodrich explains, "[t]he term 'radicalism' had been applied retrospectively to construct a collective English political movement oppositional to loyalism". She further argues that "English radicalism extended beyond Englishness and incorporated people and ideas from beyond the shores of the British Isles" (2019: 9).

21 Pratt (2000: 141 ff.). However, Pratt does not offer detailed information on this topic.

referring to John Wilkes, Catherine Macaulay, Henry Redhead Yorke, James Bland Burges and John Bowles.[22]

The political career of the radical John Wilkes (1727-1797) may be taken to express the "acute sense of crisis" which prevailed in the 1760s. As Kathleen Wilson has demonstrated, this sense of crisis was fuelled, on the one hand, by a rivalry with France and, on the other, by a government that tried to control the press and violently suppressed any revolt. The demonstration for "Wilkes and Liberty" of May 1768, later known as the St. George's Field Massacre, is a case in point (Wilson 1998: 213-214, 201ff.). The protest was aimed against the imprisonment of Wilkes, at that time Member of Parliament,[23] who strongly criticized George III in one of his articles published in *The North Briton*.

On June 5, 1762, the first issue of *The North Briton* was published. This radical newspaper was begun by John Wilkes in order to disparage the newly elected Prime Minister John Stuart, 3rd Earl of Bute, the first Scotsman to be announced prime minister. The anti-Scottish stance was revealed in the very title of the newspaper, which responded to the pro-governmental newspaper *The Briton*, edited by Tobias Smollett and considered to function as a mouthpiece for the whole nation. However, Wilkes accused him of selling Scottishness in the name of Britishness (see Gottlieb 2007:75). To balance this, *The North Briton* was dedicated "To the English Nation, the Glorious Protectors of CIVIL and RELIGIOUS LIBERTY".[24] The open Scottophobia was accompanied by an anti-French stance, assuming that the Scottish prime minister would rather turn to France than to defend 'England'.[25] As his letters reveal, Wilkes also looked disparagingly to Ireland (1804: 327). His "cult of *England*", as Linda Colley has called it (2009: 109; original emphasis), thus led to a conception of the nation, which excluded all Scottish and Irish traits. Naturally enough, Wilkes preferred the expression "England" over "Great Britain".[26] Furthermore, he ascribed the creation of the English nation and legitimate rule to

22 Keynes mentions Catherine Macaulay in his work only briefly, see Keynes (1999: 286).

23 Wilkes was excluded from parliament twice in his career.

24 See dedication in Wilkes (1764).

25 See Wilkes (1764: 30), No. 6 (published on July 10, 1762): "[...] with what unfeigned rapture will France receive the news, that there is no longer a first minister in this island from their ancient enemy England, but from their firm and unshaken ally, SCOTLAND." He also assumes that other European powers, such as Russia and Prussia, would be on good terms with this British government.

26 Colley (2009: 116). During his exile, he even started to write a three-volume history of England, of which he only completed the first volume (2009: 110). Colley further points

Alfred's reign. Thus, in a letter written in 1762, where he praises the achievements of Prime Minister William Pitt, he uses the image of the passing of "the sceptre of Alfred" from one king to the next in order to describe legitimate rule (see Wilkes 1767: 272).

One of the great admirers of Wilkes was Catherine Macaulay (1731-1791), a radical author and historian. Macaulay belonged to a group called the Real Whigs, whose members supported American independence and considered liberty the highest virtue.[27] In her *History of England* (1763-1783), which was "a best-seller among radical circles" (Hill 1958: 94), she does not pay much attention to the period covering the Saxon dominion over the British Isles. Nonetheless, she accepted Alfred as an ideal ruler, keeping a bust of the Wessex king in her study.[28] To honour her birthday in 1777, a compilation of six odes was published which included extensive references to Alfred. The first ode, entitled "Hortensia's Birth-Day", recalls a stereotypical representation of Alfred – he is called "Great patriot King" and is praised for his justice, his support of the arts and the sciences, and his assumed foundation of the University of Oxford (Anon. 1777: 17). However, it is the last ode called "Britannia's Reward – A Vision" which deserves special attention. It envisages a personified 'Britannia' who addresses herself to 'British' women in general by referring to important female writers of the eighteenth century. These include the poetess Anne Laetitia Barbauld, who is praised for her piece on the Corsican revolutionary Pasquale Paoli, Hester Chapone, a writer of conduct books for women and member of the so-called Bluestockings, Lady Mary Wortley Montagu, who is paid tribute for her critical mind, and Elizabeth Carter, whose translation of the *Discourses of Epictectus* are mentioned as a moral guide for the youth.[29] In the ninth stanza, it is Macaulay herself who is praised. By referring to Alfred, Macaulay is presented as the "Child of Liberty" (Anon. 1777: 44, 45). For 'Britannia', Macaulay best personifies the fight against 'tyranny' and for "Freedom" – a task which she sets for the rest of the British population as well (Anon. 1777: 43). As the poem attempts to celebrate 'British' achievements,

out that, on several occasions, Wilkes stressed the difference of Scottish people and, at the same time, of the primacy of England within Great Britain (2009: 118).

27 Cash (2006: 234). Benjamin Franklin was also among the group's members.

28 Keynes (1999: 286). She also called her home "Alfred's House".

29 Anon. (1777: 41 ff.). Barbauld wrote a story for children entitled "King Alfred the Great", using the then already notorious myth of Alfred burning the cakes as topic, printed in *Evenings at Home* – a series of six volumes for family reading which she published together with her brother John Aikin between 1792 and 1795.

it contributes to the new sense of 'Britishness' rather than to the older concept of 'Englishness'.

One of the later radicals, who worshipped the ideal of liberty, was Henry Redhead Yorke (1772-1813). According to Amanda Goodrich, Yorke ranks among the most important radicals of the late eighteenth century (2019: 8). He led the Sheffield Constitutional Society and supported the idea of arming for insurrection. For this, he was pursued by the Home Office and finally arrested in 1794. Despite the radical ideas he had pronounced to this point, it was during his trial, as Amnon Yuval demonstrates, that he began to turn towards more moderate positions, ultimately becoming even an "ultraloyalist".[30] Attacking his former friend Thomas Paine for his criticism on the English constitution,[31] he would defend the "magnanimous government which we derived from our Saxon fathers, and from the prodigious mind of the immortal Alfred" (Yorke 1795: 128). In 1803/1804, Henry Redhead Yorke published letters in *The Star* under the pseudonym of either "Alfred" or "Galgacus". Both historical figures served as a symbol for liberty: While Alfred had defeated the Danes, Galgacus (or Calgacus) was a Caledonian chieftain who had fought against the conquering Romans in the first century A.D. In one of these letters, Alfred is characterized as the founding father of the empire and linked to the ideal of liberty, supposedly having said the words: "it is right the people of England should be as free as their own thoughts".[32] By mentioning the "patriotic King" (i.e., George III) in the same sentence, Yorke established a link between the Anglo-Saxon king and the King of the United Kingdom (1804: 70). These letters, which were later reprinted in a volume entitled *The Anti-Corsican; or, War of Liberty* (1804), were intended to arouse patriotic feelings and an anti-French sentiment among readers. It is important to note that Yorke explicitly addressed his letters "to the People of the United Empire", praising the Act of Union of 1801 and calling both the Irish and the English "a people of brethren" (1804: 24). Therefore, it is not astonishing that he preferred to speak of 'Britain' rather than of 'England'

30 Yuval (2011: 615-616). Yuval borrows the term "ultraloyalist" from Stuart Semmel, who uses this expression for the older Yorke in his *Napoleon and the British* (2004).

31 See Hill (1958: 103-104). However, as Yuval demonstrates, it is very likely that Yorke turned against Paine in order to be acquitted of high treason (see Yuval 2011: 627-628). For the relation between Yorke and Paine see Goodrich (2019: 82 ff., 242 ff.).

32 Yorke (1804: 70). See also Yorke (1795: 104). In his *History of England*, Hume also quotes these lines, citing Asser's *Life of Alfred* as source (1854: 79).

(1804: Preface, 103). Unlike Wilkes a couple of decades earlier, Yorke was ready to embrace Britishness.

By the end of the eighteenth century, there existed a cohesive set of stereotypes about Alfred which most Britons were familiar with. This led to a couple of publications, which referred to Alfred in their titles but did not deal with the Anglo-Saxon king directly. Two interesting examples are James Bland Burges's *Alfred's letters, or a Review of the Political State of Europe to the End of Summer 1792* (1793), and the anonymously published *Letters of the Ghost of Alfred* (1798). Unlike Wilkes, Macaulay and the early Yorke, however, these two authors readily accepted the policies of their government and used Alfred primarily in order to defend the *status quo*.

Alfred's Letters by James Bland Burges (1752-1824) is an informed report about the situation in various European countries towards the end of the century, including comments on their mutual relationships. The letters were originally published in *The Sun* and read by a large part of the population (Burges 1793: Advertisement, 89). Not surprisingly, one is informed about "England['s]" virtues, a country

> which [...] appeared to surrounding nations the mild but strenuous arbiter of Europe, unequalled in prosperity and resources, enjoying the purest and most perfect government which had ever blessed a people, and profiting by the arts of peace, while she possessed and knew how to use the irresistible means of war.[33]

According to Burges, England's role as leading nation and as 'saviour' of Europe is also made possible by the alliance with Prussia and Holland, founded in order to thwart the mutual plans of Russia, Austria and France to exchange territories, so that English and Prussian power would be diminished. By calling this alliance the "Germanic association" (1793: 116), Burges clearly invokes England's Anglo-Saxon past and most likely also alludes to an intrinsic link between these nations due to their common 'Germanic inheritance'.

The anonymously published *Letters of the Ghost of Alfred* consist of nine letters, four being addressed to Thomas Erskine, the rest to Charles James Fox. The author is now known to have been John Bowles, a barrister and, as Emma Vincent has put it, an ardent "'war crusading' writer" who defended the conservative politics of William Pitt the Younger (1993: 394). Both Erskine and

---

33 Burges (1793: 90). Although Burges sometimes makes use of the term Great Britain, he still prefers the term England (see for example 1793: 95-96).

Fox, on the other hand, opposed the politics of Pitt, prime minister from 1783 to 1806 (with a break between 1801 and 1804). In 1794, when Pitt's government decided to take action against those who supported parliamentary reform, Thomas Erskine defended Thomas Hardy, a shoemaker and secretary of the London Corresponding Society, whose trial was the first of the treason trials held in October / November 1794.[34] Charles James Fox, a Whig politician, was an opponent of George III, whom he regarded as an aspiring tyrant. Supporting both the American and the French Revolution, he was known to be an advocate of religious tolerance and individual liberty.

However, in his *A Protest Against T. Paine's 'Rights of Man'*, John Bowles could still speak of Fox as "[o]ne of the greatest Political Characters of the present age" (1995: 57). This protest was an address given in 1792 before a book society of which Bowles himself was a member and which had put Paine's work on a list of recommended books. In this address, Bowles criticized Paine for his attack on the monarchy in general, and the British Constitution in particular. He further proved to be an ardent advocate of the idea of "continuity" with the past: "There is no point, line, or boundary, at which one generation can be said to terminate and another to commece [sic]" (Bowles 1995: 47). Laws are therefore held to be eternal as well as universal. However, in his address, Bowles also suggested that this continuity had only begun with the Anglo-Saxon kingdom of Wessex and that many 'accomplishments' could be ascribed to Alfred the Great (1995: 53, 50). Furthermore, his address shows his aversion towards revolutions in general. Commenting on the passing of the new Polish constitution, Bowles stresses for instance that "all great and sudden changes are precarious in their effects, and that a gradual acquisition of advantages is alone to be depended upon for security and permanence" (1995: 59).

This aversion against revolutions also finds expression in his *Letters of the Ghost of Alfred*. These had originally been published in the *True Briton*, and were considered to be an important instrument in the struggle against anarchy and revolution, "the most dreadful scourge that ever afflicted the human race" as the editor put it.[35] Although these letters do not explicitly refer to Alfred, the preface presents him as the originator of the English constitution. Bowles' fear is that this constitution is now in danger to be overthrown (see Anon.

34 It is in this context that Henry Redhead Yorke's trial took place. Thomas Erskine also defended Yorke in his sentencing hearing in November 1795 (see Yuval 2011: 635).

35 Anon. (1798: vii). The fact that Yorke was part proprietor of the *True Briton* bespeaks his conservative turn.

1798: vii). By defending it, he also intends to demonstrate his support of the monarchy:

> [A]ccording to both the letter of Law, and the genuine spirit of the Constitution, all Power, Dignity, and Political Excellence, centre in the King. He is the Sun of the System, communicating light, life, motion, and energy, to every part, and maintaining the whole in order, harmony, and cohesion. (Anon. 1798: 78)

Bowles did not believe in the sovereignty of the people and in a control of the government through the people (Anon. 1798: 8). For these reasons, he interpreted the French Revolution as a "deep and vast conspiracy against all the ancient institutions of Europe, civil, political, and religious" (Anon. 1798: 49), threatening all Europe. Because both Erskine and Fox supported the Revolution, he accused them of inciting "Rebellion", "Anarchy", "the growth of Treason, and the breaking out of War" (Anon. 1798: 9, 59). In his *A Dispassionate Inquiry into the Best Means of National Safety* (1806), he even compared the rivalry of "[r]evolutionary France" and Great Britain to that of Rome and Carthage, and warned against the danger of sharing "the fate of the latter city".[36]

6. Conclusion

Beginning with the Act of Union in 1707, national debates centred around the question of how to define national identity, either pointing to a supremacy of Englishness or giving way to a new sense of Britishness. Both camps saw fit to call on Alfred, either as representing the "true English", i.e., Anglo-Saxon, spirit, or as a 'unionist' who first achieved to unite different kingdoms under one reign.

These practices of comparisons had different effects. First of all, these comparisons served the organisation of historical events and interpreted the eighteenth century as a direct consequence of the Medieval times. This created an idea of a linear development of national history. By directly linking the Saxons of the fifth to the eleventh centuries to the British population of the eigh-

36 Bowles (1806: 27-28). See Vincent (1993: 404). In a similar vein, the anonymously published *Alfred's Address to the Ladies of England* (1803) evokes the image of Carthage in order to press its appeal for "female Patriotism" against Napoleon and the French, Anon. (1803: 13, 19-20, 24).

teenth century through the comparison of contemporary politics with those of the times of Alfred, the idea of an Anglo-Saxon community was created. These "Anglo-Saxons" resembled what Benedict Anderson would later describe as an "imagined community" (1983). However, before politicians could refer to this stereotypical notion of Anglo-Saxonism and Alfredianism, it had to become part of the British cultural memory. Literary writings such as Blackmore's epic poem *Alfred* and Mallet and Thompson's play *Alfred – A Masque* certainly had a great influence on the formation of this cultural memory.

At the same time that Alfred was used as a role model, the linear conception of time was dissolved into a hierarchical relation which set the early Medieval times above the eighteenth century. This is especially true for the radical discourse. When looking at the political discourse about the ideal of liberty in connection with the reign of Alfred the Great, comparisons with the Anglo-Saxon king were used in order to foster change. Thus, the radical movement promoted the concept of 'liberty' in order to criticize governmental and royal politics and to achieve political reform. At the end of the century, the reference to Alfred rather served as a warning against a national decline which authors such as Bowles and Burges expected if the English were once more submitted to the 'French' yoke. The fear of an impending French influence, either indirectly, through revolutionary tendencies, or directly, by military force, helped evoke the idea of liberty as a traditional English concept in order to rouse patriotic feelings and anti-French sentiments. Through de- and recontextualization, the *comparatum* 'Alfred' thus served a conservative purpose. The pursuit of national reform in earlier decades was now mainly abandoned for the sake of defending the status quo. This was accompanied by a confirmation of the Hanoverian rulers, whose status had been rather precarious during the first half of the century. In the nineteenth century, comparisons with Alfred were even more common and mainly served two purposes: the legitimation of the reign of Queen Victoria (see Parker 2007: 82ff.) and the establishment of an Anglo-Saxon community which was characterized by an (aggressive) expansionism and by the idea that it would outlast all times.

Bibliography

Anderson, Benedict. *Imagined Communities: Reflections on the Origin and Spread of Nationalism*. London: Verso, 1983.

Anon. *Six Odes Presented to the Justly-Celebrated Historian, Mrs. Catherine Macaulay on her Birthday, and Publicly Read to a Polite and Brilliant Audience, Assembled April the Second, at Alfred-House, Bath, to Congratulate that Lady on the Happy Occasion*. Bath: R. Cruttwell, 1777.

Anon. [Bowles, John]. *Letters of the Ghost of Alfred, Addressed to the Hon. Thomas Erskine and the Hon. Charles James Fox, on the Occasion of the State Trials at the Close of the Year 1794, and the Beginning of the Year 1795*. London: J. Wright, 1798.

Anon. *Alfred's Address to the Ladies of England*. London: W. Marchant, 1803.

Blackmore, Richard. *Prince Arthur. An Heroick Poem. In Ten Books*. London: Awnsham and John Churchil, 1695.

Blackmore, Richard. *Alfred, an Epick Poem. In Twelve Books*. London: James Knapton, 1723.

Bowles, John. *A Dispassionate Inquiry into the Best Means of National Safety*. London: J. Hatchard, 1806.

Bowles, John. *A Protest Against T. Paine's 'Rights of Man': Addressed to the Members of a Book Society, in Consequence of the Votes of their Committee for Including the Above Work in a List of New Publications Resolved to Be Purchased for the Use of the Society*. 1792. *Political Writings of the 1790s*. Vol. 6: *Loyalism: Response to Paine, 1792-1793*. Ed. Gregory Claeys. London: William Pickering, 1995. 38-63.

Burges, James Bland. *Alfred's Letters, or a Review of the Political State of Europe, to the End of the Summer 1792. As Originally Published in* The Sun. London: B. Millan, 1793.

Cash, Arthur H. *John Wilkes – The Scandalous Father of Civil Liberty*. New Haven: Yale University Press, 2006.

Colley, Linda. *Britons: Forging the Nation 1707-1837*. Revised Edition with New Introductory Essay. New Haven: Yale University Press, 2009.

Conway, Stephen. "War and National Identity in the Mid-Eighteenth-Century British Isles." *The English Historical Review* 116.468 (2001): 863-893.

Defoe, Daniel. *An Essay at Removing National Prejudices against a Union with Scotland. To be Continued During the Treaty Here. Part I*. London, 1706a.

Defoe, Daniel. *Jure Divino: A Satyr. In Twelve Books*. London, 1706b.

Defoe, Daniel. *Union and No Union. Being an Enquiry Into the Grievances of the Scots. And How Far They are Right or Wrong, Who Alledge That the Union is Dissolved*. London: John Baker, 1713.

Defoe, Daniel. *A True-Born Englishman. A Satire*. London: M. Wilson, 1835.

Eggers, Michael. "Outlines of a Historical Epistemology of Comparison: From Descartes to the Early Nineteenth Century." *The Force of Comparison: A New Perspective on Modern European History and the Contemporary World*. Ed. Willibald Steinmetz. New York: berghahn, 2019. 33-52.

Epple, Angelika and Walter Erhart. "Die Welt beobachten – Praktiken des Vergleichens.“ *Die Welt beobachten – Praktiken des Vergleichens*. Ed. Angelika Epple and Walter Erhart. Frankfurt: Campus Verlag, 2015. 7-31.

Epple, Angelika. "Doing Comparisons – Ein praxeologischer Zugang zur Geschichte der Globalisierung/en." *Die Welt beobachten – Praktiken des Vergleichens*. Ed. Angelika Epple and Walter Erhart. Frankfurt: Campus Verlag, 2015. 161-199.

Epple, Angelika and Walter Erhart. "Practices of Comparing – A New Research Agenda Between Typological and Historical Approaches." *Practices of Comparing – Towards a New Understanding of a Fundamental Human Practice*. Ed. Angelika Epple, Walter Erhart, and Johannes Grave. Bielefeld: transcript, 2020. 11-38.

Erhart, Walter. "'Beobachtung und Erfahrung, Sammeln und Vergleichen' – Adelbert von Chamisso und die Poetik der Weltreise im 18. und 19. Jahrhundert.“ *Die Welt beobachten – Praktiken des Vergleichens*. Ed. Angelika Epple and Walter Erhart. Frankfurt: Campus Verlag, 2015. 203-233.

Glickman, Gabriel. "Parliament, the Tories and Frederick, Prince of Wales." *Parliamentary History* 2 (2011): 120-141.

Goodrich, Amanda. *Henry Redhead Yorke, Colonial Radical. Politics and Identity in the Atlantic World, 1772-1813*. London: Routledge, 2019.

Gottlieb, Evan. *Feeling British. Sympathy and National Identity in Scottish an English Writing, 1707-1832*. Lewisburg: Bucknell University Press, 2007.

Hill, Christopher. *Puritanism and Revolution. Studies in the Interpretation of the English Revolution of the 17th Century*. London: Secker & Warburg, 1958.

Hume, David. *The History of England from the Invasion of Julius Caesar to the Revolution in 1688. A New Edition with Author's Last Corrections and Improvements to Which is Added a Short Account of His Life, Written by Himself.* In Six Volumes. Vol. 1. Boston: Little, Brown and Company, 1854 [1754].

Keynes, Simon. "The Cult of King Alfred the Great", *Anglo-Saxon England* 28, 1999. 225-356.

Liss, Oskar W. *Die Arthurepen des Sir Richard Blackmore*. Straßburg, 1911.

Lowenthal, David. "British National Identity and the English Landscape." *Rural History* 2 (1991): 205-230.

MacDougall, Hugh A. *Racial Myth in English History: Trojans, Teutons, and Anglo-Saxons*. Montreal: Harvest House, 1982.

Mallet, David and James Thomson. *Alfred: A Masque. Acted at the Theatre-Royal in Drurylane, by His Majesty's Servants*. London: A. Millar, 1751.

Parker, Joanne. *'England's Darling'. The Victorian Cult of Alfred the Great*. Manchester: Manchester University Press, 2007.

Pratt, Lynda. "Anglo-Saxon Attitudes? Alfred the Great and the Romantic National Epic." *Literary Appropriations of the Anglo-Saxons from the Thirteenth to the Twentieth Century*. Ed. Donald Scragg and Carole Weinberg. Cambridge: University Press, 2000. 138-156.

Solomon, Harry M. *Sir Richard Blackmore*. Boston: Twayne Publishers, 1980.

Steinmetz, Willibald. "Concepts and Practices of Comparison in Modern History." *The Force of Comparison: A New Perspective on modern European History and the Contemporary World*. Ed. Willibald Steinmetz. New York: berghahn, 2019. 1-32.

Vincent, Emma. "'The Real Grounds of the Present War': John Bowles and the French Revolutionary Wars, 1792-1802." *History – The Journal of the Historical Association* 78.254 (1993): 393-420.

Wilkes, John. *The North Briton*. Revised and Corrected by the Author. Illustrated with Explanatory Notes, and a Copious Index of Names and Characters. In Two Volumes. Vol. 1. Dublin: John Mitchell & James Williams, 1764.

Wilkes, John. *A Complete Collection of the Genuine Papers, Letters in the Case of John Wilkes, Esq.* Paris: J. W. Imprimeur, 1767.

Wilkes, John. *Letters from the Year 1774 to the Year 1796, of John Wilkes, Esq., Adressed to his Daughter, the late Miss Wilkes*. Vol. 3. London: Longman, Hurst, Rees, and Orme, 1804.

Wilson, Kathleen. *The Sense of the People. Politics, Culture and Imperialism in England, 1715-1785*. Cambridge: Cambridge University Press, 1998.

Yorke, Henry Redhead. *The Trial of Henry Yorke*. London, 1795.

Yorke, Henry Redhead. *The Anti-Corsican; or, War of Liberty: A Series of Letters Adressed to the People of the United Empire, First Published in The Star, Under the Signature of Galgacus: Revised and Corrected by the Author*. London: R. Taylor, 1804.

Yuval, Amnon. "Between Heroism and Acquittal: Henry Redhead Yorke and the Inherent Instability of Political Trials in Britain During the 1790s." *Journal of British Studies* 3 (2011): 612-638.

The Circulating Library, the Novel, and Implicit Practices of Comparing in Eighteenth-Century England: Assembling 'Middle-Class' Literariness

Ralf Schneider

> Mr. Bennet was glad to take his guest into the drawing-room again, and, when tea was over, glad to invite him to read aloud to the ladies. Mr. Collins readily assented, and a book was produced; but, on beholding it (for everything announced it to be from a circulating library), he started back, and begging pardon, protested that he never read novels. Kitty stared at him, and Lydia exclaimed. Other books were produced, and after some deliberation he chose Fordyce's Sermons. Lydia gaped as he opened the volume, and before he had, with very monotonous solemnity, read three pages, she interrupted him [...].
>
> *Jane Austen, Pride and Prejudice [1813] 2001: 47*

1. The Circulating Library, Literary Sociology and the Sociology of Associations

The scene from Austen's classic novel, *Pride and Prejudice*, can be read as an invitation to disentangle the reasons for both Mr Collins' horror at the sight of a book from the circulating library which he immediately identifies as a novel, and the Bennet girls' dismay at his choice of an alternative. I will return to the joke, which Austen makes at the expense of the young clergyman in this scene, later. For the present, I take the passage from an early nineteenth-century novel as a starting point for a retrospective enquiry into the origins of the complex connections it contains. The short scene involves issues of class, gender, age, material culture, ideology, sociability, book format and literary genre, and I will argue in this essay that in the course of the 'long' eighteenth century, the circulating library, as an institution and as a public space, was closely associated both with the performance of a new class identity and the development of the new literary genre of the novel;[1] furthermore, the material and ideological conditions of book-lending, the bodily presence of the novel-reading public, and the physical materiality of the books were centrally involved in this association. I propose to look at these phenomena from a perspective that combines impulses from historical literary sociology and from Actor Network Theory, because I consider such an alignment best suited to assess their complexity.

Much evidence survives on the eighteenth-century circulating library: historians of the book and the literary system have assessed and interpreted the libraries' catalogues, business papers, subscription books, advertisements and trade cards, reports about circulating libraries in diaries and letters as well as mentioning of and invectives against them in pamphlets, sermons, letters to journal editors, caricatures, novels and plays.[2] Instead of buying novels, most readers would subscribe to a circulating library that allowed them to take out a volume or two at a time, for a fee levied annually or per quarter that amounted to just twice the sum one would have to expend on a single printed and bound novel. The phenomenon had its roots in Restoration England, when Francis Kirkman opened the first commercial circulating library in 1661 (Feather 1988: 57), but it first became a wide-spread institution after Alan Ramsay had opened his library in Edinburgh in 1725 and Samuel

1 The label 'novel' can be applied to prose narratives from the largest part of the 18th only retrospectively, since the word only slowly gained prominence among other genre classifications such as 'romance', 'history', 'live', 'adventure', 'account', 'tale', 'memoir', etc. (Hunter 1996: 9). On the mixture of genres from which what we now recognize as novels emerged, see the classical study by Hunter (1990) and the more recent one by Stein (2020).

2 Among the early contributions are McKillop (1934) and the meticulous study by Hamlyn (1946), as well as Kaufman (1967); see also Stewart-Murphy (1992) and the helpful articles by Jacobs (1995, 2003, 2006). Much information on the statistics, economics, and practices pertaining to the circulating library can also be found in Erickson (1990), Skelton-Foord (1998 and 1999) and Manley (2000). See also the extensive assessment of the production and distribution system for fiction between 1770 and 1779 by Raven (2000), which is also informative on circulating libraries, their owners and business practices, and on the economic and material conditions under which novels found their readers. See also Raven's other indispensable contributions to the history of the circulating library (1990, 1996), the private subscription library (2006) and the economy of book production, distribution and reception in the period under scrutiny (2009).

Fancourt his London establishment in 1740. When the idea of the circulating library caught on, many more were opened in London and then in almost every other major English city and town, particularly from the 1750s on. It is uncertain whether the number of such libraries across Great Britain actually reached the astonishing "not less than one thousand" in the provinces at the end of the century that the *Monthly Magazine* mentioned in April 1801, or how many "more than 100 in London" there actually existed in the end (qtd. in Kaufman 1967: 10; Brewer 1997: 178). But there is no doubt that the institution was both widespread and its establishments numerous.[3] There were also other types of libraries, such as the subscription library and the book club, "the former specialising in serious non-fiction, and only few novels, the latter usually featuring the small pamphlets and printed ephemera in which contemporary religious controversies were vehemently rehearsed" (Brewer 1997: 180).[4] When the term 'library' is used hereafter, it refers exclusively to the commercial circulating library. Towards the end of the century, readers could get access to fiction in three ways, "the purchase of new novels, the purchase of novels second-hand, and the renting of fiction" (Skelton-Foord 1998: 349). However, all scholarly contributions on the topic agree that the standard mode of accessing newly printed titles, especially novels, throughout the period was by frequenting circulating libraries. Furthermore, there is much agreement that the libraries developed into social meeting places for the well to-do and fashionable society, not only in London but also in the provincial libraries and particularly in holiday resorts (Manley 2000: 32). The economic, spatial, and

---

3 Jacobs, using figures quoted by Hamlyn (1946) and Kaufman (1967) summarizes that already "by the 1750s there were at least nine circulating libraries in London", adding that "here as elsewhere records surely underestimate numbers. By 1780 there were at least nineteen and by 1800 at least twenty-six libraries in London [...]." (2006: 5) Manley (2000: 35) counts "three circulating libraries in Bath" alone in 1750, and adds that "by 1800 there were ten, plus a music library".

4 See also Manley (2000: 29): "Book clubs were usually temporary collections, where the books were sold off each year. Proprietary subscription libraries and book clubs were almost always organizations in which the members held shares in a common stock and collected usually, but not exclusively, the better class of non-fiction for the benefit of all." The type of sociability associated with the subscription library was different from that of the circulating library, because membership in the former was more expensive and mostly restricted to men; see Raven (2006). For general information on the relationship between the book market and libraries, see Feather (2006).

social aspects of these libraries were, as I will demonstrate below, instrumental in the production of the middle-class literary sphere.

Although approaches such as Book History (or History of the Book), Bibliography, Sociology of Texts, Sociology of Authorship and Reading constitute a broad and varied field, they share the conviction that the literary sphere is fundamentally shaped by the intermingling of the personal, material and economic factors of book production, distribution and reception.[5] Historical Literary Sociology, to use an umbrella term for the approaches just mentioned, has reminded scholars in literary hermeneutics time and again of the intricate connectedness between what is *in* a book and how that book comes into being, how it reaches readers, and how it exists as a material artefact that implies ideas and evaluations beyond the content-level of the book.[6] Within the social sciences, the study of phenomena of the past and the present has increasingly taken material artefacts seriously, not merely as products or tools, but as unities that are fundamentally and actively involved in social phenomena, just as people, discourses, and practices are. For the purposes of the present essay, Actor Network Theory (ANT) is particularly attractive because of its predilection for complex phenomena in the process of their emergence, for fuzzy fields of social activity in which agents, or actors, of different kinds – human beings and their bodies, material artefacts, practices, and ideas – create associations. In them, none of the actions or actors precede, predetermine, or fully explain any of the others, but they may emerge locally, spontaneously, and temporarily (Latour 1996, 2005). Felski summarizes the central idea of ANT as follows: "The social [...] is not a preformed being but a doing, not a hidden entity underlying the realm of appearance but the ongoing connections, disconnections, and reconnections between multiple actors" (2015: 158). An actor, she clarifies later, "is anything that modifies a state of affairs by making a difference" (163), which refers also to non-human entities, without, however, implying that non-human actors have intentionality or follow a purpose. What is observable as the social sphere is the outcome of connections, disconnections and reconnections, not their basis. In the words of Latour,

5 For seminal contributions to this field, see McKenzie (1986), Adams/Barker (1993), and the texts reprinted in Finkelstein/McCleery (2006). Raven (2018) gives an overview of the scope of the field.

6 To be fair, Genette's (1997) concept of the paratext must be mentioned here, since it also refers to the relationship between authors, books as material artefacts, and readers, taking also the physical appearance of the book into account.

"it's not the social that accounts for associations but rather associations that explain the social" (2005: 238).

Literary scholars may admittedly treat ANT with some suspicion. The tension between Bruno Latour's famous questioning of all component terms of the approach ("there are four things that do not work with actor-network theory: the word actor, the word network, the word theory and the hyphen!" 1999: 15) and his wholehearted defence of the project in *Reassembling the Social* (2005) may justify some reluctance to getting involved with it, as does the persistent metaphoricity and counter-intuitiveness of his language, which seems to defy clear-cut definitions and easy accessibility. However, not only are there influential supporters from within literary studies, including Rita Felski in her *Limits of Critique* (2015: 151-185). It is also especially intriguing to look at the development, features and effects of the practice of book-lending and the institution of the circulating library through an ANT lens, because neither of them, nor what one would classically call their 'social context', were simply *there*. As Bermingham (1995: 15) phrases it, "a culture-consuming public of the early modern period was there not so much to be tapped as to be created". Historians of culture such as Brewer (1997) and others (Bermingham/Brewer 1995, Hume 2006) have shown in both depth and detail that none of the many areas of cultural production (print culture, performance culture, the visual arts, music, etc.) were readily available for the broadening audiences when the (long) eighteenth century started. Rather, they co-emerged – slowly, not teleologically, in phases that saw both advances and setbacks – with and through the complex associations of concepts, bodies and artefacts, including spaces. This is of particular relevance for the emergence of the novel, which, according to Feather "is the only literary genre to have been invented since the invention of printing", so that "its literary history is inseparable from the history of its publication" (1988: 57). I take "publication" to include the mode of distribution on which I will focus below. To adopt an ANT perspective is to give precedence to the emergent and contingent, the tentative and unstable, to ties and associations that must be retrieved from the surviving data. The growth of the circulating library during the long eighteenth century and the development of the novel as a major genre, which were in turn coextensive with the social and cultural shifts towards a modern consumer society, are phenomena that lend themselves particularly well to an interpretation inspired by ANT. I will argue that access to the novel through the circulating library involved practices of performance of class identity for the emerging middle stratum of society, and that these performances possessed a crucial comparative aspect.

If there are three narratives of development – that of the novel, that of the circulating library, and that of the middle classes – none of them precedes, pre-determines, or encompasses the others. Rather, these developments can be seen as associations, or networks, which were mutually indebted to each other.

2. Social Change and Literature: Book-Lending, the Performance of Politeness, and Implicit Practices of Comparing

The eighteenth century is generally regarded as a period of drastic changes, and it is also one of considerable ambivalences. The period saw the transition of British society from a pre-modern society structured by hierarchical classification to a modern one, organized through functional differentiation.[7] It also saw the development of a modern literary system. The standard historical account of the interrelated changes put forward by historians of literature, publishing, and the book as a material artefact on the one hand, and of class, society and economy on the other, is the following: The lapse of the Licensing Act in 1695 effectively ended pre-publication censorship and stripped the London Stationers Company of its monopoly, so that both metropolitan and provincial printing businesses could flourish by and by;[8] the population grew, and education in literacy for boys and, later, also girls increased, which created a growing readership and demand for reading material, so that "[s]ome literary and cultural historians have identified alongside, and related to, the

7 This is the sociological position that, for instance, Talcott Parsons and Niklas Luhmann share. See, e.g., Parsons (1969) and Luhmann (1977).

8 See Feather (1988: 67-125) for an account of the development of the market for printed material; Belanger (1982) and Benedict (2004) provide concise overviews. While the number of master printers in London had been restricted to twenty under the Licensing Act, when Samuel Richardson set up shop in the 1720s "there were already more than seventy-five master printers in London; at his death in 1761 more than 120 were at work, and their premises grew as their work and numbers expanded" (Brewer 1997: 137). This multiplication of producers of printed material also occurred in the provinces, so that for instance in the larger town of Newcastle upon Tyne, in 1790 as many as twenty printers were at work (ibid.). Although not all printing houses produced novels, these figures give a good impression of the scope of the more general development of the printing press, from which the novel also profited.

social changes of the eighteenth century a 'reading revolution'" (Williams 2017: 6).[9]

Grounded in a mentality of improvement that dates back to the seventeenth century (Slack 2015), a set of further 'revolutions' marked Britain's shift from a pre-modern to a modern society: the financial, the agrarian, the consumer, and eventually the beginnings of the industrial revolution. All in all, since the number of ways in which people could acquire wealth and status multiplied, these developments can be understood to be the foundation upon which a social stratum below the upper gentry and above the labourers developed.[10] It is debatable whether the term 'revolution' is the best designation for all of these developments, each of which had its own phases of advancement and regression, success and failure. There is no doubt however, that we are looking at a multifactor dynamic of substantial changes between the late seventeenth and the early nineteenth centuries.

There has been a tendency in literary and cultural history to link the dissemination of print with the rise of a bourgeois mentality since Jürgen Habermas' study of the public sphere (1989). The novel in particular has been understood to be involved in this process, as Watt (1957) stated in his classical study, which was critically revaluated by McKeon ([1987] 2002), a classic by now, too. The 'middling sorts' can be regarded as an emerging social group whose moral ideals, opinions, and habits needed constant formulation and

9 For England alone, Hunt (1996: 17) quotes a growth in population between 1700 and 1800 "from approximately five million to eight and one-half million". Raven summarizes that the British population more than doubled in the period under consideration: "The British Isles in 1695 comprised three kingdoms with a total population of just over 8 million. In 1814 a United Kingdom of Britain and Ireland contained a population of some 19 million" (2006: 243). According to Hunter (1996: 21), by the mid-eighteenth century "at least 60 percent of the adult men in England (and perhaps more) could read and write", while "literacy increased among women faster than among men", starting from a lower percentage and reaching at least 40 percent by mid-century. The articles in Rivers (1982) demonstrate the breadth and variety of sections of publishing and readership, from religious, political, scientific and philosophical to belletristic reading. See Colclough (2007: 1-117) for a general history of reading practices in eighteenth-century England, based on the analysis of individual cases.

10 For general historical surveys of the socio-economic changes, see Earle (1989) on the early decades, and Davidoff/Hall (1987) on the period since 1750; further standard sources include Porter (1991), Barry/Brooks (1994), Smail (1994), Hunt (1996), and Langford (1989 and 2010); see also Barry's extensive review (1991).

affirmation, and the novel can be understood as a platform for the negotiation of that mentality (Langford 2010: 390-398). However, as a period of transition, the long eighteenth century presents a much more ambivalent and heterogeneous picture both socioeconomically and culturally. The time was still characterized by serious political and religious rifts, and though the middling sorts may have been rising, the political and economic primacy of the aristocracy and the landed gentry was not simply replaced (see, e.g., Spurr 1998). As with the 'rise' of the middle classes, we need to bear in mind that the novel also 'rose' slowly, and most perceptibly in the second half of the eighteenth century. Daniel Defoe stands out as a fairly solitary figure for the first half of the century, while the bulk of male and female authors who are now regarded as 'fathers' and 'mothers' of the English novel are located in the second half, with Samuel Richardson (*Pamela* 1740, *Clarissa* 1748) and Henry Fielding (*Shamela* 1741, *Joseph Andrews* 1742) as the early figures of that group, followed by Laurence Sterne (*Tristram Shandy* from 1759 on), Oliver Goldsmith (*Vicar of Wakefield* 1766), Tobias Smollett (*Humphry Clinker* 1771), and Frances Burney (*Evelina* 1778), as well as the Gothic novels reviving after Horace Walpole's *Castle of Otranto* (1764) towards the end of the century (Ann Radcliffe: *Mysteries of Udolpho* 1794, Matthew Lewis: *The Monk* 1796).

In the transition from the post-Restoration period to the eighteenth century, more ranks slowly joined the upper gentry as audiences for cultural products, which created new markets: "The economic history of the eighty years at issue here [i.e., 1660-1740; RS] is essentially the story of how the buying power of citizens and the lesser gentry increased to the point at which serious money could be made by appealing to the taste of what we would now call middle class consumers" (Hume 2006: 498). Novel production boomed in the later part of the century, and the canonical classics of eighteenth-century literature just mentioned were drastically outnumbered by the flood of new fashionable novels, most of which were romantic or gothic fictions.[11] That the boom of the circulating library occurred from the 1750s on can be aligned with this time frame. However, it is the point of an ANT-informed approach that we should not first reconstruct the 'social structure' of the period from documents and history books, to see how the practice of book-lending then 'fits' in

11 For the sheer scope of the output of various types of prose fiction that can be classified as 'novels', see the astonishing number of 1.421 titles of first publications listed by Garside, Raven and Schöwerling (2000) for the last three decades of the eighteenth century, which amounts to one new novel almost every week.

this framework. Rather, we need to understand what people did, thought and felt when they frequented the circulating library, how they interacted there, how they handled the artefacts, and how they evaluated their own and other people's behaviour.

British society at the time pondered a lot about, and spilled much ink on, precisely the question who constituted the 'middle classes', and modern scholarship has also been split over the issue as a consequence. The term 'class' itself became a common reference to contemporary society at the time, and it was variously defined and re-defined, as is to be expected from a period of transition and change.[12] Hume (2006: 496) speaks of the "scholarly wars of the last forty years concerning the existence or non-existence of a 'middle class'" in Early Modern England. While he is convinced that "[n]o such thing was recognized during the period 1660-1740 in any modern sense of that phrase" (ibid.), many other studies use the terms 'middle class' or 'middling sorts' in their titles (see, e.g., Davidoff/Hall 1987, Earle 1989, Barry/Brooks 1994, Smail 1994, Wahrman 1995, Hunt 1996). The absence of an explicit concept and widely used label for the middle classes until the mid-eighteenth century that Hume notes does not mean that ranks and their relations were stable. The processes of social change produced a shift in the evaluation of behaviour, with a concomitant change in the meaning of such terms as 'gentle' and 'gentleman'. The semantics of these words turned from being associated with noble birth, leisure and conspicuous consumption, to being applied to a mode of conduct and a disposition towards polite sociability (Corfield 1991: 106-107; Klein 1995: 364 and 2002: 872; Carter 2001: chapters 1 & 2). I will argue below that the circulating library helped in the creation of polite sociability which covered ranks from the lower middle to the upper classes. Adding yet another item to the list of revolutions mentioned above, Raven claims that "there was a library revolution in eighteenth-century England" (1996: 175). Those members of British society that can in retrospect be termed 'the middle classes' were the ones who frequented the circulating libraries, because (1) they wanted to read novels, (2) they could afford to do so, and (3) they had something else to gain from it: an opportunity to publicly perform a middle-class lifestyle. To

12 See Corfield (1991 and 1996) and Wahrman (1995) on the shifts in social hierarchies and their designation throughout the eighteenth century. Downie (2003) points out that Habermas unduly locates the structural changes of British society at the beginning of the period, while they really took the entire eighteenth century, and in particular the second half, to develop.

be sure, the bulk of the stock of circulating libraries would actually be non-fiction: figures quoted by Erickson (1990: 580 and 589, n. 34) suggest that the larger libraries held up to 80% of non-fiction titles. However, the smaller the businesses were, the more the balance was in the opposite direction, and the majority of titles that subscribers actually checked out were fiction; what is more, the figure of only 20% fiction titles "probably understates somewhat the libraries' emphasis upon novels, since large enterprises would stock multiple copies of recent fiction" (ibid: 580). Since new titles would be returned and could be handed out again within a few days, the actual reach of a new novel must be regarded as considerable.

Throughout the long eighteenth century, the price of a new printed and bound book deterred even affluent readers from wanting or being able to possess many. While classical literature, educational or religious works were usually deemed worthy of being purchased, books that were regarded as more ephemeral, such as novels, did not generally justify the expense. This was certainly true for workers: "*Robinson Crusoe* in 1719 cost five shillings (the book-stall price for its 364 pages in unbound sheets), and that was the equivalent of almost a week's wages for a young labourer" (Hunter 1996: 25). How did this apply to those who earned more than a young labourer? Assessments of the social composition of the circulating library clientele are somewhat contradictory. On the one hand, there are hints towards a democratisation of reading supported by the library: "Servants and other people of lower classes were beginning to read books, which they never would have bought but now could rent for a few pennies per week" (Kaufman 1967: 23). Book lending thus looks like the solution to the problem of exorbitant book prices. Charlotte Stewart-Murphy also lumps together various social strata who, according to her, congregated in "a new popular culture", to which the circulating libraries contributed:

> For the first time, the subscribers to the libraries – the well-to-do, the middle-class professionals, working-men, merchants, shopkeepers, domestic servants, and their families – shared a common literary interest and began to develop a similar set of social values. (1992: 49)

On the other hand, however, scholars have calculated that "[m]embership fees and borrowing charges for commercial circulating and proprietary libraries were hardly affordable for most" (Raven 2000: 111), and that "[t]he patrons of the circulating libraries were not poor" (Brewer 1997: 177). Raven explains that "although such institutions [i.e., the commercial circulating libraries; R.S.]

were notably cheaper than the expensive annual private subscription and proprietary libraries, cost remained prohibitive to all but the middle-class customers" (2006: 253), and Jacobs states: "Only middle and upper-class readers could reasonably afford circulating library fees before the twentieth century" (2006: 6).[13] Manley situates the clientele even higher on the social scale: "Many of these libraries would have been beyond the means of a large number of people, and their advertisements are aimed at the higher classes" (2000: 40). It is safest, then, to think of the middle class as the most important patrons. A market for élite cultural products, such as paintings, the theatre, and the opera, continued from the Restoration period well into the eighteenth century, as Hume (2006) has shown: "Opera and painting were stratospherically expensive; theater was pricey; and books of the sort that contained plays and poems were by no means readily affordable by those of the 'middling sort'" (529). I would argue that this is precisely one reason for the success of the circulating library with its focus on the novel.

Beside the pecuniary aspect, it makes sense to associate the libraries with the middling sorts, broad as that spectrum was, because novel reading and the use of the circulating library depended on the availability, or lack, of leisure: "By allowing middle-class readers to consume hundreds of books for the price of buying two books, circulating libraries were key to the creation of a modern popular culture of reading, in which *reading new books became a form of leisure activity*" (Jacobs 2006: 6; my emphasis). True leisure, i.e., the absence of the necessity to pursue a profession for one's income, was still what differentiated the highest classes from the middle. However, to be seen lending or even possessing books could be a signal that just *enough* leisure was available to be associated with the 'better' sorts of people. To be seen in public with books thus came to metonymically signify class, and the women of the middle-class family, who had the most leisure-time to spend, were the ones who mostly performed that class association. Erickson sums up that "[i]n many respects, then, books and an apparent interest in them were signs of gentility and often

13 On prices see also Raven (2009: 96-102). On the general economic conditions of the production and consumption of high culture in the period between the Restoration and the mid-eighteenth century, see Hume (2006). This situation appears to have continued until the end of the period. Between the 1790s, "when prices began to rise astronomically" (Skelton-Foord 1998: 351), and the 1830s, when the first cheap reprint series were put on the market, "artisans and farm-labourers, for instance, would very rarely, if ever, have been able to afford to purchase new books" (ibid.).

displayed only for their social utility" (1990: 576). This is true for the expensive leather-bound volumes that one might keep in the house, and it is also true for the interaction with books from libraries.

My emphasis on the double function of the circulating library as a book-distribution institution and a place of class performance rests on a speculation that combines the concept of politeness with that of comparative behaviour. The ideal of politeness functioned as a guiding principle for a society that was perhaps not willing to dissolve hierarchies of class and status, but sought ways to bridge the differences (Langford 1989, Carter 2001, Klein 2002). Spurr (1998) contends that though the eighteenth century was one of major social, religious and political divides, the English managed to contain the differences by developing standards of social interaction, rational and civilized behaviour; and the shifting semantics of concepts such as 'gentle' or 'gentleman' mentioned above also point in the same direction. As Klein has shown, "what made eighteenth-century Britain a polite society was not its horizontal division between polite and non-polite persons, but rather the wide access of a range of persons to activities and competencies that contemporaries considered 'polite'" (2002: 869). Politeness was an ideal that related to decorum, restraint, pleasantness and sociability in life-style, habits and interpersonal communication, and it also affected matters of taste and fashion (ibid.: 874). The association of fashion and politeness is crucial here, because, as Klein stresses repeatedly, "a concern with the manner in which actions were *performed*, was perhaps the most important component of the meaning of politeness", and "[i]nfusing all was a strong dimension of *display*" (ibid.: 874 and 888; my emphasis).[14] Performance and display only make sense in a public arena in which the standards of adequate behaviour either exist, or, as I claim for the emergence of a middle-class code of conduct, still need to be negotiated. I suggest that in a phase of emergent sociability, practices of comparing serve the function of negotiating the standards of adequacy or inadequacy of behaviour.

---

14 On the relevance of fashion in the eighteenth century, see Nunn (2000: 75-103) and Ribeiro (2002). The fact that upper-class dress became increasingly less ceremonious helped promote an "effacement of social distinction" and a "common genteel style of dressing" that the ranks below the aristocracy could adopt and afford (Klein 2002: 883). This tendency towards a democratisation of fashion has also been explored by Styles (2007).

Comparing is a basic function of the human mind, and the wide-spread use of practices of comparing has been associated with modernity: whether in class systems, markets, or in processes of globalisation, comparing is part and parcel of the phenomena of competition, rivalry, power and dominance that are characteristic of Western, capitalist societies.[15] As critics of colonialism have pointed out, the very notion of modernity involved a Eurocentric perspective and a comparative logic of progress and technological improvement that was used as a justification for the crimes of imperialism and aggressive foreign politics in general (e.g., Cheah 2003). In our context, three observations are important. First, while many scholars have looked at intercultural practices of comparing, social differentiation *within* a society also involves comparisons; I consider the eighteenth-century formation of a middle-class consciousness an effect of such intracultural comparing. Second, comparisons are never neutral nor 'innocent', because they tend to establish differences based on evaluations. Thus, when I contend that people from the middle classes in the eighteenth century compared their own behaviour to that of others, or that of other observed persons with regard to notions of politeness, I imply that they did so to distinguish themselves from those who fell outside the realm of the polite: both the lowest classes and the highest. To speak of comparisons between the middle and the upper classes, it is not necessary to assume that the middle classes strove to adopt or imitate the manners of the upper. Quite the contrary, practices of comparing may well establish a difference based on the assumption that this difference is beneficial. The aristocracy had, after all, a reputation of lacking virtue, a trait the middle classes certainly did *not* want to imitate.[16] Third, comparing does not require explicit verbalization. Rather, I suggest that the simple act of appearing in public and displaying certain behaviours that can be associated with politeness has a comparative facet, in so far as places *were* public, i.e., if others who also performed and displayed their behaviour there, were also present. Politeness needed an audience: "The rise of politeness placed a new

15 See the contributions to Felski/Friedman (2013) for an assessment of the political history of comparisons; see Heintz (2016) for the sociological perspective. The comparative has also been a principle of literary and cultural studies since their inception, and its fruitfulness has recently been discussed and revaluated; see for instance the "Theories and Methodologies" section of issue 128 of the *PMLA* in 2013.

16 See Morse (2000) on the centrality of the ideal of virtue, and the eighteenth-century discussions about the difficulties of attaining it.

premium on decorous conversation and refined display of persons and things" (Klein 2002: 886). The idea of politeness was to efface the performativity of the behaviour, and to establish a shared assumption of in-group belonging. Although the emphasis of public display meant "a new self-consciousness, new demands for kemptness" (ibid.: 887), the concept of politeness also "included such keywords as 'easiness', 'naturalness', and 'freedom' and sought to promote an ambience of reciprocity and equality" (ibid.: 879), The ideal was therefore a vision of an inclusive social context in which the members would feel at ease and 'know' that they naturally belonged there.

I will return to the question of the visibility of behaviour in circulating libraries below; here, I wish to make two basic points. First, apparently there was a large group of people who developed a common code of conduct by performing publicly and by maintaining a high level of mutual observation and implicit comparing. Second, I contend that the implicit practices of comparing were the guiding force behind the formation of ties and associations between humans, ideas, and artefacts. Comparing allows the inclusion of particular forms of behaviour and the exclusion of others.

The practice of reading and the materiality of the book were both involved in these implicit comparisons of public performance and in the creation of social associations. While reading is now mostly perceived to be a private, silent activity, it was frequently a communal one in the eighteenth century. Reading aloud among family and friends, or the household more generally, was still a widespread leisure pursuit, as Tadmor (1996) and Williams (2017) argue. Williams criticizes the tendency to correlate the spread of literacy with increasingly individual and silent reading. The fact that Mr Collins in Austen's *Pride and Prejudice* is not at all surprised by Mr Bennet's invitation to read to the women of the house can be seen as an indicator of the continuation of the practice into the nineteenth century. If book reading was a communal practice, book lending was a public one. The late seventeenth-century coffee house, which Habermas (1989) associated with the emergence of a genuine public sphere, had introduced the tradition of publicly accessible and rentable reading material (Kaufman 1967: 7-9). It may therefore have been customary for male readers to be seen going to an institution that provided print matter which could be read on the premises or taken out. In the eighteenth century, the publicness of book-lending was much increased by the general development of a consumer society that established modern practices of shopping as a social performance.[17] It added middle-class women, in their role as shoppers, to the public scene. The display of affluence and taste became a form of self-expression and social positioning, as

> cultural sites were places of self-presentation in which audiences made publicly visible their wealth, status, social and sexual charms. The ostensible reason for an individual's presence at a cultural site – seeing the play, attending an auction, visiting an artist's studio, listening to a concert [one might add: lending books; RS] – was often subordinate to a more powerful set of social imperatives. [...] And, from the individual's point of view, access to culture and self-presentation in the cultural arena was a means of maintaining or attaining social status and social distinctions. (Brewer 1995: 348)[18]

The fact that new titles borrowed from a circulating library could be kept for as short a span as between two and six days (Erickson 1990: 580), while books that had been in stock for a while had a lease of up to a month (Jacobs 2006: 7), points to novels being much like articles of fashion, characterized by a high demand for continuous new output voiced by the consumers and satisfied by the producers.

To sum up the gist of the argument so far: Among the changes in eighteenth-century England were the simultaneous growth of consumerism, novel production and the circulating library, as well as the increasing socio-economic power and visibility of the 'middling sorts'. The circulating libraries were predominantly frequented by persons from that social section, who turned book consumption to their public activities, aiming at performing behaviour that would be considered 'polite' in comparison with others who wished to situate themselves in that class. As I will go on to elucidate in more detail, the circulating libraries, the books they stored, the producers of fiction and its readers, were all agents in a network of sociability that was characterized by implicit shared expectations. Book consumption and the institution of the circulating library were, at the same time, confronted with quite ambivalent evaluations that resulted from the tension between politeness and consumerism.

---

17 On the development of the book as a commodity embedded in the wider growth of a consumer culture, see Raven (2009).

18 For the emergence of a modern consumer society in eighteenth-century Britain, see the seminal collection by McKendrick/Brewer/Plumb (1982) and the survey by Pennell (1999). For the concept and practice of 'polite consumption', see also Berry (2002).

3. Assembling the Literary: Reciprocal Presuppositions and the Ambivalence of Novel Reading

In his sophisticated reconsideration of the emergence of a public sphere (and its relation to the private) in eighteenth-century Britain, McKeon observes that we need to consider the public sphere as the product of both the material spaces and the ideas with which people brought that sphere into being: "The emergent public sphere was understood by contemporaries as a virtual collectivity, a metaphorical place of assembly constituted principally by publication and its readership. But it was also associated (unlike 'the public domain') with actual spaces" (McKeon 2006: 75). The circulating library was one of those spaces of assembly, *both* metaphorically and materially, and in that space, the shifting attitudes and evaluations met and were negotiated over the century. I will first look at evidence for the emergence of ties and associations between library owners, publishers, readers, books and the libraries themselves that are indicative of a virtual collectivity, and then explore the ambivalent evaluations connected with the lending of novels from circulating libraries that gave these spaces a distinct socio-cultural quality.

Four economic circumstances suggest that circulating library owners, publishers and readers, as well as books (as non-human agents), joined each other by and by in creating an atmosphere of mutual reliance. First, the practice of financing a new novel by subscription points to the production and reception of literature as providing a metaphorical place of assembly. Subscribers of circulating libraries in the late eighteenth century were frequently invited to pay for another subscription that would subsidize the publication of a new volume of fiction (Skelton-Foord 1999: 106-107). When such an invitation was successful, the lists of subscribers were frequently printed in the front matter of the finished book (Raven 2000: 55-56 and 111). Readers thus became also originators, patrons and proprietors of novels, and it would be a public fact that they did. Considering that anonymity was the rule for the first publication of a novel in the period (Raven 2003), it was the book as a material artefact and the ideas it stood for that appear as agents in the constellation, rather than authors. Even if the identity of an author was discovered and his or her name became associated with the book in question – a process in which circulating libraries had a hand, as Vareschi (2012) has shown – it would be more the *idea* of that author rather than the living individual, and as such, another non-human agent. Vareschi generalizes on the role of the circulating library and the book in ways that almost evoke an ANT framework, because he highlights the connections that emerged between groups of people and things:

> As a medium for distributing texts, the circulating library is virtual and repetitive, more so than the bookshop. Selling a book entails acquiring private property, whereas renting a book involves many people in *the common enterprise of sequential possession*. Renting books carries with it the idea that books are interchangeable and exchangeable and thus function in the abstract both as commodities and as texts. Though the trade is of the material form of the book, the discrete book does not matter as much as its ability to be exchanged for another book, or [...] for other, variant editions. The distribution system contributes to the actual, physical book becoming a *virtual entity shared* among readers. (2012: 44; my emphases)

A book that people know has gone, and will continue to go, through several hands contributes to the creation of a sense of a shared social sphere; it establishes a link between the public availability of the object and the private realm of its consumption. Vareschi's notion of a "common enterprise of sequential possession" and the "virtual entity" that is "shared" can easily be understood in terms of links, ties, or associations between the people and artefacts involved in book-lending. Referring also to some other scholars who have emphasized the function of the circulating libraries to give their subscribers a feeling of belonging to an "imagined literary community", Vareschi sums up: "The circulating library, in effect, built a virtual literary public sharing a collection of texts and ideas that the library circulated" (ibid.: 45). The novel, with its focus on private lives that are turned public through the media genre itself, supported this circulation of ideas, which brought readers together also in a community of values.

Second, there were close ties between the production and the distribution of novels. Raven lists the four publishing houses that "boosted publication totals" and that later (in the last three decades of the century) dominated the market: "Thomas Hookham, the Robinsons, the Nobles (until 1789), and, from 1775, the newcomer and greatest novel manufacturer of all, William Lane" (2000: 73). Three of these enterprises (Hookham, the Nobles, and Lane) also ran circulating libraries. Thus, not all of the books they printed depended on the speculation whether a title would find a market; rather, these producers had parts of their own markets on the very premises. Although these markets did not absorb the entire production, since "400 out of every 1.000 copies of novels were sold to circulating libraries", as markets they were nevertheless "limited, but at least knowable" (ibid.: 93). Since the circulating libraries by Hookham and Lane were the largest two in London (Skelton-Foord 1999: 92), their potency should not be underestimated. Many people in the metropolis therefore met in a fairly homogeneous cultural context, where book-lending and the reception of reading material were part of a mood of social closeness and belonging.

The apparent dependability of the business model of the circulating library thirdly manifests itself in another practice by which producers of books tried to ensure further distribution. John Lane, who founded the Minerva press in the late eighteenth century and produced highly successful popular sentimental and gothic fiction, sold "complete, packaged circulating libraries to new entrepreneurs" (Erickson 1990: 582, Raven 2000: 85). This implies that by then some standardization of taste must have taken place. Much like in the case of modern franchise enterprises, no businessman would have opened up such a venture if they had not trusted in the existence of a considerable demand and at least the promise of a reliable market. And the producer Lane must have relied on knowing what the readership wanted.

Fourth, retail business in the eighteenth century in general became increasingly competitive, which led to the rise of advertizing. Many advertisements for circulating libraries, and the catalogues they published, feature engravings that display the rooms in which the books were kept, the shelves to be browsed and the volumes to be checked out.[19] As advertisements, they unsurprisingly tend to present rather idealized versions of the places, as some scholars have remarked (see Vareschi 2012: 28-30). One could compare this to the visual representation of modern restaurants or hotel websites on the internet: Once being confronted with the reality of a booked room or with a sophisticated dish, the premises hardly ever look exactly as splendid as the photo online did; the food on the plate in a restaurant never looks quite as tasty as the pictures that present the dishes on the venue's homepage. As advertisements, such images serve a twofold purpose. First and foremost, they present the actual space and what it has to offer in the best possible way, trying to evoke in the viewer a desire to go there. But another function is that they display both the atmosphere and the functional features of the place in a way that potential customers have an idea of the kind of place they might be visiting, and of how to behave – or, rather, perform – there. This was also

19 See the illustrations in Stewart-Murphy (1992), Raven (1996), Brewer (1997: 177-179), and Vareschi (2012).

the case with the ads for the circulating libraries: The illustrations usually depicted not only the rooms and the bookshelves, but also customers in the libraries, and their clothes would provide hints as to the social affiliation of the establishment's clientele. The advertisement thus served as another agent in the network that connected literature, style, and middle-class behaviour.

It was mentioned above that book-lending was intricately connected with a broader set of public practices the middle-classes performed, among which shopping was central (Barry 1991; Berry 2002),[20] partly because shops and libraries were public places, and partly because many circulating libraries were actually mixed businesses. A guide book on opening a circulating library from 1779 advises the entrepreneur to stock "Haberdashery, Hosiery, Hats, Tea, Tobacco and Snuffs; or Perfumery, and the sale of Patent medicines" in addition to books (qtd. in Skelton-Foord 1999: 109). Rural establishments also "often acted as ticket-selling agencies for operatic and theatrical productions in the capital" (ibid.: 107), and in seaside resorts, libraries also furnished articles that particularly the female customers desired, from trinkets and ornaments to luxury goods (see also Benson 1997). On the side of the entrepreneurs, such side lines of business may have been economically necessary in times when book-lending alone would not secure the proprietor a sufficient income.[21] On the side of the consumers, going out to get reading material was closely connected with other shopping pleasures. Such public consumption elicited a range of ambivalent emotions between desire and shame that I take to bestow the particular social quality on the circulating library and its associations and that are therefore worth exploring further.

Among the attractions that brought people to the circulating libraries was the public visibility of the practice of book-lending itself. When people went out to rent a book, they could count on being seen, and to find a stage on which they could perform polite behaviour and compare and be compared with others. This is particularly true for the establishments in spa towns. The resorts were generally regarded as the meeting places of the well-to do, as marriage markets for middle-class families willing their daughters to marry

---

20 See also Klein (2002: 882): "Consumption was an important domain for the actuation of politeness because the spread of consumerism was characterized not just by quantitative increases but by qualitative alterations in the processes and meanings of acquisition."

21 Incidentally, our contemporary bookshops have reverted to that practice of offering a rather mixed range of goods.

up the social scale, and as platforms for gossip of all kinds; the libraries provided a meeting opportunity for such purposes: "In the resorts the circulating libraries became fashionable daytime lounges where ladies could *see others and be seen*, where raffles were held and games were played, and where expensive merchandise could be purchased" (Erickson 1990: 576; my emphasis).[22] Skelton-Foord remarks: "Time and again in accounts of late eighteenth- and early nineteenth-century library history it is written that popular fiction was being 'read to pieces'. But fictional representations of the circulating library suggest, albeit satirically, that within library buildings themselves almost anything other than reading was taking place" (1999: 105). Erickson emphasizes just how public it was to be a circulating-library user: "Since it was the custom to subscribe to the libraries immediately upon arrival in the watering places and resorts, their subscription books became a useful guide to who was in town" (1990: 567). Skelton-Foord also argues that the subscription book, which "was a customary record of business kept by the librarian [...] could also serve, like a register of fashionable society, to inform curious subscribers as to whom [sic] else was visiting the resort that season" (1999: 106). Even if not seen in person in the rooms of the library at all times, that is, people would still be publicly 'there' in their roles as subscribers, and as members of a community of fellow patrons, forming an imagined community. The social impact of this institution was helped by the sheer size of some establishments. One report from Margate, the fashionable watering resort, dating from the 1790s, praises a newly built circulating library featuring "a noble room" that was "large enough to contain between three and four hundred people" (qtd. in Kaufman 1967: 20). Late in the century, it appears, entrepreneurs could rely on an impressive demand from customers to have access to circulating library buildings.

Another desire, beside that to be seen, must have resided in the pleasures of shopping itself, which were closely associated with the sphere of literature, as was demonstrated above. These pleasures were, however, quite generally

22 On the watering places, see also Langford (2010: 395): "Between fashionable society with its ritual divisions of the of the year and its court-orientated timetables, and the despised fairs and holidays of the lower sort, there was a considerable gap, a gap which the new resorts filled with immense success and profit. They were essentially middle-class, [...] the bourgeois equivalent to the aristocrat's retreat to country-house life. Their underlying basis was the generally felt need for distinctively middle-class recreations. The use of fees and subscriptions ensured respectable company and a decently moneyed atmosphere."

an ambivalent issue in the period, for consumption was fundamentally linked with guilt: The same period that championed a moral codex based on moderation, virtue and decency, which also fed into the concept of 'politeness', also saw the development of a culture of consumer good consumption and commodification, that was, in strictly moralist and religious terms, despicable or outright sinful. Nobody could deny that the cardinal sins of gluttony, greed, envy, and pride were dangerously close to the human motivations that make capitalism and consumer culture possible. The desire to possess things for their beauty rather than their necessity may have been considered frivolous, and the middle classes may have despised the aristocracy for their inclination towards luxury. But the many dressmakers, peruke-makers, milliners, hosiers, gold- and silversmiths, cabinet-makers, glass-blowers, potters, etc. who catered to the needs of the middle classes could not have thrived, had they not had customers both inclined and able to buy their wares.[23]

Another potential reason for a circulating-library user's guilty conscience was that guardians both of morality and literary quality looked down both upon the circulating library and the books they offered. According to Kaufman, the institution was regarded with some caution already when it first emerged: "As a new phenomenon it was automatically suspect" (1967: 23). The suspicion was perhaps due to the moral indignation about the other practices of public amusement practised there: "In fact, librarians organized a range of games and leisure pursuits in their establishments, including billiards, musical recitals, and balls, particularly in those libraries which were situated in large Assembly Rooms at fashionable resorts" (Skelton-Foord 1999: 108). This association of libraries with other amusements occurred not only in fact, it also affected the public perception of book lending. John and Francis Noble, who dominated the output of popular romance novels between the late 1730s and the late 1780s (see Raven 1990 and 2000: 74-75) were the victims of much moralising criticism, and were in the process lumped together with other activities that annoyed the moralizers: "Vilified as 'novel manufacturers' and hawkers of immoral and licentious literature, the Nobles were the literary equivalents of the managers of Ranelagh gardens or the masters of ceremonies at [...] spa resorts" (Raven 2000: 75). The reference to the Ranelagh pleasure gardens in Chelsea here is significant, because that place underwent

23 For a comprehensive discussion of the ambivalence between politeness and commerce in the development of modern English society in the eighteenth century, see Langford (1989); the issue is also discussed by Brewer (1995) and Klein (1995 and 2002).

a process of 'gentrification' like many other forms of public entertainment throughout the century. While pleasure gardens in the early decades of the eighteenth century were associated with excessive drink, prostitution and violence, and regarded as "dangerous, disreputable, and therefore unfashionable" (Brewer 1997: 65), later in the century Ranelagh was considered to be "a sober and respectable venue" (ibid.). It was the most expensive of the establishments of this kind in and around London, its price of 2 shillings and sixpence more than doubling that of the rivalling Vauxhall pleasure garden in Kensington (ibid.: 66). The pleasure gardens were usually called "Ranelagh Gardens" or "Vauxhall Gardens" only – i.e., with the significant omission of the word "pleasure", perhaps to tone down the inutility of what would certainly be considered their attraction by their visitors. They would attract paying customers with the presentation of picture galleries, artistic performances, fireworks, dancing and other musical presentations. At Ranelagh, "[a]n orchestra and organist played music while fashionable men and women promenaded round the floor" of the main hall, and an eight-year old Wolfgang Amadeus Mozart performed his feats on the piano and organ there in 1764 (ibid.). It is difficult to assert to what extent the reputation of lowliness persisted and clung to the institution, even though, as the century proceeded, the customers of such sites were recruited increasingly from higher social strata.

Perhaps to counter such cultural depreciation, advertisements from circulating libraries did not tire of emphasizing their adherence to highest standards of quality and virtue (Manley 2000: 36-37 and 39-42). As the 1759 catalogue from a library in Kendal formulates it: "Several Books of Entertainment lately Published of which this Catalogue in part consists, are enrich'd with beautiful Examples, which by Vice's Folly are expos'd and appear in their natural deformity: from Books of this kind may be reaped great Advantages, by impressing right Principles with respect to Virtue, good sense and Manners" (qtd. in Manley 2000: 37). To argue that reading about the vices of others turns a person into a virtuous one would be to argue that nowadays people watch crime movies for the sake of learning how not to turn criminal. While it may have caused some subscribers considerable embarrassment that the circulating library was an institution associated with 'low' forms of public amusement, others were above such qualms, at least towards the end to the century. In a letter to her sister Cassandra of 18th December 1798, Jane Austen famously wrote:

> I have received a very civil note from Mrs. Martin requesting my name as a Subscriber to her Library which opens the 14th of January, & my name, or rather Yours is accordingly given. My mother finds the Money. – Mary subscribes too, which I am glad of, but hardly expected. – As an inducement to subscribe, Mrs. Martin tells us that her Collection is not to consist only of Novels, but of every kind of literature, &c. &c. – She might have spared this pretension to *our* family, who are great Novel-readers and not ashamed of being so; – but it was necessary I suppose to the self-consequence of half her subscribers. (qtd. in Erickson 1990: 579; original emphasis)

The circulating library made the most recent fiction titles available, as well as classics, and it held many titles that were beyond all blame, generally offering a broad mixture that contained "good, bad, and indifferent" books, as many commentators had it in the late eighteenth century (Skelton-Foord 1999: 93). However, the negative judgment inherited from the early part of the period seems to have prevailed. Between the late seventeenth century and the middle of the eighteenth, the genre of prose fiction was predominantly associated with narratives of amorous intrigue, frequently translated from French or Italian, whose erotic appeal was deemed dangerous in particular to young female readers (Warner 1998) and the critical disdain for popular narratives also persisted in the second half of the century, as Taylor's early study (1943) shows. Female, young and uneducated readers were allegedly most susceptible to the lure of these novels, falling prey to confusing the unrealistic storyworlds of novels with their lived experience. It was against the backdrop of such widespread cultural vilification, as Warner (1998) argues, that writers like Henry Fielding and Samuel Richardson were able to create a morally elevated type of prose fiction. This suggests that towards mid-century, very different types of novels, linked to very different evaluations, coexisted on the British print market and on the shelves of the circulating libraries. The renting and reading of novels was thus a highly ambivalent social practice.

Public admittance of pursuing pleasures in a context that regards such pursuits as shameful requires strategies of justification: "Popular novel readers, insisting […] on the improving qualities of their occupation, usually constructed defensive explanations for novel consumption" (Raven 2000: 113). I believe that the circulating library was a place in which admittance and justification, desire and shame management coexisted very closely. From a pragmatic point of view, book-lending did offer readers an opportunity to check out new novels instead of, or before, buying them. Clients could thus save money instead of wasting it on books that might turn out not to correspond to their tastes. A late eighteenth-century catalogue for John Bell's London circulating Library advertizes this by saying: "To enable every reader to form a proper judgment of Books before he becomes a purchaser of them" (qtd. in Skelton-Foord 1998: 350). This is just in keeping with ideals of parsimonious housekeeping and moderation that were widespread at the time. However, one could also always justify a visit to the circulating library by merely *pretending* to choose from a range of books that might be worth buying, even if one went there precisely for the thrill of taking out and reading the 'wrong' ones, i.e., the books one never planned to purchase and display on the bookshelves at home.

Mr Collins' choice of an alternative reading diet in the scene from *Pride and Prejudice* scene quoted at the beginning of this chapter is telling with regard to the alignment of the circulating library with desire and shame: James Fordyce was the very man who, in his two-volume work *Sermons to Young Women* of 1766, had ranted at novels for women as "an infernal brood of futility and lewdness" and stipulated that "she who can bear to peruse them must in her soul be a prostitute" (167-177; qtd. in Benson 1997: 205). Mr Collins' choice appears to him as an antidote to the potential infection through the lending-library book from which he recoils. Kitty and Lydia, however, are aghast at being expected to feel ashamed for the borrowed book, which to them looks perfectly innocent, while to Collins it signifies illicit desire. The scene taking place roughly half a century after Fordyce's outburst, Austen's readers will have recognized how utterly out of date, unfashionable and unattractive – unsexy, in modern terms – this makes Mr Collins as a potential suitor to one of the Bennett daughters, to say nothing of the chauvinistic patronising his outrageously exaggerated reaction implies. Austen must have relied on the efficiency of this indirect characterization of the young clergyman.

A final important issue implied in this scene is that this duality of desire and shame is inherent in the material artefact of the book itself, which would then affect the perception of the novel as a genre. The fact that "everything announced it to be from a circulating library", leading Mr Collins to shy away from it instinctively, refers to the fact that library novels with their "marble covers, spine-labels, and book plates, declared very clearly their origins" (Skelton-Foord 1998: 352, see also Erickson 1990: 573). The artefact can easily be slotted in the (imaginary) cultural hierarchy. The "marble bindings" are cheap pasteboard covers with a marble pattern, and only the spine was covered in leather, in contrast to the expensive leather binding that would cover the entire board of a book considered valuable enough to deserve such luxury. The alignment of knowing what type of book one held in one's hands and evaluating it touches upon more than the book cover: "the popular novel was judged in terms of the quality of its material existence – the clarity of its printing, the size and style of type and ornaments, their composition and arrangement on the page, and other design issues, including wrapping and binding" (Raven 2000: 103). As an agent in the nexus between public performance of polite sociability and the circulating library, the book itself appears as an ambivalent agent.

4. Conclusion

In eighteenth-century England, the development of the novel and the development of a middle-class mentality were closely associated. While literary and cultural historians have discussed this connection intensively, a look at the actual practices through which people got hold of books adds a fresh perspective to that connection. Members of the middle classes positioned themselves increasingly as 'polite shoppers' in the public sphere in that period, and I have argued that this public appearance was embedded in a framework of mutual comparison, in which practices of consumption were checked with regard to their meeting ideals of politeness. The rental of books and book distribution through the circulating library was one of the of areas that invited the comparison of behaviour deemed adequate for the broad and diverse social group that came to be called the middle class. The guiding principle of politeness was the ground for comparison, i.e., the *tertium comparationis*, while the two compared items, the *primum comparandum* and the *secundum comparatum*, were the observed behaviours of two agents; the *primum comparandum* could also be the observed behaviour of only one agent, while the ideal of polite behaviour constituted the *secundum comparatum*. Politeness was a central issue in the development of the social structure, because it helped to diffuse the boundaries between the upper classes and the middle: "While it was certainly easier for the gentleman of lineage and land to be polite, the individual who lacked those criteria for gentility might achieve or enhance a claim to gentility through his or her politeness himself" (Klein 2002: 876). Importantly, as an ideal, politeness was an abstract value that needed concrete practical realisations, and public arenas for the display of behaviours that could be classified as meeting the requirements. I have shown that the circulating libraries, with the ambivalent associations with elevated culture and entertainment, fashion, consumption and sociability it carried, emerged as exemplary arenas for the comparative performance of behaviour that straddled the divide between the middle and the upper classes. The involvement of the novel in this emerging arena, not only as a literary genre but, in its printed form as a material artefact, calls for an approach that goes beyond both established literary history and literary sociology.

From the perspective of literary scholarship, the social history of the book, Actor Network Theory and the study of practices of comparing may not be the most obvious candidates for an integrated approach, since they come from different disciplinary backgrounds, are based on different meta-theoretical positions and conceptual frameworks, and do not merge easily with the hermeneutic tradition of literary analysis and interpretation. As is obvious, in this article I have not even tackled the role that the contents and narrative strategies of eighteenth-century English novels played in the developments described.[24] I have, however, tried to demonstrate that a literary-sociological perspective that is aware of the relevance of practices, material artefacts, bodies, and ideas, directs our attention to the links between them, which account for the emergence of 'the social'. In the spirit of Actor Network Theory, I have therefore tried to shed light *not* on how book consumption happened 'in' eighteenth-century middle-class society, but on how a network of ties and associations between human and non-human agents – the clients of the circulating libraries, the libraries as social spaces, and the books themselves – as well as the practices linked with them emerged in the period under consideration, brought middle-class literariness into existence, and shaped it in particular ways that were different from both previous and later developments.[25] As the observation of the changes in the period have shown, the circulating library and the novels it distributed made significant contributions to the emergence of a sphere in which the middle classes could increasingly

24 I do so elsewhere; see the contribution by Hartner/Schneider in this volume.

25 The nineteenth century saw a significant mainstreaming of the genre of the novel, of the institution of the circulating library, which became dominated by the two rivalling enterprises of Charles Edward Mudie and W. H. Smith, and of the material format of the novel, which was standardized into three volumes; at the same time, serial publication either in periodicals or individually sold installments, as well as one-volume cheaper reprints which became available at increasingly shorter distances from the first publication, multiplied the channels for the publication of fiction. For a concise survey of these developments, see Feather (1988: 129-179).

rely on all actors being interested in establishing standards of politeness and maintaining the matching behaviour.

Bibliography

Adams, Thomas R. and Nicolas Barker. "A New Model for the Study of the Book." *A Potencie for Life: Books in Society*. Ed. Nicolas Barker. London: British Library, 1993. 5-43.

Austen, Jane. *Pride and Prejudice*. Ed. Donald Gray. New York: Norton, 2001 [1813].

Barry, Jonathan. "Consumers' Passions: The Middle Class in Eighteenth-Century England." *Historical Journal* 34 (1991): 207-216.

Barry, Johnathan and Christopher Brooks, eds. *The Middling Sort of People: Culture, Society and Politics in England, 1550-1800*. London: Palgrave Macmillan, 1994.

Belanger, Terry. "Publishers and Writers in Eighteenth-Century England." *Books and their Readers in Eighteenth-Century England*. Ed. Isabel Rivers. Leicester: Leicester University Press & St. Martin's Press, 1982. 5-25.

Benedict, Barbara M. "Readers, Writers, Reviewers, and the Professionalization of Literature." *The Cambridge Companion to English Literature, 1740-1830*. Ed. Thomas Keymer and John Mee. Cambridge: Cambridge University Press, 2004. 3-23.

Benson, Mary Margaret. "Parasols & Gloves & Broches & Circulating Libraries." *Persuasions* 19 (1997): 205-210.

Bermingham, Ann. "Introduction. The Consumption of Culture: Image, Object, Text." *The Consumption of Culture, 1660-1800: Image, Object, Text*. Ed. Ann Bermingham and John Brewer. London: Routledge, 1995. 1-20.

Bermingham, Ann and John Brewer, eds. *The Consumption of Culture, 1660-1800: Image, Object, Text*. London: Routledge, 1995.

Berry, Helen. "Polite Consumption: Shopping in Eighteenth-Century England." *Transactions of the Royal Historical Society* 12 (2002): 375-394.

Brewer, John. "'The most polite age and the most vicious': Attitudes toward Culture as a Commodity, 1660-1800." *The Consumption of Culture, 1660-1800: Image, Object, Text*. Ed. Ann Bermingham and John Brewer. London: Routledge, 1995. 341-361.

Brewer, John. *The Pleasures of the Imagination: English Culture in the Eighteenth Century*. London: Harper Collins, 1997.

Carter, Philip. *Men and the Emergence of Polite Society: Britain 1660-1800*. London: Routledge, 2001.

Cheah, Peng. "Grounds of Comparison." *Grounds of Comparison: Around the Work of Benedict Anderson*. Ed. Jonathan Culler and Peng Cheah. London: Routledge, 2003. 1-20.

Colclough, Stephen. *Consuming Texts: Readers and Reading Communities, 1695-1870*. Houndmills: Palgrave Macmillan, 2007.

Corfield, Penelope J. "Class by Name and Number in Eighteenth-Century Britain." *Language, History, and Class*. Ed. Penelope J. Corfield. Oxford: Oxford University Press, 1991. 101-130.

Corfield, Penelope J. "The Rivals: Landed and Other Gentlemen." *Land and Society in Britain, 1700-1915: Essays in Honour of F.M.L. Thompson*. Ed. B. Harte and R. Quinault. Manchester: Manchester University Press, 1996. 1-31.

Davidoff, Leonore and Catherine Hall. *Family Fortunes: Men and Women of the English Middle Class, 1750-1850*. Chicago: University of Chicago Press, 1987.

Downie, J. A. "How Useful to Eighteenth-Century English Studies is the Paradigm of the 'Bourgeois Public Sphere'?" *Literature Compass* 1 (2003): 1-19.

Earle, Peter. *The Making of the English Middle Class: Business, Society and Family Life in London, 1660-1730*. London: Methuen, 1989.

Erickson, Lee. "The Economy of Novel Reading: Jane Austen and the Circulating Library." *Studies in English Literature, 1500-1900* 30.4 (1990): 573-590.

Feather, John. *A History of British Publishing*. London: Routledge, 1988.

Feather, John. "The Book Trade and Libraries." *The Cambridge History of Libraries in Britain and Ireland*. Ed. Giles Mandelbrote and K. A. Manley. Vol. 2: *1640-1850*. Cambridge: Cambridge University Press, 2006. 301-323.

Felski, Rita. *The Limits of Critique*. Chicago: Chicago University Press, 2015.

Felski, Rita and Susan Stanford Friedman. "Introduction." *Comparison: Theories, Approaches, Uses*. Ed. Rita Felski and Susan Stanford Friedman. Baltimore: Johns Hopkins University Press, 2013. 1-12.

Finkelstein, David and Alistair McCleery. *The Book History Reader*. 2nd ed. London: Routledge, 2006.

Garside, Peter, James Raven, and Rainer Schöwerling. *The English Novel 1770-1829: A Bibliographical Survey of Prose Fiction Published in the British Isles*. Vol. 1: *1770-1799*. Oxford: Oxford University Press, 2000.

Genette, Gérard. *Paratexts: The Thresholds of Interpretation*. Trans. Jane E. Lewin. Cambridge: Cambridge University Press, 1997.

Habermas, Jürgen. *The Structural Transformation of the Public Sphere: An Inquiry into a Category of Bourgeois Society*. Trans. Thomas Burger. Cambridge: MIT Press, 1989.

Hamlyn, Hilda M. "Eighteenth-Century Circulating Libraries in England." *The Library*, 5th Series, 1 (1946): 197-222.

Heintz, Bettina. "'Wir leben im Zeitalter der Vergleichung': Perspektiven einer Soziologie des Vergleichens." *Zeitschrift für Soziologie* 45.5 (2016): 305-323.

Hume, Robert D. "The Economics of Culture in London, 1660-1740." *Huntingdon Library Quarterly* 69.4 (2006): 487-533.

Hunt, Margaret R. *The Middling Sort: Commerce, Gender, and the Family in England, 1680-1780*. Berkeley: University of California Press, 1996.

Hunter, J. Paul. *Before Novels: The Cultural Contexts of Eighteenth-Century English Fiction*. New York: W. W. Norton, 1990.

Hunter, J. Paul. "The Novel and Social/Cultural History." *Cambridge Companion to the Eighteenth-Century Novel*. Ed. John Richetti. Cambridge: Cambridge University Press, 1996. 9-40.

Jacobs, Edward. "Anonymous Signatures: Circulating Libraries, Conventionality, and the Production of Gothic Romances." *ELH* 62.3 (1995): 603-629.

Jacobs, Edward. "Eighteenth-Century British Circulating Libraries and Cultural Book History." *Book History* 6 (2003): 1-22.

Jacobs, Edward. "Circulating Libraries." *The Oxford Encyclopedia of British Literature*. Vol. 2. Ed. David Scott Kastan. Oxford: Oxford University Press, 2006. 5-10.

Kaufman, Paul. "The Community Library: A Chapter in English Social History." *Transactions of the American Philosophical Society* (new series) 57.7 (1967): 2-67.

Klein, Lawrence E. "Politeness for the Plebes: Consumption and Social Identity in early Eighteenth-Century England." *The Consumption of Culture, 1660-1800: Image, Object, Text*. Ed Ann Bermingham and John Brewer. London: Routledge, 1995. 362-382.

Klein, Lawrence E. "Politeness and the Interpretation of the British Eighteenth Century." *The Historical Journal* 45.4 (2002): 869-898.

Langford, Paul. *A Polite and Commercial People: England 1727-1783*. Oxford: Clarendon Press, 1989.

Langford, Paul. "The Eighteenth Century, 1688-1789." *The Oxford History of Britain*. Ed. Kenneth O. Morgan. Updated edition. Oxford: Oxford University Press, 2010. 390-469.

Latour, Bruno. "On Actor-Network Theory: A Few Clarifications." *Soziale Welt* 47.4 (1996): 369-381.

Latour, Bruno. "On Recalling ANT." *Actor Network Theory and After*. Ed. John Law and John Hassard. Oxford: Blackwell and the Sociological Review, 1999. 15-25.

Latour, Bruno. *Reassembling the Social: An Introduction to Actor-Network Theory*. Oxford: Oxford University Press, 2005.

Luhmann, Niklas. "The Differentiation of Society." Trans. Stephen Holmes and Charles Lamore. *Canadian Journal of Sociology* 2.1 (1977): 29-53.

Manley, K. A. "Booksellers, Peruke-Makers, and Rabbit-Merchants: The Growth of Circulating Libraries in the Eighteenth Century." *Libraries and the Book Trade*. Ed. Robyn Myers, Michael Harris, and Giles Mandelbrote. Newcastle: Oak Knoll Press, 2000. 29-50.

McKendrick, Neil, John Brewer, and J.H. Plumb. *The Birth of a Consumer Society: The Commercialisation of Eighteenth-Century England*. Bloomington: Indiana University Press, 1982.

McKenzie, D. F. *Bibliography and the Sociology of Texts*. London: The British Library, 1986.

McKeon, Michael. *The Origins of the English Novel, 1600-1740*. Baltimore: Johns Hopkins University Press, 2002 [1987].

McKeon, Michael. *The Secret History of Domesticity: Public, Private, and the Division of Knowledge*. Baltimore: Johns Hopkins University Press, 2006.

McKillop, Alan. "English Circulating Libraries, 1725-1750." *The Library*, 4th Series, 14 (1934): 477-485.

Morse, David. *The Age of Virtue: British Culture from the Restoration to Romanticism*. Houndmills: Palgrave Macmillan, 2000.

Nunn, Joan. *Fashion in Costume, 1200-2000*. 2nd ed. Chicago: New Amsterdam Books, 2000.

Parsons, Talcott. *Politics and Social Structure*. New York: Free Press, 1969.

Pennell, Sara. "Consumption and Consumerism in Early Modern England." *Historical Journal* 42.4 (1999): 549-564.

Porter, Roy. *English Society in the Eighteenth Century*. 2nd ed. Harmondsworth: Penguin. 1991.

Raven, James. "The Noble Brothers and Popular Publishing." *The Library*, 6th Series, 12 (1990): 293-345.

Raven, James. "From Promotion to Proscription: Arrangements for Reading and Eighteenth-Century Libraries." *The Practice and Representation of Read-*

ing in England. Ed. James Raven, Helen Small, and Naomi Tadmor. Cambridge: Cambridge University Press, 1996. 175-201.

Raven, James. "Historical Introduction: The Novel Comes of Age." *The English Novel 1770-1829: A Bibliographical Survey of Prose Fiction Published in the British Isles*. Vol. 1: *1770-1799*. Ed. James Raven and Antonia Fraser. Oxford: Oxford University Press, 2000. 15-121.

Raven, James. "Libraries for Sociability: The Advance of the Subscription Library." *The Cambridge History of Libraries in Britain and Ireland*. Vol. 2: *1640-1850*. Ed. Giles Mandelbrote and K. A. Manley. Cambridge: Cambridge University Press, 2006. 241-263.

Raven, James. "The Book as a Commodity." *The Cambridge History of the Book in Britain*. Ed. Michael F. Suarez and Michael L. Turner. Vol. 5. Cambridge: Cambridge University Press, 2009. 85-117.

Raven, James. *What is the History of the Book?* Cambridge: Polity Press. 2018.

Ribeiro, Aileen. *Dress in Eighteenth-Century Europe, 1715-1798*. Rev. ed. New Haven: Yale University Press, 2002.

Rivers, Isabel, ed. *Books and their Readers in Eighteenth-Century England*. Leicester: Leicester University Press & St. Martin's Press, 1982.

Skelton-Foord, Christopher. "To Buy or to Borrow? Circulating Libraries and Novel Reading in Britain, 1778-1828." *Library Review* 47.7 (1998): 348-354.

Skelton-Foord, Christopher. "Surveying the Circulating Library Scene: Popular British Fiction, 1770-1830." *Bibliotheken in der literarischen Darstellung: Libraries in Literature*. Ed. Peter Vodosek and Graham Jefcoate. Wiesbaden: Harrassowitz, 1999. 89-113.

Slack, Paul. *The Invention of Improvement: Information and Material Progress in Seventeenth-Century England*. Oxford: Oxford University Press, 2015.

Smail, John. *The Origins of Middle-Class Culture: Halifax, Yorkshire, 1660-1780*. Ithaca: Cornell University Press, 1994.

Spurr, John. "England 1649-1740: Differences Contained?" *The Cambridge Companion to English Literature 1650-1740*. Ed. Steven N. Zwicker. Cambridge: Cambridge University Press, 1998. 3-32.

Stein, Jordan Alexander. *When Novels Were Books*. Cambridge: Harvard University Press, 2020.

Stewart-Murphy, Charlotte. *A History of British Circulating Libraries: The Book Labels and Ephemera of the Papantonio Collection*. Newton: Bird and Bull Press, 1992.

Styles, John. *The Dress of the People: Everyday Fashion in Eighteenth-Century England*. New Haven: Yale University Press, 2007.

Tadmor, Naomi. "'In the even my wife read to me': Women, Reading and Household Life in the Eighteenth Century." *The Practice and Representation of Reading in England*. Ed. James Raven, Helen Small, and Naomi Tadmor. Cambridge: Cambridge University Press, 1996. 162-174.

Taylor, John Tinnon. *Early Opposition to the English Novel: The Popular Reaction from 1760-1830*. New York: King's Crown, 1943.

Vareschi, Mark. "Attribution and Repetition: The Case of Defoe and the Circulating Library." *Eighteenth-Century Life* 36.2 (2012): 36-59.

Wahrman, Dror. *Imagining the Middle Class: The Political Representation of Class in Britain, c.1780-1840*. Cambridge: Cambridge University Press, 1995.

Warner, William. *Licensing Entertainment: The Elevation of Novel Reading in Britain, 1684-1750*. Berkeley: University of California Press, 1998.

Watt, Ian. *The Rise of the Novel: Studies in Defoe, Richardson and Fielding*. London. Chatto & Windus, 1957.

Williams, Abigail. *The Social Life of Books: Reading Together in the Eighteenth-Century Home*. New Haven: Yale University Press, 2017.

Comparing Conduct: English Novels of the Long Eighteenth Century and the Formation of Ideals of Social Behaviour

Marcus Hartner & Ralf Schneider

1. Introduction

Literary studies are in many ways a comparative practice. Scholars compare different texts and authors, they compare genres and literary figures, and they compare motifs, stylistic devices and national literatures, to name only a few of the most obvious examples. In the works of literary scholars, in other words, "comparisons are everywhere" (Erhart 2020: 111). However, despite such widespread academic practices of comparing, comparatively little attention has been devoted to the staging of comparisons in literary works themselves. Some aspects, as, for instance, the inherently comparative nature of stylistic devices such as the metaphor, have been thoroughly investigated. Yet, the various ways in which comparisons are deliberately enacted in literary works of all genres, i.e., the question in how far comparative practices play a constitutive role in literary texts themselves, remains profoundly understudied.

In this context, our article aims at making a contribution to the nascent field of research on literary practices of comparing.[1] Taking our cue from historical narratology and the recent surge of academic interest in comparative practices in the humanities, we turn to British novels from the long eighteenth century and argue that comparisons specifically revolving around ideas of social and moral behaviour constitute an integral component of narrative fiction

1 On the study of (literary) practices of comparing, see Erhart (2020), Kramer et al. (2020), and the introduction to this volume.

in this period. While aspects of comparison can be relevant on different analytical levels, we are primarily interested in the ways texts 'compare' their literary figures. Put differently, our focus is on narrative practices that perform and/or induce comparisons specifically between fictional characters.[2] For this purpose, we examine novels from Defoe to Inchbald and Edgeworth and show that those texts often do not (primarily) stage comparisons in a direct, explicitly articulated way. They rather tend to rely on various indirect strategies that prompt the reader to perform multi-layered comparisons him- or herself.

Moreover, we show that the eighteenth-century novel and its indirect strategies of figural comparing, by and large, display a general preoccupation with questions regarding social norms and behaviour. The genre of the novel, which emerges as the dominant literary medium over the course of the eighteenth century, makes use of practices of comparing that have their roots in the social dynamics of that time. Grounded in the changing social structure of the period, especially the emerging middle-classes' need for guidance in questions of morality and social life, novels practice acts of comparing in their own particular, literary ways.[3] In this fashion, we argue, they make an important contribution to the historical formation of the emerging ideal of a morally superior middle class.

2. Social Comparing in Edgeworth's *Belinda* (1801)

We begin our discussion by turning to Maria Edgeworth's *Belinda* as a general introductory example for the complex strategies of comparing social conduct found in much of the period's narrative fiction. In the novel the reader encounters a failed anthropological experiment that is both the result and the

2 For the discussion of other forms of comparison in literature, see again Erhart (2020) as well as Schneider (2017).

3 Applications of the term "class" in discussions of eighteenth-century social structure come with conceptual problems and are seen by some as anachronistic. For introductions to the term and concept of class in early modern Britain, see Corfield (1987) and Cannadine (2000: 27, 31). In this article, we use the plural 'middle-classes' as a way of acknowledging that no such thing as a monolithic 'middle class' existed in the period. The term rather refers to a broad and changing spectrum of social groupings. Historically, the language of social differentiation remained contentious well into the nineteenth century (Crossick 1991).

cause of different comparative acts. As the story of *Belinda* unfolds, the eponymous heroine's suitor Clarence Hervey is revealed to have a "secret attachment" (*Belinda* 136) to a young woman, Virginia St. Pierre, whom he keeps in seclusion in a house in Windsor. It turns out that years before the events portrayed in the story, Clarence had returned from a trip to pre-revolutionary France appalled by the licentious behaviour of French women and determined to find himself a wife of different moral disposition. When soon afterwards he encounters a beautiful, innocent young girl called Rachel while riding in the New Forest, he decides to take matters into his own hands. He forms the plan of raising the girl to be his future wife. He renames Rachel, who had been kept in almost perfect isolation from the world by her grandmother, after the heroine of Jacques-Henri Bernardine de Saint-Pierre's romance *Paul et Virginie* (1788) and ensures that she is brought up in continued seclusion from the putatively corrupting influences of (polite) society.

Unsurprisingly, the experiment of creating an ideal female in the image of Rousseau's educational ideals fails. It turns into an illustration of "the long-term effects" of a general lack of social intercourse coupled with "a purely supervised education" (Gustafson 2017: 660). The novel presents the seventeen-year-old Virginia as a parody of the innocent heroine of sensibility: "a soft sighing, dying damsel who puts bullfinches in her bosom" (*Belinda* 415) and whose natural beauty and affectionate nature come at the expense of a childish and overly excited imagination and a profound lack of brains (see Gonda 1996: 216). After having done everything to shield Virginia from the world, Clarence eventually realizes that it is precisely this lack of social experience that has prevented Virginia from becoming a suitable spouse:

> In comparison with Belinda, Virginia appeared to him but an insipid, though innocent child: the one he found was his equal, the other his inferior; the one he saw could be a companion, a friend to him for life, the other would merely be his pupil, or his plaything. Belinda had cultivated taste, an active understanding, a knowledge of literature, the power and the habit of conducting herself; Virginia was ignorant and indolent, she had few ideas, and no wish to extend her knowledge; she was so entirely unacquainted with the world, that it was absolutely impossible she could conduct herself with that discretion, which must be the combined result of reasoning and experience. (*Belinda* 345-346)

While Hervey is still touched by Virginia's innocence, it is Belinda's prudence, her "conduct" and "discretion" he begins to admire. Comparing the social skills of both women Clarence is not only forced to re-evaluate his ideas about the benefits of a sentimental education, but he cannot help becoming "every day more wisely and fondly attached to Belinda" (346) and finally has to admit that "[n]othing could be more absurd than my scheme of educating a woman in solitude to make her fit for society" (432). Published at the end of the period under consideration here, this statement can also be read as an acknowledgement of the importance of the social sphere for the development of an individual.

In general, the Virginia-subplot in Edgeworth's novel serves several functions. In terms of plot, Virginia is one of the obstacles that need to be overcome for the romance to reach its happy conclusion in the prospective marriage of Belinda and Clarence. On a more philosophical level, the failed experiment is a condemnation of both Rousseau's educational philosophy (Kowaleski-Wallace 1991: 100) and the type of romance fiction represented by Saint-Pierre's *Paul et Virginie*.[4] Most importantly in the context of this chapter, however, the example illustrates a key compositional feature of the novel's narrative design: the central role comparisons play in the text's literary negotiation and didactic evaluation of contemporary norms and values of social behaviour. Clarence does not recognize the extent of Virginia's deficiencies until he begins to explicitly compare her to Belinda. Moreover, we find various other literary figures in the text also engaging in acts of social comparing. Characters compare their lovers and suitors, they compare themselves to other characters, and on occasion even engage in reflections of their own comparative practices. The novel's heroine Belinda, for example, is troubled by her own inclination to compare the qualities of her suitors with each other. "And yet," she concludes, "how are we to judge of character? How can we form any estimate of what is amiable, of what will make us happy or miserable, but by comparison?" (*Belinda* 217).

Belinda's acknowledgement of the necessity to compare touches upon a key aspect of the text. Explicitly labelled a "Moral Tale", Edgeworth's novel revolves around the question of how to judge moral character. *Belinda*, Linda Bree argues, was deliberately intended by Edgeworth to promote the discussion of "the principles of morality" (2020: xxvi). For this purpose, the text

---

4 Virginia's 'faulty' education is also signalled by her reading practices which "echo turn-of-the-century anxieties about novel reading; as soon as she learns to read, she becomes a model of the dangerously susceptible female reader" with an insatiable appetite for romance fiction (Britton 2013: 439-440).

creates a diverse set of literary characters embodying different virtues and vices; it then makes not only the protagonists but also the reader navigate the emerging tableau of human behaviour by constantly comparing those different characters with each other in both explicit and implicit ways. Inner-textual practices of comparing are thus complemented by extra-textual appeals to the readers' capacity for comparing behaviour and dispositions.

Critics have pointed out that the characters of Edgeworth's *Belinda* constitute a rather exaggerated "assortment of natural oddities" (Chalk 2014: 133). However, we believe that despite the novel's eccentric collection of characters, its structural narrative reliance on practices of comparing is neither particularly eccentric nor unusual for the literary fiction of its time. In the following section of our chapter, we will examine different novels in order to illustrate this claim. Moreover, we will suggest a heuristic distinction between two basic modes of comparing in narrative: 'direct' vs. 'indirect' comparisons.

3. Modes of Comparing in the Eighteenth-Century English Novel

We have suggested above that in both literature and literary studies comparisons are ubiquitous. Readers, for example, "constantly compare different heroes and different actions, different fictions and different reading experiences" (Erhart 2020: 114). Moreover, scholars have argued that the recipient's emotional investment in literary fiction may be (at least partially) based on the formation of analogies between the individual reader and certain aspects of the persona of one or several fictional characters. "In reading", Fluck (2013: 59) argues, "we establish analogies to those aspects that fit into our own narrative of identity or are especially meaningful or moving from the perspective of this narrative."

Yet, comparisons not only emerge in the intertextual space between different literary works or from acts of comparing that relate fictional worlds to readers' own personal experiences. They also play an important role on the level of the individual narrative; here texts can actively work to trigger or invite comparisons between different aspects or components of their fictional worlds. While such invitations take various forms, we can differentiate heuristically between two basic modes of narrative comparing in a way roughly analogous to the classical narratological differentiation between telling vs. showing.[5] First, comparisons can be enacted explicitly and directly, i.e., by mentioning at least *two comparata* (*primum comparandum* and *secundum comparatum*) or both these *comparata* and the *tertium comparationis*.[6] Much more frequently, however, comparing in narrative is done more indirectly, namely when there are no linguistic markers explicitly signalling an act of comparing, but the context makes it clear that two (or more) items are supposed to be compared to one another. While the former are more obvious and thus easier to analyze, the latter practices of comparing are in many ways more interesting for literary scholarship, as they are based on a complex semantic interplay between the producers and recipients of texts about the theme and evaluation of the comparison: the positioning of *comparata* in a novel without the explicit naming of the *tertium* can be understood as an offer by the text – and thus, by extension, the author – that is realized by readers if they see the comparability. Therefore, the more implied the comparison is, the greater must be the shared understanding between (implied) authors and readers.[7]

---

5 For an overview on the distinction of "telling" vs. "showing" and its controversial debate, see Klauk/Köppe (2014). Furthermore, our distinction between direct and indirect practices of comparing is deliberately heuristic in nature and does not do justice to the full complexity of comparative practices in literature.

6 For a more detailed account of the theory and terminology of comparing, see the introduction to this volume.

7 In our discussion of figural comparisons, we use the notion of 'narrative practices of comparing' as an emphatically *heuristic* concept that refers both to a text/author's strategic offer to the reader to establish a comparison *and* the realisation of the offer made by the reader. While naturally not every reader will follow every invitation to compare, narratives can foreground the relationship between literary figures in structural and stylistic ways, thus, making it more likely that readers will follow the cues to compare provided by the text/author (see discussion below for examples). On the general (cognitive) reception processes underlying those assumptions, see Schneider (2000) and Strasen (2008). For pragmatic reasons we do neither engage with the specifics of literary communication and reception processes nor the inherent complexity of the categories of "text", "reader", and "author" in this article. For a general introduction to and survey of the academic study of characters in fictional worlds, see Eder/Jannidis/Schneider (2010). An influential cognitive theory that conceives of processes of mental comparison ("cross-space mapping") as an integral part of meaning making in general has been proposed by Fauconnier/Turner (2002).

3.1 Direct Comparisons

As the example of *Belinda* above has shown, comparing in literature can take place on the inner-textual level of speakers: characters in novels, as well as narrators, can directly compare virtually anyone or anything that is important in the fictional world with anyone or anything else. Readers can follow suit and mentally perform the comparison. Such direct comparisons frequently occur in the eighteenth-century novel in connection with the growing class consciousness of the bourgeoisie. A classic instance of this kind of direct comparison between the classes can be found at the very beginning of Daniel Defoe's *The Life and Adventures of Robinson Crusoe* (1719). Here, Robinson's father, having been confronted with his son's plans to go to sea, exhorts Robinson to stay where providence has put him, by comparing and contrasting the middle station of life with those above and below:

> He told me it was for Men of desperate Fortunes on one Hand, or of aspiring, superior Fortunes on the other, who went abroad upon Adventures, to rise by Enterprize, and make themselves famous in Undertakings of a Nature out of the common road; that these things were all either too far above me, or too far below me; that mine was the middle State, or what might be called the upper Station of *Low Life*, which he had found by long Experience was the best State in the World, the most suited to human Happiness, most exposed to the Miseries and Hardships, the Labour and Sufferings of the mechanick Part of Mankind, and not embarrass'd with the Pride, Luxury, Ambition and Envy of the Upper Part of Mankind. (1994 [1719]: 4-5)

Robinson's father still has in mind a static model of a predestined social structure that echoes classical models and stands in contrast to the notions of social mobility and self-optimisation that would characterize later eighteenth-century society. Yet, the tendency to regard social distinctions with the help of a model of vertical stratification, as well as the middle-class contentedness with being placed in the 'best' social stratum, set the tone for much eighteenth-century writing about social classes. In this example, the three classes serve as the *comparata*, and the presence or lack of circumstances conducive to happiness as the *tertium*.

The passage from Defoe's novel is, however, a rare case of very explicit social comparing by way of discussing abstract social distinctions. More often, explicitly articulated comparisons, such as in the example from *Belinda* above, relate specific characters and/or their actions in the story with each other. In addition to such direct strategies, in which comparisons are voiced by narrators or characters, texts can work by making structural offerings to the reader. This type of comparing is by nature indirect.

3.2 Indirect Comparisons

While indirect comparisons again exist in many forms, one of the most common ways of indirect structural comparing in novels emerges from a text's constellation of characters. Classical drama analysis has long been aware of the inherently comparative aspect of presenting an arrangement of different characters (on the stage), and seminal theoretical works have drawn attention to the relations of contrasts and correspondences between the *dramatis personae* of a given work (see Pfister 1988 [1977]: 163-176). Similarly, in narrative fiction comparisons are frequently triggered by constellations of characters or perspectives that foreground aspects of similarity and difference.[8] For example, two or more literary figures can be portrayed as similar in some respects, such as age, gender, or class, but different in others, as for instance attitudes and behaviour. To see a character act in a particular way in a given situation, and then observe a different character who shares a number of traits with the first behave differently in a similar or perhaps even the same situation, initiates a comparison that draws attention to the reasons behind their respective behaviours and serves to characterize their fictional personalities. In this case, the two characters are the *comparata*, whereas the way in which they act is the *tertium comparationis*.

A good example of this kind of comparison can be found in an episode of Tobias Smollett's *The Expedition of Humphry Clinker* (1771) in which the old squire Matthew Bramble and his family travel to the city of Bath 'to take the waters'. Having arrived at the famous resort, Bramble and his young niece Lydia react in fundamentally different ways to the people they encounter and the places they visit. While Bramble is appalled by virtually every aspect of fashionable life in the city, especially by what he considers the inappropriate mixing of people from different social ranks, Lydia is delighted by this kind of unceremonious behaviour. For her, Bath is an "earthly paradise" filled with

8 Pfister defines the identity of a (dramatic) figure from a structuralist point of view as "the sum of the contrasts and correspondences linking it with the other figures in the text" (1988 [1977]: 163). On the application of Pfister's theory to character constellations in fiction, see Nünning (2001).

music and entertainment. And she is fascinated by the unconventional intermingling of people from different social backgrounds in the pump rooms (*Humphry Clinker* 68). By contrasting their different assessments of city and resort, the text thus not only invites the reader to compare the personalities and age of both characters but also to relate their points of view to different contemporary ideas about propriety and decorum.

While this comparison in Smollett's novel is triggered by a form of narrative multiperspectivity in which the same 'object' is viewed from different (character) perspectives (see Hartner 2008: 182-187),[9] a similar comparative effect can emerge from the presentation of action sequences or plot structures that share recognisable features. The relationship between comparable plot elements can be one of contiguity, i.e., it can emerge from the appearance of these elements in either spatial or temporal vicinity, as in the case of the picaresque novel. Here, the protagonist is usually placed in successive situations that are comparable, for example, in terms of the hero's capacity for suffering.[10] In general, however, structural analogies between successive parts of a story can emerge whenever novels present different characters acting differently in comparable situations or uttering different opinions about the same issue. Depending on how strongly marked or foregrounded these analogies are by the narrative, they invite readers to compare the attitudes and habits of the figures in ways that range from the blatantly obvious to the intellectually encoded. Yet, many eighteenth-century novels feature implicit comparisons so deeply ingrained into the basic structure of the narrative that we contend that it is virtually impossible for the recipient not to start comparing the respective characters during the reading process.

A case in point is the relationship between Tom Jones and Master Blifil from Henry Fielding's *The History of Tom Jones, a Foundling* (1749). Cast as boyhood companions and rivals – Tom being Squire Allworthy's ward, the

---

9 On multiperspectivity in literature in general, see also Hartner (2014).

10 See Guillén (1971), on the "loosely episodic" (84) form of the picaresque novel which is generally characterized by "recurrent motifs, circular patterns, and incremental processes" (85). According to Ehland (2003), a central aspect of the situation of the *picaro* is the dilemma that the protagonist's acceptance into society requires the sacrifice of his moral identity – a dilemma that structurally "*materialises in a repeated change of place which generates not only new spatial settings but also new human environments*" (65, original emphasis). The genre thus structurally invites comparisons between those different human environments and the protagonist's corresponding actions and strategies of survival.

other boy the Squire's nephew – they are frequently placed in comparable circumstances. Blifil's meanness and small-mindedness stand out as particularly negative in comparison with Tom's generosity and warm-heartedness, forming a central theme of the narrative. When Allworthy falls ill and is thought to be dying, Tom's only concern is his mentor's health, while Blifil is more interested in the inheritance promised by his uncle, his demonstrations of sorrow notwithstanding. The narrator's comments leave no doubt throughout the novel that the reader is supposed to compare the dispositions and actions of the two young men. One chapter in the work's third book is even entitled "Chapter 10 – In which Master Blifil and Jones appear in different lights" (116-118). In spite of Tom's naivety and his frequently rash behaviour, the evaluation of Tom as the morally superior of the two is driven home eventually when his real parentage is revealed and the narrative closure rewards Tom's honesty with an inheritance and increased social status. In fact, the whole panorama of characters in Fielding's novel can be grouped into a virtuous and a villainous cluster, respectively. Lead by Master Blifil, the villainous group containing Mr Square, Reverend Thwackum and Lord Fellamar among others,[11] is characterized mainly by hypocrisy and falseness, but also by coldness towards or abuse of their wives. In the good group are honest and charitable men, such as Tom himself and Squire Allworthy, as well as the virtuous woman Sophia Western.

Beyond portraying characters in places or situations that are arranged to trigger comparing, some novels go one step further and present structural analogies between entire plotlines. Again, we consider it practically impossible not to compare what happens to the characters in such cases. A striking example is Elizabeth Inchbald's *A Simple Story* (1791), which is neatly divided into two parts, consisting of two 'books' each, which present plotlines of a strikingly analogous nature.[12] In the first two books, the reader is confronted with the story of a young lady, Miss Milner, who is entrusted to the care of a Mr Dorriforth after her father's death. Pleasure-loving and obstinate, Miss Milner revolts continuously against the constraints society has imposed upon women by disobeying Dorriforth's rigid orders and rules. Despite her behaviour, however, Dorriforth and Miss Milner are later united in a tempestuous marriage, after the priest Dorriforth has renounced his priesthood upon inheriting a

11 The characters Lady Bellaston, Mr Nightingale and Fitzpatrick also belong to this group.

12 Mergenthal (1997: 146-151) elaborates on the structural analogies in this novel.

title. In the second half of the novel, after a time-lapse of seventeen years, the reader is presented with the life of Matilda, the daughter of Dorriforth (now Lord Elmwood) and Miss Milner, who is dead by the time the third book begins. Here the reader learns that Miss Milner committed adultery after her daughter's birth and was abandoned by her husband. In contrast to her mother, however, Matilda manages to win Dorriforth's love through utter submissiveness and obedience. The reader here finds two consecutive development plots with different outcomes which are obviously meant to be compared. Miss Milner's actions and attitudes, extremely unconventional in the context of the norms of female behaviour at the time, are contrasted to those of her daughter Matilda, whose personality is much more adapted to social expectations. In other words, the two women are the *comparata*, the *tertium* is a standard of female behaviour that is not explicitly verbalized in the novel but emerges from both Dorriforth's orders and prohibitions and from the fact that Miss Milner is punished for trespassing them. The emerging comparison, however, does not result in a simple, antithetical juxtaposition of Miss Milner and Matilda, as the daughter unites some of the aspects of both her parents (see Mergenthal 1997: 151). This hints at the overall estimation that all extremes of behaviour and opinion, those of the mother and the father, are deemed destructive.

The novels discussed so far all feature comparisons revolving around questions of social norms and values. They illustrate by way of example that many eighteenth-century works of fiction are preoccupied with aspects of social comparing. This preoccupation, we will argue in the following, emerges from a broader social concern with questions of morality, conduct and social status that play an essential role in various forms of public discourse during the period. Before continuing our discussion of comparative practices in eighteenth-century fiction, we therefore take a closer look at the changing social structures, especially the so-called rise of the middle classes, that shape manifestations of social comparing in literature and beyond in this period.

4. Social Comparing and Historical Change in Eighteenth-Century England

Social, cultural and literary historians of the long eighteenth century have long ascertained an essential link between the development of the middle classes as the culturally dominant group in modern English society on the one hand, and the development of the novel as a distinct literary medium on the fast-growing market for printed material, on the other.[13] In this context, scholars have drawn attention to the importance of various historical factors such as the financial and agrarian revolution, the emergence of consumer capitalism as the predominant life-style of large parts of the population,[14] and developments in the publishing industry (for example, the lapse of the Licensing Act in 1694), which contributed to a veritable explosion of the print market.[15]

This explosion, in which periodicals and novels joined forces in discussing matters of current social issues primarily for an emerging middle-class readership, forms a particularly important background to our discussion of comparative practices. It coincides with the emergence of a cultural discourse that promoted the idea of the middle-classes, or the 'middle order', as a social group possessing a distinct and superior (moral) quality. Building on the notion of a "virtuous social middle" (Wahrman 1995: 64) initially developed in Aristotle's *Politics*,[16] this discourse engaged in the construction of the idea of the middle classes as a distinct social group distinguished by its political, economic importance for the British nation, on the one hand, and by its superior moral qualities, on the other.

David Hume famously attempted to provide a philosophical foundation for this belief. He argued that the upper classes are too immersed in the pursuit of pleasure to heed the voices of reason and morality, while "the Poor"

---

13 These notions were proposed already in the late 1950s and early 1960s by scholars such as Watt (1957) and Habermas ([1962] 1989). Among the landmark contributions to the history of the early English novel in its socio-cultural context after Watt are the studies by Davis (1983), McKeon (2002 [1987]), and Hunter (1990); they start from fairly different theoretical premises and put different emphases on the factors for the rise of the novel. For a short summary of perspectives after Watt and Habermas, see also Cowan (2016).

14 On the importance of the Consumer Revolution, see McKendrick/Brewer/Plumb (1982), and Berg (1999; 2005). For further studies on the history of the period, see Porter (1982), McKendrick (1982), Earle (1989), Langford/Harvie (1992), Weatherill (1993), Haan/Niedhart (2002), and Beck (2003). These studies explore the changes we can summarize only sketchily here. Rogers (2016) presents a concise survey of the factors with regard to their relevance for the emergence of the novel.

15 See Feather (2006: 67-125 and 2016) as well as Hinds (2016) and Suarez (2016) for accounts of the publishing industry in the long eighteenth century.

16 See Aristotle (1984: IV.11).

find themselves entirely caught up in the daily struggle for survival and therefore have "little Opportunity of exerting any other Virtue, besides those of Patience, Resignation, Industry and Integrity" (1964 [1742]: 376). As a result, in his opinion, "the middle Station of Life [...] is more favourable to the acquiring of *Wisdom* and *Ability*, as well as of *Virtue*" (377) than any other class. "[A] man so situate[d] has a better Chance for attaining a Knowledge both of Men and Things, than those of a more elevated Station" because the middle class provides the best opportunities for the exercise of virtuous behaviour (ibid.). In Hume's opinion it exposes its members to a wider and more complex range of social life and thus forces them to develop greater moral sensitivity and power of judgement (376-377).

The idea of "the middle order of mankind" as a social sphere of particular quality, which we have already encountered in Defoe's *Robinson Crusoe* (see above), was neither entirely new nor universally acknowledged in the eighteenth century.[17] However, it provided a controversial but attractive conceptual means of ideological self-fashioning for those who saw themselves as belonging to this particular segment of society. Facilitated by the expansion of the publishing industry it consequently found its way into many contemporary texts celebrating the "generous Disposition and publick Spirit" of members of the middle classes in contrast to the "Depravity and Selfishness of those in a higher Class" (Thornton 1752: np).[18]

4.1 Social Comparing and the Middle Classes

While the well-established historical developments sketched above connect the media genre of the novel with the rise of the middle classes and the idea of the virtuous social middle, the role of practices of comparing in these processes has been largely overlooked by academic scholarship so far. Until recently, on the one hand, there has been "no reasonably coherent research tradition" that engages with the history of "comparisons as practices" in gen-

17 On competing models of the social structure of the period and the persistent traditional belief in a providentially ordained hierarchical order of social layers, see the discussion in Cannadine (2000: 24-56). In this context, see also French, who argues that the aristocracy and gentry retained their dominant economic and political power in Britain throughout the eighteenth century and beyond (2017: 269, 280). On the emergence of the "Middling Sort" as a cultural identity during the early modern period, see Muldrew (2017).

18 Quoted from the unpaginated preface of Thornton (1752).

eral (Steinmetz 2019a: 4). On the other hand, the focus of existing research on social comparing, for example in the field of social psychology, has been mainly directed at the individual. While researchers in this discipline have long been aware of comparing as a key psychological process of identity formation and self-evaluation (Festinger 1954), they have long neglected the role comparisons play in the functioning of communities, groups, and society at large (Križan/Gibbons 2014: 2). However, more recent scholarship has emphasized that the construction of the individual cannot be neatly separated from that of society:

> [S]ocial comparisons are tools that are just as important to the functioning of societies as they are to the functioning of individuals. As many great social thinkers of the 20th century have recognized, how we construe individuals and the society in which they live is mutually dependent. Our notion of the self is dependent on how we are viewed and treated by others, and our views of social groups always depend on how we view their constituent individuals. (ibid.)

In other words, social comparing is not only essential to the way individuals judge their abilities and opinions. As the "regulation of individual behavior is central to a proper functioning of a society" (ibid.), it also forms an important aspect of its (ideological) construction.

From a historiographical point of view, this means that practices of social comparing need to be understood as discursive practices that contribute to create and maintain social, legal, political, and cultural structures on the one hand, and that provide impulses for change on the other. They are therefore particularly interesting and revealing objects of study in periods of (social) transformation. This applies to Britain in the long eighteenth century – a key phase in the country's slow historical transition from a society primarily regulated by (inherited) status and rank to one based predominantly on ideas of (economic) competition.[19] As different views about social hierarchies struggle and clash with each other during the course of this development, practices of

---

19 According to Steinmetz (2019b), this transition goes hand in hand with changes in the (dominant) usage of different forms of comparison between 1600 and 1900. Next to traditional, hierarchical "above/below comparisons" (82) of social rank, the period saw the increasing appearance of two different types of comparison: (1) a form of competitive social comparing he calls "better/worse comparisons" (81; *passim*); and (2) comparisons that give "priority to individual difference" and function as "assertions of being 'simply different'" (81). He emphasizes that all three basic forms of comparison (bet-

social comparing play a key role in the self-fashioning of the increasingly self-confident eighteenth-century middle classes.

We have already seen that this process of self-fashioning goes hand in hand with a self-attribution of moral superiority based on favourable comparisons of social virtues. This self-positioning relies significantly on the way members of the middle classes relate themselves specifically vis-à-vis the upper strata. In social contacts with their 'betters', they develop strategies of behaviour aimed at toning down distinctions in rank. This includes "ingratiation", "vanity" and, most importantly, "emulation" (Porter 1982, 87-88, and see McKendrick 1982), i.e., the adoption of styles in dress, furniture, pastimes, (etc.). During the period, those who wish to find out what it means to be middle class and to adjust their behaviour accordingly would naturally resort to comparing themselves with the upper classes they attempt to emulate in appearance and habits, though not morals. The eighteenth-century middle classes cultivate a reputation of libertinage and idleness for the aristocracy and gentry that contradicts their own moral codex. Moreover, such socially 'vertical' comparing is complemented by a 'horizontal' awareness of the behaviour of members of one's own class, to which one can compare one's own actions and habits.

On another level, eighteen-century middle-class self-fashioning is complicated by the contrast between traditional (Christian) values of social behaviour and the behavioural codes inherent to a culture of competition. In the moral framework of the time, the mainsprings of consumer capitalism that increasingly secure the social position and well-being of the middle-classes are dangerously close to the cardinal sins of avarice and gluttony: the desire for, and consumption of, goods beyond necessities and subsistence, as well as the desire for profit-making. Though largely accepted as 'natural' human motives today, they are difficult to reconcile with the central ideals of decency, moderation and righteousness during the eighteenth century. Consequently, the middle classes need to constantly negotiate how to align the material side of gentility with the moral one. They need to find a way of being both a 'polite' *and* a commercial people at the same time (Langford 1989).

In sum, various modes of comparing accompany the changes in social structure in the long eighteenth century. Comparing codes of competitive behaviour on the one hand and ideals of decency and moderation on the other

---

ter/worse; above/below; simply different) have co-existed ever since "and may be re-enacted at any time" (104).

play a key role in the emergence of a general philosophical awareness of the conflict between (economic) competition and moral behaviour. Comparing other people's behaviour either between them or with reference to oneself serves as an important strategy for finding out about sanctions that are administered to deviancy from the implied norm. In this way, comparing provides a practical tool that helps individuals who are concerned and insecure about their own behaviour to navigate the social world by obtaining feedback and reassurance about the propriety and adequacy of certain actions, tastes, and moral values.

In this context, literary fiction during the eighteenth century fulfils an important function in expanding readers' horizons of personal experience and knowledge in a way that adds aesthetic and 'safe' modes of comparing to the more immediate social practices they observe in their own lives. Moreover, literature in general complements other, more openly instructive textual resources such as conduct books, sermons, and philosophical treatises. Specifically, the novel offers itself as a laboratory for social values and behaviour in accordance with bourgeois ideals by drawing on the inherent strengths of literary storytelling. In the remainder of our chapter, we suggest that it is the novel's ability to present large, heterogeneous collections of characters and to stage complex, multi-layered, and inherently ambiguous comparisons that was largely responsible for its emergence as a key medium in the negotiation of middle-class ideals of behaviour during the eighteenth century. For this purpose, we turn to two further examples: Oliver Goldsmith's *The Vicar of Wakefield* (1766) and Frances Burney's *Evelina, or the History of a Young Lady's Entrance into the World* (1778).

5. Complexity and Ambiguity in Narrative Practices of Comparing

We begin by turning to Goldsmith's *Vicar of Wakefield* as a good example of the complexity and multi-layeredness of literary practices of comparing. Chapter 16 reports the "rivalry in point of taste" (2006 [1766]: 70) that exists between the family of Dr Primrose, the Vicar of the title, and the neighbouring Flamborough family. Like many upper middle-class families at the time, the Flamboroughs had their family portrait painted by an itinerant painter, in imitation of tradition of family portraiture practiced by the nobility. The Primroses, ever eager to out-do all others in their aspiration for gentility, want to surpass their neighbours and have the painter produce a hugely dimensioned painting, cluttered with all sorts of (incongruent) mythological symbols. When the painting is finished, the family realize that it is too big to fit through any of the doors, so that it has to remain in the kitchen, where it was done, rather than be hung in some more representative room: "The picture, therefore, instead of gratifying our vanity, as we hoped, leaned, in a most mortifying manner, against the kitchen wall, [...] and the jest of all our neighbours" (71).

Comparing occurs on multiple levels in this novel generally, and in this particular scene, too. First, the Primrose family, naively caught between attempts to increase their morality on the one hand and eager to rise in the esteem of those socially above them on the other, continually compare themselves with other families, the Flamboroughs in this case. The *comparata* are the Primroses' attitudes and behaviours, and what they perceive to be the attitudes and behaviours of others; the *tertium* is the degree of respectability the Primroses assume these attitudes and behaviours demonstrate.

Since the comparison prompts the Primroses to actions that will prove ridiculous, the second level comes into play, namely the level of the text itself, understood as an act of communication between the author and his readership. The reader is invited to compare the Flamboroughs' successful imitation of an upper-class habitus with the unsuccessful one of the Primroses, and to laugh at the latter, much as their motivations may be understood. The moral of this episode appears to be partly rendered in the Vicar's acknowledgment that the function of the picture was to gratify the "vanity" of the family, and partly in the reader being led to understand that the real difference resulting from comparing the two families lies in the fact that the Primroses practice their emulation of the upper classes with a lack of moderation. The wish to have one's family portrait painted is not despicable, it seems, but to do so in excess is. Yet, the highly ironic fashion in which the novel, including this episode, is rendered, leaves considerable room for ambiguity with regard to the precise scope of the implicit comparisons offered by the text. The Primroses' failed vanity project, for example, may also be read as an ironic comment on the middle-class inclination for upward social imitation in general. This, in turn, may invite readers to reflect on their own inclination for imitation, in other words, to compare themselves to both the Primroses and the Flamboroughs in a critical fashion.

In any case, readers have to draw their own conclusions about the precise moral lessons offered by the comparisons evoked in the narrative. As Nünning (2004) has shown, the reading of *The Vicar of Wakefield* and its usage of irony, for example, are heavily influenced by the perceived reliability of the first-person narrator Primrose. Goldsmith's novel thus not only serves as a reminder of the crucial role of the narrative voice in the presentation of characters and comparisons in literary fiction. It also suggests that the semantic polyvalence generally inherent to literary texts extends to narrative practices of comparing. In fact, we believe that it is the semantic complexity of literature and its openness to interpretation that turned the eighteenth-century novel into an ideal textual medium for the staging of comparisons.

The usual length, complexity, and richness of detail of the novels from the period makes it possible for complex strings of interrelated comparisons to be woven into the narrative tapestries of their story lines. This not only leads to the inclusion of large numbers of increasingly complex comparisons. It also ensures that texts do not merely mirror the presentation of ideas about social norms and behaviour found in other types of media and public discourse during the period. The conflicts enacted in literary stories make it possible to stage colliding viewpoints in great detail and to negotiate ideological tensions inherent in contemporary ideas about social conduct in ways that force eighteenth-century readers to participate in the construction, interpretation, and evaluation of those ideas by way of comparison. Again, practices of indirect comparing play a particularly important role in this respect, as they generally required a higher degree of (cognitive) participation by the reader. Moreover, they can be evoked in many different ways, thus inviting authors to be creative in terms of the narrative structure of their works.

Complexity and ambiguity in eighteenth-century fiction, in other words, can take many forms. In the example of Goldsmith's *Vicar of Wakefield* it is closely connected to the humorous and ironic tone of the text. In Frances (Fanny) Burney's successful epistolary novel *Evelina* (2012 [1778]), our last example, ambiguity arises from a different ideological tension played out in the narrative. Presenting a heterogeneous cast of characters embodying different sets of values and/or vices, the novel features multiple sets of direct and indirect forms of comparing that attempt to convey a general moral lesson. Yet, the text's choice for the embodiment of virtue reveals an underlying ideological tension in contemporary middle-class attitudes towards the nobility.

Generally, the novel is another prime example for the key role that comparisons play in the narrative negotiation of morality and conduct. The novel's young protagonist Evelina has grown up in rural seclusion as the ward of Mr Villars, a clergyman, after the death of her mother. When invited to a trip to London, Burney casts her as an impartial observer of the habits and fashions of London society, which gives the author the opportunity to present

Evelina with all types of behaviour that she can partly understand and compare, but which partly also baffle her. Since readers get access to these behaviours through the letters she sends back home to her guardian, they are encouraged to perform a variety of comparisons.

The first characters that can be compared by the reader before Evelina arrives in London, however, are Evelina, her mother, and her grandmother, who are discussed in close succession in the letters between Villars and his acquaintance, Lady Howard, which open the novel. The implied *tertium comparationis* between the three women is a combination of prudence, decency and the danger to fall prey to dishonest men. Lady Howard tells Villars about the design of Evelina's grandmother Mme Duval, an Englishwoman pretending to be French to get Evelina to live with her in France after she has learned of her granddaughter's existence. Mme Duval had cut off all connections to her daughter, Evelina's mother, who had been persuaded into a marriage with a Lord Belmont that the dubious peer later renounced without acknowledging the daughter as his legitimate offspring. Mme Duval is described by Lady Howard as "vulgar and illiterate" (12) and by Villars as "at once uneducated and unprincipled; ungentle in her temper, and unamiable in her manners" (13) and she is associated with low social status, since as a young woman, she was "a waiting-girl at a tavern" (14). This stands in contrast to Evelina's unfortunate mother: when Evelina is allowed to go to London in the custody of Lady Howard, she is described by the lady in direct comparison with her mother: "She [Evelina] has the same gentleness in her manners, the same natural grace in her motions, that I formerly so admired in her mother" and is attested both intelligence ("excellent understanding, and great quickness of parts") and moral integrity, possessing "a certain air of innocency and inexperience that is extremely interesting" (23). The interest of this character conception for the reader lies in the question which kind of fate the innocent woman will meet in the society of the metropolis. Neither her grandmother's nor her mother's developments, which are compared succinctly over the first few pages, offer themselves as patterns.

Evelina's letter to Villars reporting the first ball she takes part in then duly delivers her impressions of the men in the city, and it initiates the next set of comparisons. Out of a group of young gentlemen with a "careless indolent manner", one person "who had for some time looked at us with a kind of negligent impertinence" and whose "dress was so foppish that I believe he even wished to be stared at" besieges Evelina with his attentions which she refuses, not least because she finds him "ugly" (32). Immediately afterwards, she is approached by "another gentleman, who seemed about six-and-twenty years old, gayly, but not foppishly, dressed, and indeed extremely handsome, with an air of mixed politeness and gallantry" (33). Subsequently, she finds that "[h]is conversation was sensible and spirited; his air and address were open and noble; his manners gentle, attentive, and infinitely engaging; his person is all elegance, and his countenance, the most animated and expressive I have ever seen" (ibid.). Although Evelina does not comment on the discrepancy between the two men in manner and dress, the immediate juxtaposition is clearly intended to provoke acts of comparing. The man who impresses Evelina so much, Lord Orville, will also prove superior to yet another suitor, Sir Clement Willoughby. Orville thus functions as the ideal potential partner of the romance plot, which indeed he proves to be after a whole series of prototypical hindrances including mutual misunderstandings, a faked letter written by a spurned rival, and the fact that as an aristocrat Orville seems to be out of reach for Evelina – until her real descendance from Lord Belmont is revealed towards the end.

As if the initial comparative constellation were not enough, Burney brings all three men together before the eyes of Evelina in quick succession two more times at places of entertainment, Drury Lane Theatre (letter no. 20) and the London Pantheon (letter no. 23) respectively. On these occasions, the impertinent fop, Mr Lovel, continues to misbehave and even offends Evelina on grounds of her inexperience and while Sir Clement oscillates between reticence and forwardness, Lord Orville again shines with "his generous conduct" (123), "his usual politeness" (133) and "a politeness which knows no intermission, and makes no distinction, is as unassuming and modest, as if he had never mixed with the great, and was totally ignorant of every qualification he possesses" (ibid.). This last characterisation is followed by a summary of another nobleman who remains unnamed in this scene and has aroused Evelina's contempt by being so utterly "deficient in *good manners*" (125, original emphasis) that "even Sir Clement Willoughby appeared modest in comparison with this person" (ibid). In comparison to Lord Orville the nameless nobleman appears as the epitome of upper classes' bad reputation. Evelina states that

> this other lord, though lavish of compliments and fine speeches, seems to me an entire stranger to real good breeding; whoever strikes his fancy, engrosses his whole attention. He is forward and bold, has an air of haughtiness towards men, and a look of libertinism towards women, and his conscious

> quality seems to have given him a freedom in his way of speaking to either sex, that is very short of rudeness. (133)

The correct version of politeness from the perspective of the novel, as the text's extensive conglomeration of direct and indirect comparisons aims to emphasize, is not naturally connected to rank, but a quality of attitude and behaviour that needs to be performed with moderation and discretion.

While clearly aware of the conventional system of class distinction by denomination, the novel's comparisons thus promote the ideal of good conduct over the primacy of birth. By means of comparing, the text sets an essentially (upper) middle-class understanding of virtue and decorum as the general standard according to which all members of society should be judged. For this purpose, it presents characters from the nobility who embody different degrees of morally deficient behaviour, thus promoting the ideology of the virtuous social middle by drawing on and reinforcing contemporary stereotypes about young noblemen. However, at the same time, the romance retains a clear fascination with the upper strata of society that subliminally undermines the notion of the middle station as "the best State in the World" (Defoe 1994 [1719]: 5). By presenting Lord Orville, the highest-ranking of Evelina's suitors, as the girl's ideal marriage partner and the male embodiment of sensible (male) conduct and good character, Burney's work makes an ambivalent statement on the position of the middle classes and their strife for gentility.

This ambivalence also extends to the figure of Evelina herself. Since none of the gentlemen in question is a writer of letters in the novel, we get access to their behaviour mainly through the perspective of the female protagonist, who, as an outsider unspoiled by the habits of London society is presented as possessing a somehow 'natural' power of judgment of morally adequate behaviour. This, in turn, differentiates her from both her mother and her grandmother, who in comparison appear to have lacked that kind of understanding. Repeatedly exhibiting this talent over the course of the novel, Evelina comes to embody a (middle-class) ideal of (female) sensibility, judgement, and conduct. However, her status as this embodiment of the virtuous social middle equally retains an aspect of ambiguity. When the plot finally confirms her noble descent as the daughter of Lord Belmont, this not only facilitates the happy ending of the romance plot. It creates a constellation of characters in which the representatives of ideal male and female behaviour both turn out to be members of the nobility. Despite all of its promotion of middle-class ideology, the text thus still implicitly raises the suspicion that nobility of character and nobility of birth may be related after all.

6. Conclusion

The eighteenth century was a period of drastic change, which included the slow emergence both of new social patterns of behaviour and of literary genres. In both areas, there was much experimentation and diversity, and there were contradictory but overlapping tendencies and ambivalences. On the social side, the composition of what can be regarded as the emerging middle classes changed throughout the century and scholars continue to disagree on how strongly this development affected other segments of society (see Corfield 1987; Cannadine 2000: 24-56; French 2017). On the literary side, the genre label of the eighteenth-century novel is a heuristic academic construct. There is no such thing as 'the' eighteenth-century English novel. Apart from the considerable confusion displayed by authors, publishers, booksellers and commentators of the period as to the name for this emerging genre,[20] the sheer polymorphism and diversity of prose narratives makes it difficult to summarize what the texts published during this period have in common that would even allow a single, unifying genre designation. There is such a variety of narrative modes and moods that lumping them together with traditional labels such as 'formal realism' and 'individualism' (Watt 1957) is seen as highly problematic by today's scholarship (McKeon 2002 [1987]). In addition, different sub-genres did not only have different readerships, but also different formulas for plot developments, character types, and character constellations. This complex situation affects the analysis of literary practices in connection with contemporary issues of social comparison quite considerably. It makes it inherently problematic to put forth comprehensive assertions about the types and performances of narrative practices of comparing, on the one hand, and to make general statements about the nature and development of different classes and their norms and values, on the other hand.

Nevertheless, despite those reservations, we believe that there is a discernible relationship between much of the period's literary fiction and con-

20 See the collection of contemporary voices, attempts at definition, and controversies collected in Williams (1970) and Richetti (2012); see also the chapter on circulating libraries by Ralf Schneider in this collection.

temporary practices of social comparing grounded in the changing social structure of the long eighteenth century, in particular, the emerging middle-classes' need for guidance in questions of morality and social life. Even though social comparing also occurred in other literary genres,[21] it was the new genre of the novel, with the multitude of characters and plotlines it usually features, that provides an ideal aesthetic framework for the literary negotiation of social values, norms, and conduct. With the examples discussed in this chapter, we have tried to suggest that novels engaging with those issues tend to rely heavily on evocations of figural comparisons, on the one hand, and on the staging of different types of indirect comparison, on the other hand. Texts also feature direct comparisons, explicitly articulated by characters or narrators. Yet, indirect strategies are often not only deeply ingrained in the narrative structure of texts, but they tend to require a higher degree of (cognitive) participation and can serve as a powerful way of prompting readers to perform multi-layered acts of comparing. With this ability to present extensive, heterogeneous character constellations and to stage ideological tension and colliding points of view by evoking complex strings of multifaceted and ambiguous comparisons, the eighteenth-century novel goes beyond the mere replication of ideas from contemporary public debates about social comparing. It historically offered itself as a literary laboratory for middle-class ideals of social values and behaviour. In this way, it made an important contribution to the contemporary formation of the emerging idea of a morally superior middle class. As the novel became the dominant literary medium over the course of the century, it provided readers with the possibility of obtaining guidance, feedback and reassurance about the propriety and adequacy of certain actions, tastes, and moral values, on the one hand, and the opportunity to engage in critical reflections of those issues, on the other. Moreover, ever since this key phase in the development of the novel, practices of comparing literary characters have arguably served as a key narrative strategy in much of literary fiction. And, as social psychology tells us, this is not surprising. Because, after all, Belinda seems to be right: "[H]ow are we to judge of character [...] but by comparison?"

---

21 Eighteenth-century drama, in particular comedy, employs contrasting characters as a standard device. Some novelists, including Henry Fielding, Tobias Smollett, Oliver Goldsmith and Fanny Burney were also dramatists, which may account for some of the parallels in the use of contrastive character constellations.

Bibliography

Aristotle. *The Politics*. Trans. Carnes Lord. Chicago: University of Chicago Press, 1984.

Beck, Rainer. "Luxus oder Decencies? Zur Konsumgeschichte der Frühneuzeit als Begin der Moderne." *"Luxus und Konsum": Eine historische Annäherung*. Ed. Reinhold Reith and Torsten Meyer. Münster: Waxman, 2003. 29-46.

Berg, Maxine. "New Commodities, Luxuries and Their Consumers in Eighteenth-Century England." *Consumers and Luxury: Consumer Culture in Europe 1650-1850*. Ed. Maxine Berg and Helen Clifford. Manchester: Manchester University Press, 1999. 63-85.

Berg, Maxine. *Luxury and Pleasure in Eighteenth-Century Britain*. Oxford: Oxford University Press, 2005.

Berry, Helen. "Polite Consumption: Shopping in Eighteenth-Century England." *Transactions of the Royal Historical Society* 12 (2002): 375-95.

Bree, Linda. "Introduction." *Belinda*, by Maria Edgeworth. Ed. Linda Bree. Oxford: Oxford University Press, 2020. iv-xxxix.

Britton, Jeanne M. "Theorizing Character in Maria Edgeworth's *Belinda*." *Nineteenth-Century Literature* 67.4 (2013): 433-456.

Burney, Frances. *Evelina, or the History of a Young Lady's Entrance into the World*. London: Penguin, 2012 [1778].

Cannadine, David. *Class in Britain*. London: Penguin, 2000.

Chalk, Dannie Leigh. "Comparative Gender in Maria Edgeworth's *Belinda*." *Studies in the Literary Imagination* 47.2 (2014): 131-152.

Corfield, Penelope J. "Class by Name and Number in Eighteenth-Century England." *History* 72 (1987): 38-61.

Cowan, Brian. "Making Publics and Making Novels: Post-Habermasian Perspectives." *The Oxford Handbook of the Eighteenth-Century Novel*. Ed. J. A. Downie. Oxford: Oxford University Press, 2016. 55-70.

Crossick, Geoffrey. "From Gentleman to the Residuum: Languages of Social Description in Victorian Britain." *Language, History and Class*. Ed. Penelope J. Corfield. Oxford: Basil Blackwell, 1991. 150-178.

Davis, Lennard. *Factual Fictions: The Origins of the English Novel*. New York: Columbia University Press, 1983

Defoe, Daniel. *Robinson Crusoe*. Ed. Michael Shinagel. New York: Norton, 1994 [1719].

Downie, J. A., ed. *The Oxford Handbook of the Eighteenth-Century Novel*. Oxford: Oxford University Press, 2016.

Earle, Peter. *The Making of the English Middle Class: Business, Society and Family Life in London, 1660-1730*. London: Methuen, 1989.

Ehland, Christoph. *Picaresque Perspectives – Exiled Identities: A Structural and Methodological Analysis of the Picaresque as a Literary Archetype in the Works of James Leslie Mitchell*. Heidelberg: Winter, 2003.

Eder, Jens, Fotis Jannidis, and Ralf Schneider, eds. *Characters in Fictional Worlds: Understanding Imaginary Beings in Literature, Film and Other Media*. Berlin: de Gruyter, 2010.

Edgeworth, Maria. *Belinda*. Ed. Linda Bree. Oxford: Oxford University Press, 2020.

Erhart, Walter. "Odysseus, Blackbirds, and Rain Barrels." *Practices of Comparing: Towards a New Understanding of a Fundamental Human Practice*. Ed. Angelika Epple, Walter Erhart, and Johannes Grave. Bielefeld: Bielefeld University Press, 2020. 111-135.

Fauconnier, Gilles and Mark Turner. *The Way We Think: Conceptual Blending and the Mind's Hidden Complexities*. New York: Basic Books, 2002.

Feather, John. *A History of British Publishing*. 2nd ed. London: Routledge, 2006.

Feather, John. "The Book Trade, 1770-1832." *The Oxford Handbook of the Eighteenth-Century Novel*. Ed. J. A. Downie. Oxford: Oxford University Press, 2016. 291-307.

Festinger, Leo. "A Theory of Social Comparison Processes." *Human Relations* 7.2 (1954): 117-140.

Fielding, Henry. *The History of Tom Jones, a Foundling*. Ed. R. P. C. Mutter. London: Penguin, 1985 [1749].

French, Henry. "Gentlemen: Remaking the English Ruling Class." *A Social History of England: 1500-1750*. Ed. Keith Wrightson. Cambridge: Cambridge University Press, 2017. 269-289.

Fluck, Winfried. "Reading For Recognition." *New Literary History* 44 (2013): 45-67.

Goldsmith, Oliver. *The Vicar of Wakefield*. Oxford: Oxford University Press, 2006 [1766].

Gonda, Caroline. *Reading Daughters' Fictions: 1709-1834: Novels and Society from Manley to Edgeworth*. Cambridge: Cambridge University Press, 1996.

Guillén, Claudio. "Toward a Definition of the Picaresque." *Literature as System: Essays Toward the Theory of Literary History*. Princeton: Princeton University Press, 1971. 71-106.

Gustafson, Katherine. "Assimilation and Indeterminacy: *Moral Tales for Young People*, *Belinda*, and Edgeworth's Destabilizing Fictions of Maturity." *Eighteenth Century Fiction* 29.4 (2017): 635-661.

Haan, Heiner and Gottfried Niedhart. *Geschichte Englands vom 16. bis zum 18. Jahrhundert.* 2nd ed. München: C. H. Beck, 2002.

Habermas, Jürgen. *The Structural Transformation of the Public Sphere: An Inquiry Into a Category of Bourgeois Society*. Cambridge: MIT-Press 1989 [1962].

Hartner, Marcus. "Narrative Theory Meets Blending: Multiperspectivity Reconsidered." *The Literary Mind* [REAL 24]. Ed. Jürgen Schlaeger and Gesa Stedman. Tübingen: Narr, 2008. 181-194.

Hartner, Marcus. "Multiperspectivity." *Handbook of Narratology*. Ed. Peter Hühn et al. 2nd ed. Vol. 1. Berlin: de Gruyter, 2014. 353-363.

Hinds, Peter. "The Book Trade at the Turn of the Eighteenth Century." *The Oxford Handbook of the Eighteenth-Century Novel*. Ed. J. A. Downie. Oxford: Oxford University Press, 2016. 5-21.

Hume, David. "Of the Middle Station of Life." *The Philosophical Works*. Vol. 4. Ed. Thomas H. Green and Thomas H. Grose. Aalen: Scientia Verlag, 1964 [1742]. 375-80.

Hunter, J. Paul. *Before Novels: The Cultural Contexts of Eighteenth-Century Fiction*. New York: W.W. Norton, 1990.

Inchbald, Elisabeth. *A Simple Story*. Oxford: Oxford University Press, 1988 [1791].

Klauk, Tobias and Tilmann Köppe. "Telling vs. Showing." *Handbook of Narratology*. Vol. 2. Ed. Peter Hühn et al. 2nd ed. Berlin: de Gruyter, 2014. 846-853.

Kowaleski-Wallace, Elizabeth. *Their Fathers' Daughters: Hannah More, Maria Edgeworth, and Patriarchal Complicity*. Oxford: Oxford University Press, 1991.

Kramer, Kirsten et al. "Vergleichen und Erzählen. Zur Verflechtung zweier Kulturtechniken." *Working Paper des SFB 1288*, No. 4 (2020). ‹https://pub.uni-bielefeld.de/record/2946608›.

Križan, Zlatan and Frederick X. Gibbons. "Communion in Social Comparison – Back to the Roots." *Communal Functions of Social Comparison*. Ed Zlatan Križan and Frederick X. Gibbons. Cambridge: Cambridge University Press, 2014. 1-8.

Langford, Paul. *A Polite and Commercial People: England 1727-1783*. Oxford: Oxford University Press, 1989.

Langford, Paul and Christopher Harvie. *The Eighteenth Century and the Age of Industry*. Oxford: Oxford University Press, 1992.

McKendrick, Neil. "The Consumer Revolution of Eighteenth-Century England." *The Birth of a Consumer Society: The Commercialization of Eighteenth-Century England*. Ed. Neil McKendrick, John Brewer, and J. H. Plumb. London: Europa, 1982. 9-33.

McKendrick, Neil, John Brewer, and J. H. Plumb, eds. *The Birth of a Consumer Society: The Commercialization of Eighteenth-Century England*. London: Europa, 1982.

McKeon, Michael. *The Origins of the English Novel, 1600-1740*. Baltimore: Johns Hopkins University Press, 2002 [1987].

Mergenthal, Silvia. *Erziehung zur Tugend: Frauenrollen und der englische Roman um 1800*. Tübingen: Niemeyer, 1997.

Muldrew, Craig. "The 'Middling Sort': An Emergent Cultural Identity." *A Social History of England: 1500-1750*. Ed. Keith Wrightson. Cambridge: Cambridge University Press, 2017. 290-309.

Nünning, Ansgar. "On the Perspective Structure of Narrative Texts: Steps Toward a Constructivist Narratology." *New Perspectives on Narrative Perspective*. Ed. Willie van Peer and Seymour Chatman. Albany: State University of New York Press, 2001. 207-224.

Nünning, Vera. "Unreliable Narration and the Historical Variability of Values and Norms: *The Vicar of Wakefield* as a Test Case of a Cultural-Historical Narratology." *Style* 38.2 (2004): 236-252.

Pfister, Manfred. *The Theory and Analysis of Drama*. Cambridge: Cambridge University Press, 1988 [1977].

Porter, Roy. *English Society in the Eighteenth Century*. Harmondsworth: Penguin, 1982.

Richetti, John. "The Novel Before 'The Novel'." *The Cambridge History of the English Novel*. Ed. Robert L. Caserio and Clement Hawes. Cambridge: Cambridge University Press, 2012. 14-29.

Rogers, Pat. "Social Structure, Class and Gender, 1660-1770." *The Oxford Handbook of the Eighteenth-Century Novel*. Ed. J. A. Downie. Oxford: Oxford University Press, 2016. 39-54.

Schneider, Ralf. *Grundriß zur kognitiven Theorie der Figurenrezeption am Beispiel des viktorianischen Romans*. Tübingen: Stauffenburg Verlag, 2000.

Schneider, Ralf. "Comparison, Analogy, and Knowledge in Literature: Basic Considerations and the Case of Early Modern English Texts." *Analogy, Copy, and Representation: Interdisciplinary Perspectives*. Ed. Christoph Haase and Anne Schröder. Bielefeld: Aisthesis, 2017. 137-154.

Smollett, Tobias. *The Expedition of Humphry Clinker*. Ed. Angus Ross. Harmondsworth: Penguin, 1985 [1771].

Steinmetz, Willibald. "Introduction: Concepts and Practices of Comparison in Modern History." *The Force of Comparison: A New Perspective on Modern European History and the Contemporary World*. Ed. Willibald Steinmetz. New York: Berghan, 2019a. 1-32.

Steinmetz, Willibald. "Above/Below, Better Worse or Simply Different? Metamorphoses of Social Comparison, 1600-1900." *The Force of Comparison: A New Perspective on Modern European History and the Contemporary World*. Ed. Willibald Steinmetz. New York: Berghan, 2019b. 81-112.

Strasen, Sven. *Rezeptionstheorien: Literatur-, sprach- und kulturwissenschaftliche Ansätze und kulturelle Modelle*. Trier: WVT, 2008.

Suarez, Michael F., S. J. "Business of Fiction: Novel Publishing, 1695-1774." *The Oxford Handbook of the Eighteenth-Century Novel*. Ed. J. A. Downie. Oxford: Oxford University Press, 2016. 22-38.

T[hornton], W[illiam]. *The Counterpoise: Being Thoughts on a Militia and a Standing Army*. London: Printed for M. Cooper, 1752.

Wahrman, Dror. *Imagining the Middle Class: The Political Representation of Class in Britain, c.1780-1840*. Cambridge: Cambridge University Press, 1995.

Watt, Ian. *The Rise of the Novel: Studies in Defoe, Richardson and Fielding*. London. Chatto & Windus, 1957.

Weatherill, Lorna. "The Meaning of Consumer Behaviour in Late Seventeenth- and Early Eighteenth-Century England." *Consumption and the World of Goods*. Ed. John Brewer and Roy Porter. London: Routledge, 1993. 206-227.

Williams, Ioan M., ed. *Novel and Romance, 1700-1800: A Documentary Record*. London: Routledge & Kegan Paul, 1970.

The Complexity of Narrative Comparisons in Wollstonecraft's *Maria; Or, The Wrongs of Woman* and Lennox's *The Female Quixote*

Anne Lappert

1. Introduction

Comparisons are omnipresent and have served as "one of the key movements of thought and method" in philosophy and the sciences since antiquity (Eggers 2019: 33). The same applies to comparative practices in literature. As a constituent part of several rhetorical devices, comparing can be traced back as far as Aristotle's *Rhetoric* (see Cope 1867: 374, 446-447). And as a rhetorical strategy, it can serve to highlight differences, to point out similarities, and of course to get argumentative points across. While this observation may seem unremarkable or even trivial, it is all the more noteworthy that a thorough analysis of the wider spectrum of comparative practices is not available as of yet. This is especially true for textual practices of comparing in the novel. While some literary 'methods' of comparing such as the rhetorical devices of metaphor and metonymy have been thoroughly investigated,[1] other aspects of comparing in literature, for example, in narrative texts such as novels, remain understudied.[2] Once we turn from the investigation of comparison as a methodological issue, for instance, to the study of comparisons as textual

1 For introductions to the study of metaphor, see Punter (2007) and Evans/Green (2006: 286-325).

2 For an introductory exploration of different aspects of comparing in literature, see Erhart (2020), who discusses a distinction between inner-textual comparisons, comparisons as narrative features, and comparisons in terms of metaphors. For reflections on the general relationship between narration and comparison and the function of comparing in literature, see also Kramer et al. (2020), Schneider (2017), and the contribution by Hartner/Schneider to this volume.

practices that serve argumentative purposes, many questions remain unasked – especially with regard to issues of ideology. As Epple/Erhart (2015: 14-15) remind us, understanding comparative practices generally requires us to take a closer look at who compares what for which purposes in order to understand the ideological premises underlying a particular practice of comparing. However, when dealing with a novel, this is not enough. In order to analyze the ideological investment underlying a particular comparative practice in narrative fiction, it is just as necessary to look at *how* the individual comparisons forming this practice function in the argumentative structure of the text.

In their contribution to this volume, Marcus Hartner and Ralf Schneider take a first step towards the investigation of narrative practices of comparing. They turn to practices that compare and/or prompt comparisons in the eighteenth-century novel and show that texts from this period display an excessive concern with manners of conduct and social customs. Applying a heuristic differentiation into direct and indirect comparisons they indicate that eighteenth-century novels show a preference for indirect comparisons that come in a variety of forms. Taking their argument as a point of departure, I attempt to add to their survey by offering an analysis of two eighteenth-century novels, Mary Wollstonecraft's *Maria; Or, The Wrongs of Woman* (1798) and Charlotte Lennox's *The Female Quixote* (1752). My analysis specifically zooms in on narrative comparisons of social practices by focusing on the novels' ways of addressing questions of female rights and education in order to foreground the complexity and interlocking nature of different practices of comparing in literature. In my contribution to this volume, I attempt to complement the distinction offered by Hartner/Schneider and, in doing so, I intend to illustrate the complex, diverse and multi-layered form of comparative practices in the eighteenth-century novel.

In the following, I will argue that with regard to *Maria; Or, The Wrongs of Woman* and *The Female Quixote*, a distinction into direct and indirect comparisons does not suffice. Instead, a differentiation into at least three basic types, namely imagery comparisons, narrative comparisons and intertextual comparisons is necessary in order to illustrate how the two works' individual practices of comparing serve the feminist arguments posed in those texts. The chapter takes a closer look at how each suggested type of comparison operates to suit its respective argumentative purpose. Based on this analysis, it suggests that it is not sufficient to study the occurrence of comparisons as rhetoric devices. Rather, to analyze comparative arguments in narrative texts, it is crucial to investigate which practices of comparing are employed and what purposes their concrete form serves in the literary construction of the presented argument. To analyze the power and complexity of comparisons in literary texts, it is not enough to look at *who* compares *what* for *which purpose*. We also need to examine *how* such comparisons work on a textual level. While the importance of the latter aspect might seem minor, I will show that the meaning retrievable from the works by Wollstonecraft and Lennox changes significantly if the full spectrum of comparative practices is taken into consideration in their analysis.

2. Types of Comparing in Mary Wollstonecraft's *Maria; Or, The Wrongs of Woman*

In *Maria; Or, The Wrongs of Woman*, the female and the male characters are connected via the novel's protagonist Maria. In the text, the latter marries George Venables to get away from her family, particularly from her despotic brother, but this plan backfires. She gives birth to a daughter that is withheld from Maria by George. He confines Maria to an asylum, where she meets and befriends a member of staff, Jemima. Maria and a male inmate, Henry Darnford, fall in love and Darnford is eventually sued by George for the seduction of his wife Maria. Maria gives birth to a child from Darnford that eventually dies. Darnford leaves both, the country and Maria.

In a first step, a number of direct and indirect comparisons on the intratextual level of communication between characters can be distinguished. According to Hartner and Schneider we can generally speak of a *direct* comparison in narrative fiction when "at least *two comparata* (*primum comparandum* and *secundum comparatum*) or both these *comparata* and the *tertium comparationis*" are explicitly mentioned in a text. In contrast, they define *indirect* comparisons as the "positioning of *comparata* in a novel without the explicit naming of the *tertium*" – a strategy that serves as "an offer by the text" inviting readers to construct comparability by searching for and adding a suitable *tertium* themselves (see the contribution by Hartner/Schneider in this volume). Despite numerous indirect comparisons both Maria and Jemima occasionally also use direct comparisons. For example, Maria compares her own situation to that of Darnford. Darnford and Maria are both inmates in the asylum when Maria finds notes by Darnford in one of the books she received from Jemima. These notes are read by Maria as secret messages and establish a first communication between Maria and Henry Darnford before they are able to meet in person. Thus, a link is created between the two characters via Darnford's secret message in the book that is eventually read by Maria (18). Jemima also repeatedly uses direct comparisons to illustrate her situation as an orphan being treated like an animal by her foster family. She describes being kicked about "like a dog or cat", or "like a mule", and being "view[ed] [...] as a creature of another species" (*Maria*, 48-49; see also 18-19). But while the distinction into direct and indirect comparisons can be a helpful means of a first general orientation, it tells us little about the complex structures and interrelations of different comparative practices at work in a specific text. While Jemima uses direct comparisons to illustrate how she has been treated, for instance, she simultaneously indirectly compares her own situation to that of an imaginary girl that enjoys the protection of a loving mother. When she states that it was the lack "of the grand support in life – a mother's affection" that was her greatest misery, she invites the reader to imagine how different her life could have been with a loving mother by her side (see 37, 40). Though not directly or explicitly comparing her situation with that of a daughter protected by a loving mother, the daughter position as such serves as the shared feature, the *tertium comparationis*, of this indirect comparison; she implies that the daughter protected by a mother and the daughter who must make do without such protection have very little in common. However, the passage can also be read as a warning that a girl has hardly any protection but her mother; the argument is thus geared to demand a better protection for girls and women.

Jemima's comparisons of her situation as an orphan in a foster family, in general, and of an orphan *daughter*, in particular, to a child protected by a loving mother can be differentiated according to the categories 'direct' and 'indirect'. However, the example already makes apparent the problem of this kind of distinction. Both types of comparison can be differentiated according to the absence or presence of comparative particles. Yet, it would be a mistake to read both cases as separate from each other. Instead, the example illustrates that both types work together. While the direct comparison paints an image of Jemima's situation as a motherless child, the indirect comparison complements her descriptions by drawing on said image to bring in a gender aspect and to create a harsh contrast between an orphan *girl* and a beloved *daughter*. In other words, the direct comparison of Jemima to animals is related to the indirect comparisons which contrasts the level of protection enjoyed by a beloved daughter in the care of her mother to that of an orphan girl. Furthermore, both comparisons work by inviting images of the actual living situation of orphan girls and protected daughters. Hence, the warning against a lack of protection for girls is constructed by a complex network of direct and indirect comparisons that both heavily rely on creating an image of the suffering of orphan girls for the reader. This indicates that both, direct and indirect comparisons can be embedded in larger structures of meaning, but the distinction alone does not offer much insight in terms of what functions a comparison serves in these structures.

Another problem with the straightforward characterization of comparisons as either direct or indirect is that it narrows down the attention to the presence and absence of linguistic markers instead of highlighting the more subtle comparative structures embedded into a text. In the case of *Maria; Or, The Wrongs of Woman* the narrative structure of the novel is of interest, considering that two passages are set off from the rest of the text by their narrative voice, but also in terms of genre, because they offer two embedded narratives in the form of autobiographies. Jemima narrates her life story shortly before Maria narrates her own (*Maria*, 36-52, 59-109). At these two successive points the narrator changes from an extradiegetic, heterodiegetic to an intradiegetic, autodiegetic narrator thereby inviting a comparison between both text passages. These deviations from the initial heterodiegetic narrative situation highlight the two text passages. The recognition that Jemima and Maria are telling their own stories is indispensable to understand the plot and this realization can only be arrived at by way of comparing. At this point any attempt at figuring out why and in how far these passages are different immediately invites a further and more detailed comparison between both passages and between each part with the rest of the narrative. This then leads to the recognition that both embedded narratives share certain narrative, generic, and plot features: they are narrated by a woman sharing her story autobiographically in first person: both narratives revolve around an unhappy childhood and youth that places both women in the asylum. The accounts relate how both women's lives become unbearable after the deaths of their mothers. Both women experience rejection by their fathers and abuse. Jemima is physically abused by her father and her stepmother (38-39) and her later master (40-41). Maria is emotionally abused by her despotic brother and her ill-tempered father (70-72). Neither of them is protected by their fathers and both women can only escape from those forms of abuse to other forms of abuse (71). Jemima must leave her master's house after she is found pregnant with his child (42). She works as a prostitute and eventually becomes a servant to a master who keeps her for pleasure (44-45). After his death, she starts working in the asylum. Maria escapes her tyrannic brother by marrying George Venables (73), who betrays Maria and bankrupts her. Before Maria has a chance to get a divorce, George confines her to an asylum to get unhindered access to the money she inherited from her uncle. What is interesting is that the autobiographies, because of their succession and their similarities in content and narrative structure, question the status of marriage as a protection for women. Both Jemima and Maria are raped by men who presumably 'own' them. Jemima is 'owned' by her master; Maria is 'owned' by her husband. Both narratives employ a language that frames women as possessions by stating that the female characters are "introduced as an object" or, "born a slave", and the female characters lament that they are "a common property", or "the property of their husbands" (*Maria* 39, 40-43, see also: 78). Hence, the novel discusses questions of absolute authority between social classes as well as between men and women and can be classified as a Jacobin novel.

By vividly portraying the cruel fate of the two characters, Wollstonecraft's novel criticizes the fact that 'wife' and 'servant' are legally speaking in a similar position. They are the 'goods' of men and completely depend on the kindness and favour of the men who 'keep them'.[3] This connects to the author's arguments in her essay *A Vindication of the Rights of Woman* (1792), where she demands that women should not be regarded as the property of their husbands but as independent human beings worthy of a rational education; it also connects to *A Vindication of the Rights of Men* (1790) where Wollstonecraft attacks what she sees as an unjust class system under the absolute authority of a monarch. By comparing the narratives of Jemima and Maria, along with the arguments proposed in Wollstonecraft's two earlier political texts, the reader is thus invited to compare marriage to servanthood – a comparison that simultaneously criticizes the inhumane class system of contemporary society and the legal situation of women in marriage (*Maria* 52, 67, 87, 104; *Rights of Men* 95; Taylor 2003: 64). While *A Vindication of the Rights of Woman* and *A Vindication of the Rights of Men* are political and philosophical essays, *Maria; Or, The Wrongs of Woman* is a novel. This generic difference allows the novel to take up

3 See, Hale (1736: 629): "The husband cannot be guilty of a rape committed by himself upon his lawful wife, for by their mutual consent and contract the wife hath given up herself in this kind unto her husband, which she cannot retract." Here it suffices to acknowledge that this argument was posed in public discourses and that the first recorded prosecution of a husband for raping his wife is dated no earlier than 1949 after a prior separation of the two and no earlier than 1991 while the marriage was still upheld (Han 1989: 113). For a more detailed discussion of the subject, see King (1998).

the arguments developed in Wollstonecraft's two earlier essays, as the reader is invited to reconstruct and relate those arguments in the comparison between Jemima's and Maria's autobiographies. Hence, the comparison between those passages prompted by the novel's narrative structure is closely interlinked with an intertextual comparison between the text and the author's two political works. By drawing attention to the similar situation of both women despite their difference in social class, the novel reveals Wollstonecraft's feminist arguments and her political argument against monarchy to form related issues.

However, intertextual comparisons in *Maria; Or, The Wrongs of Women* are by no means limited to Wollstonecraft's own texts; they also relate to popular (literary) works by other writers.[4] So, for instance, an intertextual link can be discerned between Maria's and Darnford's relationship and that of the characters Armida and Rinaldo in Torquato Tasso's epic poem *Jerusalem Delivered* (*Gerusalemme liberata*, 1581). Again, this link makes use of complex interlocking structures of comparing in order to pose an argument against marriage as a form of protection for women. The heterodiegetic narrator in Wollstonecraft's novel describes the connection between Maria and Darnford as so strong that "paradise bloomed around them; or they, by a powerful spell, had been transported into Armida's garden" (*Maria* 35). This reference points to Tasso's epic poem, in which the sorceress Armida abducts the Christian knight Rinaldo and takes him to her enchanted garden where they fall in love.[5] Once the spell is broken Rinaldo leaves Armida heartbroken to continue the crusade. Armida becomes suicidal and is eventually saved by Rinaldo, who also convinces her to become Christian.

Armida's garden thus stands for a love that is illusional. Even though in Tasso's narrative Armida and Rinaldo end up together, the garden remains a general image of being deceived and under somebody's spell and thereby already installs a flicker of intertextual doubt as to the sincerity and endurance of Maria's and Darnford's relationship. The foreshadowing of disappointment

4 Theories of intertextuality, a term initially coined by Julia Kristeva, suggest that intertextually forms an essential aspect of all (literary) works. Texts never stand alone but are always interlinked with other texts. For an introduction to the history and theory of intertextuality, see Allen (2000).

5 While the remark of Armida's garden might not be immediately apparent nor resonate with contemporary readers, it is important to keep in mind the popularity of the Tasso's epic all across Europe well into the eighteenth-century (Durant/Durant 1961: 260-1).

by comparing their current situation to Armida's garden is then fulfilled in the story when Venables successfully files a lawsuit against Darnford for the seduction of Maria (126). Darnford eventually leaves for another country (136) and after the death of her and Darnford's child Maria becomes suicidal. In one fragmented version of the ending she eventually takes her own life, while in another version, like with Armida and Rinaldo, Maria is rescued by Jemima (*Maria* 136-137). Armida's garden thus serves as a metaphor for a state of (romantic) illusion.[6] George Lakoff and Mark Johnson define a metaphor as "understanding and experiencing one kind of thing in terms of another" (5) assuming that "every experience takes place within a vast background of cultural presuppositions" (57). Here Maria's relationship with Darnford is made sense of in the context of the magical garden of Armida. The metaphor implies that Maria does not see the situation clearly. Once the metaphor successfully invites the reader to reflect Maria's and Darnford's relationship in terms of Armida's garden, it also, in a second step, invites the reader to compare her relationship with Darnford to her marriage with Venables. Both men deceive Maria to take advantage of her. Her husband Venables takes advantage of Maria financially, while Darnford takes physical advantage of Maria leaving her with a dead child (131-132, 136). Both men benefit from her only to leave her in delicate situations. Marriage is not a protection for Maria, but the prerequisite for her exploitation in a moral and legal sense. In her relationship to Venables, her possessions become his property once they are married. Darnford's relationship with Maria leads to her committing adultery, which frees him from any moral responsibility towards her as it renders him liable to Venables for having violated the latter's 'possession'. Hence, the final example combines four different forms of comparing: first, Armida's garden is a metaphor for a state of romantic illusion, secondly it offers a comparison by use of imagery taking an enchanted garden as a representation of love. Here, the meaning constructed from metaphor and imagery overlap because with regard to Armida's garden the enchanted garden *is* an illusion, yet they form distinct comparative practices. Finally, by using Armida's garden as a

6 Here it is not necessary to debate if a metaphor is always a comparison, but it suffices to point out that certain metaphors are employed to invite comparisons following Walter Erhart's argument that "comparing is the key element and an essential dynamic operation in the practice and rhetoric of metaphors, tropes, and similes alike" (2020: 123).

framework for making sense of the relationship between Maria and Darnford, their relationship is linked to Tasso's epic poem *Jerusalem Delivered*. The relationships between Armida and Rinaldo and between Maria and Darnford invite an intertextual comparison by explicitly mentioning Armida's garden.

The fact that both texts share narrative and plot features – such as the aspect of imprisonment, or the notion of love as a struggle for power over someone else and as a trap that leads to confinement, isolation, and even (attempted) suicide – invites a closer analysis. The different types of comparison outlined with the help of the first novel do not only co-occur but are entangled and work together to create ever more complex structures. Only the combination of all four comparative practices enables a reading of the text passage as an argument against marriage. Linking love to an illusion (metaphor) can only be understood as an argument against a power imbalance in marriage if the enchanted garden (imagery) is linked to the character Armida in Tasso's epic poem (intertextual) and the relationship of Maria and Darnford is read in the context of the narrative of Armida and Rinaldo (narrative). Only if all four comparative practices come together, a feminist argument can be constructed from the passage. If the intertextual or the narrative comparison are eclipsed or missed by the reader, the argument will not work anymore because elements such as the imprisonment in the garden are eliminated from the act of reasoning; Hence, the link to marriage cannot be made. While the narrative of Tasso's epic offers reconciliation at the end, Maria is not saved by a knight in shining armour but by a fellow woman (137). The romantic reconciliation of the epic remains a fantasy whereas the female protagonist of the novel can find comfort only by those in a similar situation, if at all. The harsh contrast only becomes apparent if all four forms of comparing are combined in a reading of the passage. On the other hand, it is also impossible to grasp only one of these types of comparing due to their interdependence and overlapping.

3. Types of Comparing in *The Female Quixote* by Charlotte Lennox

The second novel under consideration here, *The Female Quixote* by Charlotte Lennox, revolves around the incapability of the protagonist Arabella to compare and to differentiate her own situation from that of the protagonists in the French romance novels she consumes in great numbers. Arabella confuses the ontological levels on which she and these characters exist. Other characters in the text, such as the Doctor who admires Arabella's virtues yet tries to argue against romance fiction (374-375), compare her behaviour to an ideal standard of female conduct against which she is ridiculed and derided. The novel's plot thus displays a clear preoccupation with the topic of comparing – a preoccupation that is further highlighted by the title which provides an intertextual link to Miguel De Cervantes' *Don Quixote* (1605/1615). This link invites the reader to compare both texts and both protagonists, the male and the female Quixote. For this kind of reinvention of one character in terms of another (of Don Quixote in Arabella as a female Quixote), Walter Erhart, drawing on the example of Homer's *Odyssey*, argues that

> variations of themes and figures in world literature constitute a practice of comparing not by mere transfer or 'adaptability' of famous literary characters, but by a comparative action that puts the traditional figure in relation to the newly invented figure through an established *tertium comparationis* that sorts out similarities and differences [...]. [T]he variations of figures and characters in world literature, their mythical qualities, are triggered by the dynamics of comparative practices. The *Odyssey* becomes a pre-text when its actions and characters, already borne out by comparative practices, appear in a new context, a post-text or – according to Genette's terminology – in a 'hypertext' in which similarities and differences are worked out through a common framework, be it the theme of suffering or ingenuity or the narrative structure that the two texts have in common: sufferings with a happy ending, man fighting against natural powers, culture conquering the 'other,' homecoming. (2020: 118)

In other words, by installing Arabella as a female Quixote, the reader is immediately invited to compare both protagonists and to look for a shared framework in which both characters can be placed. To find this framework and to make sense of the relation between Arabella and Don Quixote, both texts must be compared in more detail to elucidate the numerous similarities in their narrative and plot structures: Both novels are cases of heterodiegetic narration and both protagonists have severe problems realizing the difference between the literary fiction they read and the reality of the storyworlds they inhabit.[7] Both of them expect to find in 'real life' elements of the fictions they

7 Both texts are narrated from outside the story world and hence constitute heterodiegetic narratives. However, in the case of *Don Quixote* occasional breaks in the narrative in the form of metalepsis have been discussed. For a discussion of metalepsis in *Don Quixote*, see Levin (2016) and Patrick (2008).

consume and based on this premise misinterpret the events they encounter. Finally, both texts can be considered metafictional because they discuss the power and the danger of fiction *in* fiction; both novels employ a humorous and occasionally ironic tone when talking about the virtues employed by the protagonists in accordance with the fictions they consumed (see Close 1973: 242; Mandel 1958: 161-162; Waugh 2011: 2). As we have seen, the title of *The Female Quixote* sets the novel into relation with De Cervantes' *Don Quixote* and invites the reader to compare both texts. This invitation to an intertextual comparison then calls for other literary practices of comparing in order to capture the full spectrum of the connection between both works that the title only hints at. The invitation to compare is thus not limited to one form of comparing, but rather invites diverse comparative practices in order to highlight similarities and difference between both texts. Here, especially narrative comparisons (including comparisons on the level of plot and narrative situation) support an intertextual comparison invited by the title and its variation of Don Quixote in the form of the female Quixote.

However, the intertextual comparison between *Don Quixote* and *The Female Quixote* not only highlights the similarities between both texts but also draws attention to their differences. In *Don Quixote* the reactions of the other characters towards Don Quixote's misconceptions tell us something about the protagonist. For instance, the reaction of the boy named Andrew whom Don Quixote meets along the way does not serve to indicate Andrew's level of serenity but highlights the level of Don Quixote's confusion (*Don Quixote* 265). The other characters serve as a canvas against which Don Quixote's ignorance is played out. Comparing both texts, it becomes clear that this situation is reversed in *The Female Quixote*. The other characters correct Arabella's mistake and speak out against the risk of consuming too much romance fiction. Yet, while they do ridicule her ignorance towards the distinction of fiction and reality, a distinction that requires comparing, they meet her with admiration and do not speak out against the virtues depicted in the romance fiction she consumes (*The Female Quixote* 148-150, 376-377, 379-381). Their response highlights the paradox of the romance novel in *The Female Quixote* that is, much like Arabella, both valued and ridiculed by the other characters. Hence, the focus is moved away from the female Quixote to the perception of her confusion by the other characters within the story. In other words, the novel can not only be read as a parody of *Don Quixote*, but also as a comment on its perception in eighteenth-century British cultural discourses (see More 1799: 20-23). Arabella's misunderstanding serves as a comment on the society around her. The characters installed around Arabella openly mock her for taking her French romance novels as historically accurate (*The Female Quixote* 121-122, 142). However, the mockery remains ambiguous, and is not directed exclusively at Arabella. Instead, the reaction of the other characters to Arabella's obsession with romance novels reflects the perception of the genre of the novel, in general, and *Don Quixote,* in particular, by eighteenth-century British society – a society that, while increasingly consuming novels, also warned against the dangers of this new genre (see More 1799: 23, 31; Watt 2006: 22, 42-43). This ambiguous positioning towards fiction is highlighted by inviting comparisons between both novels, between Arabella and the other characters' response to her, and by contrasting fiction with the expectations of a society that is nevertheless considerably shaped by the fictions it consumes (see More 1799: 20-23; Martin 1997: 57-58). Yet, even harsh criticism of romance novels did not necessarily imply a rejection of the novel or even the genre as such, as becomes apparent in Hannah More's *Strictures on the Modern System of Female Education* (1799). More warns of the "thousand mischiefs" of romance novels and yet praises the virtues depicted in these novels as having "formed the ancient texture of British manners" (20-23). In other words, *The Female Quixote* addresses expectations that are shaped by fictions, by comparing fiction and the expectations it installs. It reveals that Arabella is not the only character whose expectations are shaped by fiction albeit Arabella takes things to an extreme. The novel continuously coquettes with the blurring of fictional narratives and social expectations, constructing a *tertium comparationis* in the form of Arabella's virtue that is a shared element between the two.

Arabella does not blindly copy the female conduct displayed in romance novels but does so for specific purposes. This is highlighted when Arabella instructs her maid on how to tell her narrative (121-122) and when Miss Glanville directly brings up the topic of comparison (142-143). While the former part unmasks Arabella's behaviour as a performance carefully constructed in accordance with what she *assumes* is expected, the latter contrasts her performance with her capabilities and warns against taking Arabella's performance of the presumably expected for naivety or simple-mindedness. Martin convincingly argues that

> as Miss Glanville gaily displays her ignorance, becoming the unwitting object of her own raillery, Arabella's status in the satire is shifted, and new value granted to her learning and intelligence. While Arabella is admittedly sometimes foolish, she is never a fool. (1997: 55)

Arabella's response to Miss Glanville's mockery, which is going too far and eventually turns against herself, invites a comparison between both characters' reactions. It offers similar structural elements. Both women find themselves in powerful positions because the respective other made a mistake and both women can openly point out this mistake to put the respective other down. Miss Glanville makes use of this opportunity, but Arabella is "unwilling to expose her Cousin's Ignorance, by a longer Dispute upon the Subject", which puts Arabella in the morally higher position (*The Female Quixote* 143). Whereas Miss Glanville takes the opportunity to ridicule Arabella, Arabella does not belittle Miss Glanville and once made aware of her mistake in taking romance novels as historically accurate, she accepts Mr Glanville in marriage (379).

Arabella's mistake was not that she did not behave as was expected of her, or that her assumption of these expectations was wrong, but that she overdid it and thereby rendered these expectations ridiculous. All the while the society that seemingly condemns romance novels as a young woman's guilty pleasure holds on to the virtues proclaimed by romance novels (370-371, 374). Arabella does not fall out of favour for copying and performing these virtues in social contexts, but because she does so in a way that betrays romance novels as their source and by doing so questions the virtues she performs by the very act of their performance. She destabilizes the social order by openly performing a masquerade of the fiction of womanhood, yet presumably not for the purpose of protesting against the existing social conventions but by mere accident. However, the accident only occurs because she does not know any better. Once the mistake is pointed out to her and Arabella 'learns' about her misunderstanding she immediately takes up her predestined position in society as Mr Glanville's wife (383; see Meyer Spacks 1988: 536). The moment Arabella realizes her mistake is a turning point in the novel separating the narrative and her behaviour into before and after this realization (376-378), which invites a comparison between the uniformed and the informed Arabella. With this, the novel suggests that an uneducated woman might be an even greater risk to society than an educated one. Lennox certainly does not speak up for female education with the same rigour as Mary Wollstonecraft in *Maria; Or, The Wrongs of Woman*, but her novel nevertheless offers an experiment of a young woman exposed to British eighteenth-century society without receiving the necessary education to manoeuvre herself safely through this environment. This poses an antithesis to the concept of an educated woman as a risk to the social order and offers an image of education as enabling women to take up their position in society (Wyett 2015: 9).

4. Types of Comparing and Their Function

My exploration of the different forms of comparing in the two novels by Wollstonecraft and Lennox has revealed three recurring types of comparisons, namely narrative comparisons (including comparisons on the level of discourse, story, plot, etc.), imagery comparisons (including comparisons triggered by simile, metaphor, parables, etc.), and intertextual comparisons (invited by different types of references to other texts). The three types of comparing I have identified in the two novels are not mutually exclusive nor exhaustive, but they offer a preliminary overview of the comparative practices employed in both texts. All three mainly fall under the category of indirect comparisons and thus illustrate that the distinction between direct and indirect comparisons is too simple and needs to be further refined. Moreover, especially intertextual comparisons and comparisons by narrative structure seem to have a high likelihood of working together to construct more complex meanings not just from each individual comparative practice, but by creating a surplus of meaning exactly in the entanglement of both practices. In such cases narrative comparisons might therefore appear as a subcategory of intertextual comparisons. However, not all narrative comparisons need to point at other texts as was indicated by the autobiographic narrative of Jemima and Maria in Wollstonecraft's novel. Thus, the relation of narrative and intertextual comparison must be a more complex one. The relation of narrative comparisons and intertextual comparisons needs further research and at this point can only be hinted at. Most importantly, it needs to be tested in the context of a bigger corpus.

My findings indicate that comparisons of one type often invite other types of comparisons, as was the case with Armida's garden in *Maria; Or, The Wrongs of Woman* where the recognition of Armida's garden as a metaphor for romantic illusion automatically points the reader to the epic by Tasso and invites a narrative and intertextual comparison. Occasionally, however, certain practices are employed individually in order to support certain arguments posed by the text. In the imbedded narratives of Maria and Jemima, only a narrative comparison between the two is invited. While other comparative practices are employed especially in Jemima's story, the comparison of both women is limited to their life stories. Here, in what Erhart (2020: 117) terms an inner-textual comparison, the comparison is kept simple to foster the construction of the relationality between Jemima and Maria. The narrative structure highlights their shared struggles as women which are exacerbated by an unbalanced power relation to men either modulated by family structures, class structures or marriage. It poses an argument against class injustice and gender divides by constructing a relation between womanhood and slavery in the autobiographies of both women (*Maria* 11). If the comparison between the two women is not established, even the genre ascribed to the novel can change. The categorisation under a specific genre influences how a novel is perceived, as becomes apparent in More's (1799) discussion of *Maria; Or, The Wrongs of Woman*. While critical of romance novels, More speaks out vehemently against Wollstonecraft's novel. In the case of *Maria; Or, The Wrongs of Woman* the novel can be read as a romance novel based on the unhappy love plots between Maria and George and between Maria and Darnford. However, especially when a greater focus is put on the two women narrating their life stories, the socio-political argument against absolute authorities is foregrounded and the novel can be read as a Jacobin novel. Jacobin novels evolved at the end of the eighteenth-century and were "inspired by the events in France and fuelled by the controversies which followed Burke's *Reflections on the Revolution in France*" (Watson 1992: 146). Jacobin novels posed social political arguments against monarchy and absolutism. Hence, depending on the focus of the reader the novel is turned from a Jacobin novel engaging with matters of class and gender divides, to a romance novel (Johnson 2004: 103). Here, the feminist argument against marriage is linked to an argument against Absolutism. The power position of the husband over wife and children is linked to the power of the monarch over the state. Thus, the practices of comparing employed are decisive for the meaning construction and positioning of the argument structure of the novel in the discourses of its time. Only if read as a Jacobin novel based on the narrative comparison of both women can the criticism of the novel by Hannah More be contextualized (1799: 31).

In the case of the *The Female Quixote*, one aspect needs further attention before closing the discussion, and that is the relation between comparison and parody. A parody always invites a comparison between the parody and that which is parodied. Gray, Jones and Thompson distinguish between satire which "draws on social conventions" and parody which "draws on aesthetic ones" (2009: 17). According to this approach, when looking at parody one looks at formal features in a text and how these features are enacted. The parody must repeat these formal elements of that which it parodies yet it must walk the fine line between repeating these elements without becoming that which it parodies. This can be achieved by repeating some, but not all elements or by rearranging or recontextualising the repeated elements. Hence, if the(se) shared elements are added in great number, the parody paradoxically deviates and repeats the original simultaneously. Since a parody repeats mainly formal features, it might be considered a performative practice of literature. The repetition invites readers to compare and the deviation in the performance has the potential to subvert the argument of the parodied text. Phiddian pays tribute to this dilemma when he states that, in order to succeed, "Parodies can't live with their host discourses, and they can't live without them" (1997: 682). For this intermediate position of parody between deviation and repetition, Laurent argues that parody can be seen as a technique to "keep meaning from becoming lethargic" (59). It is a way of negotiating meaning by the comparative confrontation of the parody with its source texts. Parodies in novels according to the suggested grouping above fall under intertextual comparisons and support the statement by Angelika Epple and Walter Erhart that comparisons are "instruments of power" (2015: 15) and as such ideologically charged. However, Lennox's novel is a complex intertextual comparison because it does not limit itself to two *comparata*. Instead, it simultaneously draws on romance novels, *Don Quixote* and the perception of both in eighteenth-century British society, hence creating a relation between four entities. The complex meaning can only be constructed from this comparison by making oneself familiar with all four sources. It is not enough to be familiar with romance novels, *Don Quixote* and the text by Lennox, but rather the public discussion of all three such as offered by More (1999) must be taken into consideration as well.[8] The ambiguity of her remarks about romance novels and the praise of *Don Quixote* offer a tension of rejection and admiration that is echoed in the argumentative structure of the *The Female Quixote*. Hence, it critically highlights that Arabella is ridiculed

8 More's text was published in 1799 and *The Female Quixote* 1752 hence, it would be misleading to argue that Lennox took the text by More into consideration when writing her novel. However, More's text can be taken as exemplary for the ambivalent discourses on romance novels at the time. It was chosen for the paper because it addresses female education in *Maria; Or, The Wrongs of Women*, romance novels and *Don Quixote*, and hence offers a particularly suiting source for a discussion of both novels in terms of the arguments they pose on female education.

for taking romance novels as historically accurate yet idolized for upholding the virtues of these novels.

5. Conclusion

This chapter analyzed practices of comparing in *Maria; Or, The Wrongs of Woman* by Mary Wollstonecraft and *The Female Quixote* by Charlotte Lennox to argue that the comparative practices employed in novels are not innocent but are invoked in support of certain ideologically charged arguments. In *Maria; Or, The Wrongs of Woman*, the narrative comparison between Jemima and Maria turns the novel from a romance to a Jacobin novel, conveying a feminist argument against marriage that is entangled with an argument against the political order and in favour of a better position for women in eighteenth-century British society. Hence the narrative comparisons between Jemima and Maria do not just support the arguments presented in the novel; rather, the comparative practices employed in the text provide no less than the basis on which the arguments of the novel are built upon. In *The Female Quixote*, the intertextual comparison between Lennox's novel and *Don Quixote* by De Cervantes offers the framework in which the novel parodies romance novels and their perception in eighteenth-century Britain.

Certain arguments developed in the novels analyzed here are difficult to construct from the text unless comparative practices receive more attention and are included in the examination of those texts. Based on the heuristic distinction between direct and indirect comparisons suggested by Hartner and Schneider with an added subgrouping into narrative, imagery and intertextual practices of comparing, the chapter suggested that literary practices of comparing can co-occur and build complex networks that can contribute to creating multi-layered argumentative structures within a novel. By taking into consideration not just who compares what, and for what purpose, but taking a closer look at the textual practices employed in a literary work, the underlying ideological premises of the ideas posed in a novel can be addressed. In Wollstonecraft's novel marriage is compared to a form of slavery, while Lennox employs intertextual comparisons and narrative comparisons to outline the ambiguous position in British society towards romance novels and the female virtues they propagate. Both novels pose strong feminist arguments, and both do so by employing certain practices of comparing. Thus, to outline the underlying ideological investment in a novel, it is necessary to analyze *how* novels compare.

Bibliography

Allen, Graham. *Intertextuality*. New York: Routledge, 2000.

Aristotle, W. R. Roberts, Ingram Bywater, Friedrich Solmsen, and Aristotle. *Rhetoric*. New York: Modern Library, 1954.

Close, Anthony J. "Don Quixote's Love for Dulcinea: A Study of Cervantine Irony." *Bulletin of Hispanic Studies (Liverpool)* 50.3 (1973): 237.

Cope, Edward Meredith. *An Introduction to Aristotle's Rhetoric: With Analysis, Notes and Appendices*. Macmillan, 1867.

De Cervantes, Miguel Saavedra. *The Ingenious Hidalgo Don Quixote De La Mancha*. Trans. John Rutherford. Penguin, 2003.

Durant, Will and Ariel Durant. *The Age of Reason Begins*. Simon and Schuster, 1961.

Eggers, Michael. "Outlines of a Historical Epistemology of Comparison: From Descartes to the Early Nineteenth Century." *The Force of Comparison: A New Perspective on Modern European History and the Contemporary World*. Ed. Willibald Steinmetz. New York: berghahn, 2019. 33-52.

Epple, Angelika and Walter Erhart, eds. *Die Welt beobachten – Praktiken des Vergleichens.* Frankfurt: Campus Verlag, 2015.

Erhart, Walter. "Odysseus, Blackbirds, and Rain Barrels." *Practices of Comparing*. Bielefeld University Press, transcript, 2020. 111-136.

Evans, Vyvyan and Melanie Green. *Cognitive Linguistics: An Introduction*. Edinburg: Edinburg University Press, 2006.

Gray, Jonathan et al. *Satire TV: Politics and Comedy in the Post-Network Era*. New York: New York University Press, 2009.

Hale, Matthew, George Wilson and Sollom Emlyn. *The History of the Pleas of the Crown*. Vol. 1. T. Payne et al., 1778.

Han, Tan Cheng. "Marital Rape-Removing the Husband's Legal Immunity." *Malaya Law Review* 31 (1989): 112-128.

Johnson, Nancy E. *The English Jacobin Novel on Rights, Property and the Law: Critiquing the Contract*. Basingstoke: Palgrave Macmillan, 2004.

King, Rebecca Frances. *Rape in England 1600-1800: Trials, Narratives and the Question of Consent.* Durham theses, Durham University, 1998.

Kramer, Kirsten et al. "Vergleichen und Erzählen. Zur Verflechtung zweier Kulturtechniken." *Working Paper des SFB 1288*, No. 4 (2020). Accessed online, 15 August 2021. ‹https://pub.uni-bielefeld.de/record/2946608›.

Lakoff, George and Mark Johnson. *Metaphors We Live By.* Chicago: University of Chicago Press, 2003.

Laurent, Jenny. "The Strategy of Form." *French Literary Theory Today: A Reader.* Ed. Tzvetan Todorov. Cambridge: Cambridge University Press, 1982. 34-63.

Lennox, Charlotte and Margaret Dalziel. *The Female Quixote, or, The Adventures of Arabella.* Oxford: Oxford University Press, 2008 [1752].

Levin, Yael. "Metalepsis and the Author Figure in Modernist and Postmodernist Fiction." *Twentieth Century Literature* 62.3 (2016): 289-308.

Mandel, Oscar. "The Function of the Norm in *Don Quixote*." *Modern Philology* 55.3 (1958): 154-163.

Martin, Mary Patricia. "High and Noble Adventures: Reading the Novel in The Female Quixote." *Novel: A Forum on Fiction.* 31.1 (1997): 45-62.

Meyer Spacks, Patricia. "The Subtle Sophistry of Desire: Dr. Johnson and "The Female Quixote"." *Modern Philology* 85.4 (1988): 532-542.

More, Hannah. *Strictures on the Modern System of Female Education: With a View of the Principles and Conduct Prevalent Among Women of Rank and Fortune. By Hannah More. In Two Volumes.* Vol. 1. T. Cadell jun. and W. Davies, 1799.

Patrick, Brian D. "Metalepsis and Paradoxical Narration in Don Quixote: A Reconsideration." *Letras Hispanas* 5.2 (2008): 116-132.

Phiddian, Robert. "Are Parody and Deconstruction Secretly the Same Thing?" *New Literary History* 28.4 (1997): 673-696.

Punter, David. *Metaphor.* London: Routledge, 2007.

Schneider, Ralf. "Comparison, Analogy, and Knowledge in Literature: Basic Considerations and the Case of Early Modern English Texts." *Analogy, Copy, and Representation: Interdisciplinary Perspectives.* Ed. Christoph Haase and Anne Schröder. Bielefeld: Aisthesis, 2017. 137-154.

Tasso, Torquato. *Jerusalem Delivered: An English prose version.* Detroit: Wayne State University Press, 1987.

Taylor, Barbara. *Mary Wollstonecraft and the Feminist Imagination.* Cambridge: Cambridge University Press, 2003.

Watson, J. R. "The Jacobin Novel." *A Handbook to English Romanticism.* Ed. Jean Raimond. London: Palgrave Macmillan, 1992. 146-149.

Watt, Ian P. *The Rise of the Novel: Studies in Defoe, Richardson and Fielding.* Berkeley: University of California Press, 2006.

Waugh, Patricia. *Metafiction: The Theory and Practice of Self-Conscious Fiction*. London: Routledge, 2011.

Wollstonecraft, Mary. *The Vindications: The Rights of Men and The Rights of Woman*. Peterborough: Broadview Press, 1997.

Wollstonecraft, Mary. *Maria; Or, The Wrongs of Woman*. New York: W. W. Norton, 1994 [1798].

Wyett, Jodi L. "Quixotic Legacy: The Female Quixote and the Professional Woman Writer." *Authorship* 4.1 (2015): 1-19.

"'tis by Comparison we can Judge and Chuse [sic!]": Incomparable Oroonoko

Monika Class

1. Introduction

Aphra Behn's *Oroonoko, or The Royal Slave, a True History* was first published in early summer of 1688 less than a year before the author's death. The novel narrates the short life of a royal West African general. It delineates how it comes about that this prince, who starts his military career successfully defending his kingdom at the age of seventeen, who undergoes experiences of forbidden love, kidnapping, and enslavement, and who leads a slave rebellion that fails, ends up dismembered in the British colony of Surinam. The British had colonized the territory in 1652, but the Dutch usurped the colony in 1667 (Hughes 2007: xxxi). Aphra Behn probably resided on a Surinamese sugar plantation in the early 1660s, but there is no extant trace of the enslaved figure whose free name was Oroonoko and slave name Caesar; nor is there documentary evidence of a slave rebellion on a British Surinamese plantation at the time (Britland 2019).

Since the mid-1980s, *Oroonoko* has been elevated to the status of a canonical work of English prose fiction (Aravamudan 2014: 27). Some scholars have designated *Oroonoko* the origin of the English novel and the first American novel as well (Azim 1993: 35; Doyle 2008: 97; Spengemann 1984; Schabert 1997: 305). While the scholarship on *Oroonoko* is vast, the ideology of the novel is particularly contested partly because the ambiguous configuration of the text – a dialogization of multiple discursive practices – resists a translation into stable ideologies (Athey and Alarcón 1993: 417). Central to this body of scholarship is the question to what extent Oroonoko's struggles work as a surrogate for late seventeenth-century and early eighteenth-century dominant British historiography. This focus can be traced back to Laura Brown and Felicity Nussbaum's *The New Eighteenth Century* (1987). Building on New Historicism, the edited volume played an important role in the integration of gender, race, class and empire studies into (American) eighteenth-century scholarship (Alkon 1989: 581). In her essay, Laura Brown influentially established the reading that the figure of Oroonoko alias Caesar stands in for the Stuart monarchs and by extension for Behn's allegiance with them.[1] Accordingly, Anglocentric Restoration politics have served as the major *tertium comparationis* for analyses of Behn's powerful work of literature. Commentators disagree about the colonial significance of *Oroonoko*: Some scholars regard the narrative as an endorsement of plantation slavery (e.g. Moira Ferguson 1992: 356), others as a denouncement (e.g. Goreau 1980: 289) and many address the intrinsic ambivalences about colonial power, the slave trade, race and gender within the text (Griffin 2019: 107; Lipking 2004: 175; Morrissey 2016: 11; Margaret Ferguson 1991: 159; Hughes 2002: 1).

In light of these developments in eighteenth-century studies, the present essay contributes to the investigation of the practices of comparing in long eighteenth-century Britain by examining the comparisons and the rhetorical suspension of comparability in the narrative configuration of Behn's *Oroonoko*. In the preface, dedicated to the Scottish nobleman Richard Maitland, Behn draws attention to the importance of comparison for the "*Critical Reader*" (*Oroonoko*, 1995: 56): "'*tis by Comparison we can Judge and Chuse* [sic!]" (55). At the same time, however, Behn configured reversals of the eponymous hero's fate in ways that complicate and postpone comparability. Scholars have noted that analogies between Behn's text and British historiography of the period include inconsistencies. They observe, for instance, that this "hybrid masterpiece" (Botelho 2014: 34) contains "contradictory" combinations of rhetorical patterns (Chibka 1998: 513).

In this spirit, this essay follows a hermeneutic-phenomenological approach by analysing the operations of comparability and incomparability within the emplotment based on Paul Ricoeur's theory of triple mimesis (Ricoeur 1984). Broadly speaking, the approach means that readerly embodiment plays a vital role in the signification process that results from the encounter of readers with the text (Ricoeur 1988). Not only is meaning constituted through the intellectual fusion of horizons (Gadamer 1989), the

1 According to Sal Nicolazzo, the collection has had the adverse effect of priming "eighteenth-century scholarship to understand race and empire primarily as topics that politicized enquiry might peruse, rather than as foundational material structures that implicate us and our work in objects of study" (Nicolazzo 2020: 233).

signification of fiction also depends on readers' emotions and affects according to Ricoeur (1988: 137). Author's compositions play an important role in such embodied reading experiences. Ricoeur theorizes such representations under the heading "emplotment".

The term "emplotment" designates "the operation that draws configuration out of a simple succession" (Ricoeur 1984: 65). Emplotment (*mise en intrigue*) creates narratives by lending a mere sequence of events a coherent form that encompasses a beginning, a middle and an end. The entire level of configuration within Ricoeur's mimetic model consists of this narrative operation (i.e., emplotment). Besides configuration, there exist two further levels in the mimetic process, namely prefiguration and refiguration. Configuration, which is synonymous with narrative composition, is the middle part of the model, preceded by the prefiguration and followed by refiguration. Ricoeur bases emplotment on the Aristotelian notion of "muthos", modifying the latter in two ways that are relevant for the present argument. First, emplotment ultimately serves the development of fictional character and not vice versa (Ricoeur 2005: 216). Second, Ricoeur generalizes "muthos" to such an extent that it characterizes narrative *per se* and not only dramatic art (Bläser 2015: 18).

On the one hand, emplotment accounts for coherence inasmuch as the former synthesizes heterogeneity. On the other hand, emplotment also creates pathos and emotionality in the widest sense of catharsis (Ricoeur 1984: 43). Therefore, Ricoeur speaks of two opposing poles at work in emplotment: concordance (synthesis of heterogenous elements) and discordance (unresolved dissonances). The notion of discordance includes reversals (peripeteia) in the story that inflict an unexpected turn on the hero or heroine: The "play of discordance internal to concordance" is the "internal dialectic of poetic composition" (38). Derived from Aristotelian tragedy, Ricoeur's narrative theory, then, can be said to be interwoven with emotionality (especially with pity and fear): "By including the discordant in the concordant, the plot includes the affecting within the intelligible" (44). These reversals trigger readers' emotions for the hero and, in doing so, hamper his comparability insofar as the figure's sustained struggles reinforce readers' imaginings of the very characters as if he were an individual (Ricoeur 2005: 216). In brief, the discordant elements of the emplotment do much to rhetorically suspend the hero's comparability and thus reinforce Oroonoko's literal persona, namely the enslaved African prince.

That discordance outweighs concordance in the case of *Oroonoko* underpins my argument about the dynamics of comparability and incomparability. I contend that three reversals in the narrative suspend comparability momentarily, emphasize the hero's action and suffering irrespective of the narratorial commentary, and, in doing so, recalibrate otherwise Eurocentric analogies inherent in the novel. The first part of this article focuses on three major analogies with the Stuart monarchy and Roman history and the second half highlights three major peripeteia – from bliss to sullenness, from enslaver to the enslaved, and from martyrdom to infrahuman spectacle – each of which suggest that the emplotment ultimately transcends Eurocentric analogy. The contradictions in the plot cluster around the materiality of plantation slavery. Instantiating rhetorical incomparability mainly through sullen bliss, the enslaved enslaver, and unwitnessed martyrdom, I propose that Behn makes a virtue out of discordant configuration by constructing her eponymous hero as an exceptional human being (as opposed to a moral exemplar or racialized type). The figure of the entitled West African leader of a slave rebellion galvanizes singularity. In so doing, Behn's tale can be said to establish a hallmark of the novel as a literary genre in terms of formal realism (Watt 1957).

By "rhetorical incomparability", I mean certain textual devices that effectively postpone or suspend comparability. Jean-Jacques Rousseau rightly observed that "[w]hoever sees only a single object has no occasion to make comparison" (qtd. in Cheah 1999: 3). The same applies to whoever only imagines a single person. Having said this, rhetorical incomparability does not rule out the structural ubiquity of comparability (Sass 2020: 94). Rhetorical incomparability in this essay should not be conflated either with "the line of argument – popular within literary studies, where it [...] repeats the discipline's self-defining reverence for the unique, the particular and the incomparable, while making it seem that the dislike [of comparability] itself is anti-imperialist by its very nature" (Robbins 2013: 191). Anything and anybody can be compared in principle, but one of the innovative virtues of early eighteenth-century novels (and novellas) was the introduction of fictional characters that strikingly resembled real-life people. John Bunyan's allegory *The Pilgrim's Progress* (1678, 1684) features figures that stand in for certain moral types or abstract ideas such as the main character "Christian". By contrast, early novels in English are invested in the imitation of human beings (Bode 2005: 127; Auerbach 1946). Such a fleshing out of fictional character is more likely to occur in text-reader interaction "if no information is presented that would allow easy initial categorization" or comparison (Schneider 2013: 123). For life-like characters to emerge from prose fiction, it is vital to postpone comparability to some degree. The rhetoric of incomparability in novels resembles "the suspension of structurally possible comparisons [in other fields such as] in morals and public life as well as in intimate contexts" (Sass 2020: 94). After all, rhetorical incomparability is, Hartmut von Sass notes, a "highly important institution" (ibid.). Eighteenth-century critical readers and philosophers like Rousseau emphasized comparability (Epple/Erhart 2020: 25), but early anglophone novelists nonetheless made a virtue out of postponing comparability by narrative means that evoke the hero's seeming incomparability. In brief, the demands that early novelists made on their readers allowed and even encouraged them to simply follow the life and adventures of their hero. In Behn's case, I propose in Part II of the present essay, such followability does not suspend comparisons for good but reinforces Oroonoko's non-European persona as a West African prince: The peripeteia of the emplotment – sullen bliss, the enslaved enslaver, and unwitnessed martyrdom – are effective in mainly three ways: First, they postpone and arguably even occlude Eurocentric comparisons; second, they evoke Oroonoko as a strong man of action, and, third, they make room for comparisons with the transnational history of slavery. In so doing, they evoke Oroonoko's literal persona, namely as a West African warrior-prince who is unjustly sentenced to be dismembered in the British colony Surinam.

Comparability plays a vital role in the vast scholarship on Behn's foundational novella. "Comparative work", Pheng Cheah notes, "is generally understood as a mode of analysis that begins from one given national or cultural case of subject of legitimate interest, X, which is the basis for forming a provisional hypothesis or working idea about this subject that serves the *tertium comparationis*" (1999: 3). Methodologically speaking, the grounds of comparison inevitably shape the results and therefore call the "objective basis" of comparisons into question (ibid.). "In the past, the grounds of comparison were undeniably Eurocentric", Cheah claimed in 1999 (3). Part I "The Analogies of Plot" supports Cheah's hypothesis that the bias of comparison in Behn's case is Eurocentric on two levels: that of the primary text, i.e., Behn's novella, as well as that of the critical intervention made by Laura Brown and others.

Drawing on Geoffrey E. R. Loyd, some scholars agree that comparisons can be classified along the axes of five valences: (1) one's own superiority claims, (2) other's superiority, (3) priority of communalities, (4) insurmountable of differences and concomitant incomparability, and (5) novelty (Epple/Erhart 2020: 23). By opposing "the theoretical pitfalls of the 'other'" (1987:

185), Brown prioritized above all the third valence, namely the communalities between the African hero and the Stuart Monarchs. In this line of argument, scholars have shown how the similarities exoticize the protagonist. My point in Part I is that such an emphasis on communalities with European monarchs unwittingly or wittingly reinforces the Eurocentric bias of comparisons; indeed, the emphasis on communalities with the Stuarts has effectively occluded the novella's potential for lateral comparison, for instance, the work's comparability with the transnational history of slavery (even if Brown tried to salvage the latter). By "lateral comparison", I mean the modes of comparability that "balance the 'frontal comparisons' of 'us' and 'them' as practiced in much traditional as well as in postcolonial anthropology" (Epple/Erhart 2020: 17). As an alternative to Brown's communality-focused comparisons, Part II of this essays suggests that the novelty of Oroonoko's story at the time warrants a lateral comparison with the transnational history of slavery.

2. The Analogies of Plot

The narrative configuration of *Oroonoko* partly does run parallel to the historiography of the Stuart Monarchs, with Charles I and also with Charles II and James II. In its beginning, middle and end, the short novel establishes suggestive analogies between the murdered West African crown prince and English historiography from the Civil Wars to the Glorious Revolution. Charles I features initially in the narrator's reference to Oroonoko's aristocratic breeding and education. Much narratorial emphasis is placed on Oroonoko's knowledge of "the late Civil Wars in England, and the deplorable Death of our great Monarch" and Oroonoko's moral judgement that this execution means an "Abhorrence of the Injustice" (*Oroonoko*, 1995: 62). The hero's knowledge of British politics and his evaluation thereof operate as narratorial recommendations. They work as attempts to assimilate Oroonoko's manner and moral compass into some equivalent of "some European Court" (ibid.). These statements thus seemingly align Oroonoko with Restoration ideology: first, the royalist position in mid-seventeenth-century English politics; secondly, the indefeasibility of the monarchy; and, thirdly, the glorification of Charles I.

Parts of the middle section in the narrative reinforce this parallel. Upon arrival in British colonial Surinam, which completes a series of events consisting of the kidnapping, the Middle Passage, the enslavement and commodification of the African prince, readers learn that the overseer of the Lord

Governor's plantation gives Oroonoko a new name as a rite of passage into enslavement: "Mr *Trefry* gave Oroonoko that of Caesar, which Name will live in that Country [Surinam] as long as that (scarce more) glorious one of the great Roman" (*Oroonoko*, 1995: 88). It is commonly accepted that "Caesar" is the code name Behn used for the Stuart kings in her other writing (Doyle 2008: 103). Long after the death of Charles I in 1649, Behn and her audience had lived under the rule of Charles II until he passed away in 1685 and James II succeeded to the throne. Charles II is Caesar in Behn's "poem 'A Farewell to Celladon on His Going Into Ireland' (1684) as is James II in her poem 'Poem to Her Sacred Majesty Queen Mary' (1689)" (Brown 1987: 199). Analogous to that, Oroonoko alias Caesar can be said to personify three English monarchs at once while the analogies match above all the two failed kings in need for mystification, Charles I and James II.

Progeny features as a thematic catalyst for the intradiegetic crisis in a way that compares to the Glorious Revolution. It is Imoinda's pregnancy that precipitates Oroonoko's rebellion since revolt offers the only option for escape from the enslavement of their offspring (Sussman 1993). Central as reproduction is to dynasties, this emplotment has been said to run parallel to the birth of James II's son in 1688 and the Catholic king's deposition (Guffey 1975; Miller 1982: 541). This analogy fails to consider the unpopularity and arbitrariness of this British ruler, who according to Whig and Tory parliamentarians had "tried to destroy the constitution and impose popery and absolutism" (Miller 1982: 545). Nonetheless, it is fair to say that the birth of James' heir spurred on the rebellion (against James II) since the male progeny entailed the threat that the next ruler of England "would be, not one of James' Protestant daughters, Mary or Anne, but a Catholic son" (Page/Sonnenburg 2003: 236). In addition, Surinam belongs to the British history of Dutch usurpation. The intradiegetic location thus aligns the English colonial defeat in 1667 with William of Orange's, "the Dutchman's", seizing the English throne in 1688.

If we read *Oroonoko* as such an allegory for the Glorious Revolution, the signification of the eponymous hero is reduced to universalist claims of royal bloodlines and the meaning of his enslavement by white colonisers dwindles into a hazy figure for the threat of illegitimate rule, social unrest in the wake of the deposition of the legitimate monarch, and the jeopardy of the "patrilineal ideology" of landownership (Pacheco 1994: 500). This reductive analogy can be extended to the indefeasibility of the English monarchy even at the expense of Anglican Protestantism, which opens up questions concerning the author's biography and her loyalism to the Stuart kings that lie outside of the theoretical frame of the present analysis of narrative configurations.

The beheading of Charles I has served as a *tertium comparationis* for the brutal, graphic ending of *Oroonoko*. "For Behn and others", Brown notes, "the colonies stage an historical anachronism, the repetition of the English revolution, and the political endpoint of Behn's narrative is the re-enactment of the most traumatic event of the revolution, the execution of Charles I" (Brown 1987: 197). In the novella's final section, Behn's principal character is confined to Parham Hill and thus protected from his persecutors so that he can recuperate as far as possible from the horrific torture the British inflicted on him after the revolt. However, as the personification of evil tyranny, the Deputy Governor Byam calls in his council consisting of "notorious villains" from Newgate prison (*Oroonoko,* 1995: 112), sentences Oroonoko to death, kidnaps him once again and has him quartered at the hands of the Irish henchman Banister. As Oroonoko is being brutalized to death, he remains stoic "without a Groan, or a Reproach" (118).

These events correspond roughly with the execution of the English king in 1649. Charles I was imprisoned, tried for treason, and beheaded by a small group of Members of Parliament called the "Rump" following his defeat in the Civil Wars. Behn's configurations echo, according to Doyle, the "language used in sympathetic Restoration histories and biographies of Charles, revealing the close connection" (2008: 103). These texts represent Charles I as the heroic martyr, who betrays no sign of fear at the verge of imminent death (Brown 1993: 58). Moreover, the figure of the "wild" Banister resembles the descriptions of the "absolute barbarity" of the king's executioner (Doyle 2008: 103). Inasmuch as these royal hagiographies recount the dismemberment of the king's corpse and the parading of his body parts in London streets, Behn's narrator recalls how the pieces of Oroonoko's remains, the "frightful spectacle of a mangle'd king" (*Oroonoko,* 1995: 118), are sent across South American plantations. Along these lines, the fictional life narrative of Oroonoko appears basically as a surrogate for the commemoration of English kings and English glory in the 1640s, 1660s, and 1680s. In these terms alone, the narrative configuration of *Oroonoko* would amount to an exoticized version of the English trauma of regicide.

But "there is no simple political allegory in Behn's novella" (Brown 1987: 197). Critics tend to overlook that, irrespective of Behn's codename, Julius Caesar was also "the perhaps most celebrated victim" of kidnapping from a coastal region (Patterson 1982: 115). Ransom was paid and Caesar freed. But

Caesar stepped in, according to Plutarch, to crucify his captors himself once they had been caught (Osgood 2010). Oroonoko's fate matches Plutarch's historiography insofar as the narrative configuration begins with the analeptic representation of Oroonoko's royal ancestry and military achievements in the storyworld called Coromantien, continues on the slave ship and then in Surinam with Oroonoko's failed attempts to negotiate his release and that of others against a ransom – "either Gold, or a vast quantity of Slaves" (*Oroonoko,* 1995: 93) – and ends with his thwarted plan to take revenge on the villain Byam and "all those he thought had inrag'd him [sic!]" (113).[2] Crucially, the analogy with Julius Caesar's kidnapping does not extend to the Roman's liberation and revenge on the captors. It is Oroonoko who is quartered in the end. Nonetheless, Plutarch's subtext opens up an analogy that casts not only the villains, Byam and Banister, but also the supposed colonial benefactors, the plantation overseer Trefry and Colonel Harry Martin, into the mould of a band of mean pirates.

The significance of the narrative incorporation of Plutarch's histography leads beyond the analogy with late seventeenth-century domestic politics since it provides a subtext for the re-enactment of British imperial history of enslavement and slave revolt in the West Indies and Guiana. That Roman history and in particular the English version of Plutarch's *Lives of the Noble Grecians and Romanes* (1579) offers parallels for the intradiegetic slave rebellion is a rhetorical move that features prominently in Oroonoko's important anti-slavery speech. Oroonoko appropriates the legend of Hannibal for his revolt (see also *Oroonoko,* 1995: 93). The assimilation of Hannibal is part of the rhetorical feat that helps Oroonoko to regain the support of his former slaves and fellow Africans (453, fn. 93). For Oroonoko compares himself to Hannibal and the flight from the plantation to Hannibal's crossing of the Alps: "He told them that he had heard of one *Hannibal* a great Captain, had Cut his Way through the Mountains of solid Rocks; and shou'd a few Shrubs oppose them; which they cou'd Fire before 'em [sic!]?" (106). The significance of this comparison is disputed. Commentators have explained Oroonoko's summoning of Hannibal in terms of racial identity: "*This is a black pride incarnate*" (Polk 2000: 158; see also Margaret Ferguson 1994: 170). Derek Hughes notes that "Hannibal, however, was not black, or even African. The Carthaginians were

2 I will discuss the enslaved enslaver in detail in the second part of the present essay.

Phoenician colonists in North Africa" (2002: 9).[3] What remains undisputed, however, is Hannibal's reputation as one of the great military leaders of antiquity and as the most dangerous obstacle to Roman global dominance during his lifetime. The comparison thus flatters both parties: the African rebels and the British slaveholders.

The comparison with Hannibal highlights a virtue of the African prince that tends to be overlooked, namely Oroonoko's military prowess. Critical assessments largely focus on Oroonoko's whitewashed physiognomy, Eurocentric education, and commodification as a pet slave (Aravamudan 1999: 29-70; Brown 1987: 187). But the length of narratorial commentary dedicated to European assimilation should not distract scholarly attention from Oroonoko's military achievements in Coromantien at a very young age. After all the African backstory begins with Oroonoko's military promotion to the rank of general in the army and his victorious intervention in a two-year war at the tender age of seventeen. This is to say that in contrast to court-centred medieval romances like *Roman de la Rose*, Behn's novella begins with the hero's absence from court. Overall, the young prince spends more than ten years in the company of "fighting Men, or those mangl'd, or dead; who heard no Sounds, but those of War and Groans" (*Oroonoko*, 1995: 62). What underpins the narrative discourse on Oroonoko's looks and gallantry is the emplotment of his leadership legitimized not only by royal birth but also earned by military merit and his other pursuits of honour. Having said this, the comparison with Hannibal does not only help to throw Oroonoko's bellicose acumen into relief, but the analogy also keeps counterhegemonic formations in check: the comparison signals that the enslaved African general will be the defeated by the British colonisers, inasmuch as Hannibal ultimately loses his battles against Rome.

3. The Peripeteia of Plot

New Historicism has taught us that a work of literature does not exist in a vacuum (Greenblatt 1995). Through this lens claims of incomparability *per se* become indefensible. However, New Historicism has a blind spot insofar

3 Derek Hughes reviews key texts from Sepúlveda and Las Casas through Arthur, Comte de Gobineau on the discursive formation of "race" in the late seventeenth century (2012).

as fictional narratives like Behn's powerful novella also convey a pathos that interrupts and recalibrates underlying comparability. In this regard, the remainder of this essays departs from the New Historicist analysis in the wake of Braun's influential essay. I provide instead an alternative interpretation of Behn's novella by combining the premise of what Sass has called "the dimension of an ethics of comparison" and the ethics of reading based on Ricoeur (Sass 2020: 95; Ricoeur 1988).

Rhetorical or "performative incomparability implies [as mentioned] structural comparability" (Sass 2020: 95). Incomparability in a work of literature is rhetorical insofar as it suggests a refusal to compare while the structural comparability of the work persists. If incomparability is a matter of rhetoric, as Sass claims, it is also a matter of affect. Brown largely failed to take the role of affects into consideration. Paying close attention to the ways in which emplotment stirs affects, I argue that Behn's emplotment (1) engages readers so thoroughly in the hero's action and suffering through the horrific trials he encounters that it reinforces the African hero's literal persona and, in doing so, undermines Eurocentric comparisons and (2) redirects them towards lateral comparisons such as with the transnational history of slavery.

Central to the present interpretation is my contention that incomparability in the case of Behn's novel is rhetorical and evokes primarily an affective disposition. "Nothing compares to you" is not only the title of Prince's pop song covered by Sinéad O'Connor (Sass 2020: 91), the *Oxford English Dictionary* also tells us that one of earliest recorded meanings of "incomparable" is meant in the affective sense of "matchless", "peerless", and "transcendent" such as the record dated to 1662 in Thomas Elyot's *The Castle of Helthe*: "She was afterwards his incomparable wife" (OED 2021). Behn composed the plot in such a way that readers follow Oroonoko's trials and tribulations in the narrated world and not Charles I's tribunal and execution. The emplotment conveys rhetorical incomparability insofar as the novelistic evocation of pity and fear depends on Oroonoko's actions. The peripeteia direct readers' attention away from Eurocentric comparisons inasmuch as these moments of sudden reversal in the hero's fortunes compare above all to specific elements of West African culture as well as plantation slavery.

By tracing Oroonoko's action and suffering in the second part, my essay contributes to a specific debate in Anglo-American literary criticism. Current scholarship about the role of affect and Ricoeurian hermeneutics is embroiled in the debate about "postcritical reading" spearheaded by Rita Felski's *Uses of Literature* and other publications (e.g. Anker/Felski 2017; Felski 2020). "Postcritical reading" is defined by a goal rather than a methodology, namely "to do better justice to the transtemporal liveliness of texts and the coconstitution of texts and readers – without opposing thought to emotion or divorcing intellectual rigor from affective attachment" (Felski 2015: 154). The proponents of postcritique broadly follow Eve Kosofsky Sedgwick's shift from paranoid to reparative reading, intending to recast literary criticism as an affective and critical practice (Sedgwick 2002). My line of argument is sympathetic to this aspect of "postcritical reading" but not the entire polemic (see Landy 2020). I agree "that critique is as much a matter of affect and rhetoric as of philosophy or politics" (Felski 2015: 3). In this spirit, my interpretation of *Oroonoko* suggests that the lateral comparisons in Behn's novel are reinforced and even driven by Oroonoko's rhetorical incomparability insofar as it focuses attention on his character development. At the same time, however, my uses and understanding of "neophenomenology" (Felski 2015: 191) are diametrically opposed to Felski's reduction of Ricoeur's hermeneutics. Felski caricatures Ricoeur as a hardened hermeneut in whose view "[m]eaning can be retrieved only after arduous effort; it must be wrested from the text, rather than gleaned from the text" (Felski 2015: 31). From the vantage point of postcritical reading, the hermeneutics of suspicion serves merely as a foil in the recalibration of literary criticism. Collapsing Ricoeur's entire theory of narrative into the hermeneutics of suspicion, postcritical reading has so far failed to consider Ricoeur's *Time and Narrative* and other writings that actually elucidate affective styles and modes of reception. In this respect, I emphatically depart from postcritical reading and draw on Ricoeur's narrative and reception theory, conceptualising the rhetorical incomparability in Behn's novel in the aforementioned terms of emplotment as the interplay of concordance and discordance (Ricoeur 1984, 1985, 1988).

Emplotment suits the analysis of Behn's contradictory novella because the Ricoeurian concept provides insights into the internal dynamic of the narrated actions independent from narratorial commentary. The homodiegetic white female narrator in *Oroonoko* colours the events in the shades of western standards of evaluation (see Nadine Boehm-Schnitker's article in this volume). The present essay focuses instead on Oroonoko's actions as presented in the narrative composition in order to eschew the opinionated narrator. It is Oroonoko's actions that provide readers with a perspective that leads beyond the comparisons with British and Roman historiography; indeed, it is Oroonoko's actions and suffering that transcend an allegory of the Glorious Revolution. This excess of meaning erupts above all at the points of configuration of plantation slavery. These unsettling formations take primarily the shape of three important reversals: sullen bliss, the enslaved enslaver, and unwitnessed martyrdom.

It is at midpoint in the novella that the testimonial configurations clash head-on with Eurocentric history and romance. Consequently, incomparability begins to outweigh comparability within the overall narrative configuration. Crucially, the supposed happy ending of the conventional marriage plot – Oroonoko and Imoinda's wedding – entails a perfidious reversal: the incompatibility of slavery and marriage turns bliss into "sullenness" (*Oroonoko,* 1995: 93). This incompatibility has to do with the material conditions of slavery.

According to Orlando Patterson, enslaved persons are alienated from their social order. This alienation is the reaction to and result of their coercion into total submission to the master. Patterson's "celebrated" comparative study of slavery is designed to identify the "inner dynamics" and "institutional patterns" of slavery (Patterson 1982: ix; Gilroy 1993: 63). The sociologist influentially theorized slavery as the state of social death: "the man who was enslaved was in a permanent condition of liminality and must forever mourn his own social death" (Patterson 1982: 60). Slaves are socially dead to the extent that they are "alienated from all 'rights' or claims of birth" and thus cease to belong in their own right to "any legitimate social order" (5). Enslavement involves the loss of social existence other than under the master's dominance and thus "the incorporation of the slave into the marginal existence of the permanent alien" (54). That this alienation extends to marriage rights is dramatized in *Oroonoko*.

When Oroonoko and Imoinda marry and conceive a child, marriage fails one of its main purposes: the legitimisation of progeny and of the custodial powers of parents. The hereditary status of slavery precludes marriage from fulfilling these very functions (Patterson 1982: 187). One of the crucial differences between Oroonoko's parentage situation and that of the English king James II lies in the fact that plantation slavery contributed substantially to the erasure of family trees among the descendants from enslaved Africans in the West Indies: "One of the most important findings of Michael Craton's study of the oral history of the descendants of the Worthy plantation slaves of Jamaica" (6) was the near impossibility "to trace precise lineage" (Craton 1978: 374-375). In the storyworld, the dissolution of the parental rights, which marriage otherwise secures, contributes to the social death of slavery, too: "This Thought made him [Oroonoko] very uneasy and his Sullenness gave them [the enslavers] some Jealousies of him" (*Oroonoko,* 1995: 93). The pregnancy brings the alienation inherent in slavery into focus and renders Oroonoko and

Imoinda's happiness sullen. Behn configures the masculine drive to preserve patrilineal ancestry as a major cause for Oroonoko's decision to challenge his British enslavers after all: "This new Accident [Imoinda's pregnancy] made him more Impatient of Liberty" (ibid.). The collision of the romance configurations of the Anglo-Roman comparison with the testimonial configurations of hereditary plantation slavery thus marks a major turning point within the emplotment of *Oroonoko*. This discordance tends to move readers and inspire compassion.

Another reversal that distinguishes Behn's novella consists in the enslavement of the enslaver. Commentators have regarded the fact that Oroonoko "is described as having captured and sold black slaves in African wars before he himself was enslaved" as an ideological indicator for the whole work of fiction. Margaret Ferguson, for instance, interprets such "'civilised' doubleness" as an endorsement of "the privileges of the nobility with the profits of the slave trade" (Margaret Ferguson 1994: 179). This argument disregards the heterogeneity of slavery, overlooks the exceptional brutality of plantation slavery in the West Indies and reinforces the Western polarisation of "slaves and nonslaves" (Patterson 1982: 27; Patterson 1967; Mintz 1986: 48-51).

Historians of slavery conceive of a spectrum between two extremes of slavery. In his foundational monograph *Many Thousands Gone*, Ira Berlin distinguishes between a "society with slaves", where slavery exists but does not function as the dominant labour system, and a "slave society", where slavery represents the dominant form of labour and shapes every other social relationship within that society (between man and women, parents and children, husbands and wives, workers and bosses, as well as rulers and rules). Far from justifying slavery, the distinction offers a way to differentiate between West Indian plantation slavery and certain forms of African slavery rather than conflating them as the same evil. The abolitionist pamphlet, written by the former slave trader John Newton and published in 1788, compared British with African slavery as follows:

> The state of Slavery, among these wild barbarous people, as we esteem them, is much milder than in our colonies. For as, on the one hand, they have no land in high cultivation, like our West-Indian plantations, and therefore no call for that excessive, unintermitted labour, which exhausts

our Slaves; so on the other hand, no man is permitted to draw blood, even from a Slave. (1788: 15-16)[4]

According to Newton, enslaved labour at the sugar plantations in the Caribbean was merciless whereas slavery among Africans was "much milder". Newton's pamphlet appeared in 1788, but the use of African labour at sugar factories and plantations was already in place since the middle of the seventeenth century. Sidney W. Mintz has established the argument in economic history that the preindustrial state of seventeenth-century British society does not preclude the "recognition of the industrial aspects of plantation development" in the West Indies during the period (1986: 49). Slaves in the sugar factories, for instance, worked "continuously in shifts lasting all day and part of the night, or the whole of every second or third night" (50). The homodiegetic narrator describes this economy: "Those then whom we make use of to work in our Plantations of Sugar, are Negro's [sic!], Black-Slaves altogether" (*Oroonoko*, 1995: 60). The configurations of Oroonoko as the enslaved enslaver, which the eponymous "royal slave" anticipates, captures the heterogeneity of slavery mentioned by Newton and studied in the history of slavery. The figure of enslaved African enslaver points to aspects of the African practice of slavery in terms other than those of the Western ideology of freedom.

Oroonoko features initially as an enslaver of Africans when he presents the prisoners he has taken in battle to the daughter of the general who gave his life in order to save the prince: "Oroonoko coming from the Wars [...] thought in Honour he ought to make a Visit to Imoinda, the Daughter of his Foster-father, the dead General [...] to present her with those Slaves that had been taken in this last Battel, as the Trophies of her Father's Victories" (*Oroonoko*, 1995: 63-64). The scene configures the enslavement of the defeated soldiers as an act of honour attributed to both the killed general and to the victorious prince. The figuration suggests that Oroonoko's reputation as an African hegemonic male depends on the number of dependents he can obtain. It matches the sociological data for sub-Saharan Africa gathered by Patterson, who shows that power and honour are intricately linked in enslavement practices (1982: 79, 11). According to Patterson, slavery served as a means alongside kinship and

4 For a discussion of the contemporary relevance of the conflation of different types of slavery see Akala's *Natives: Race and Class in the Ruins of Empire* (2019: 139). For more information about John Newton see the entry in Postma's *The Atlantic Slave Trade* (2003: 95-96).

affinal relations for an "ambitious man" to acquire prestige, which is "critical in *all* African societies" (1982: 83; see Athey and Alarcón 1993: 443, fn. 41). The dishonour experienced by the enslaved prisoners of war directly serves the prince's honour, bolstering his social status and appeal for his love interest Imoinda. Her appreciation reinforces the hero's honour rhetorically.

Furthermore, the figure of the enslaved enslaver contains configurations of African cultures, probably those of the Ashanti people. Scholars have observed that Oroonoko's invented homeland is named after a West African trading post formerly used by English and Dutch slave merchants (Hughes 2012: 127). According to Susan Andrade, "Coromantien, also spelled Coromantyn and Koromanty, was the name given in the New World to ethnic groups like the Ashanti, who came from the interior of the African Gold Coast, now Ghana" (1994: 209). Moira Ferguson notes that "people from that region in question would have spoken Ashanti, Fanti, and possibly some less widely spoken languages such as Twi or Ga" (1992: 342). The configuration of Oroonoko's social relations in Coromantien and in particular his enslavement of prisoners of war runs parallel to customs in a society with slaves like the early Ashanti kingdom in West Africa, also known as Asante.[5]

The author-narrator describes Oroonoko above all as "Prince" and "General" (*Oroonoko,* 1995: 63). The configuration of Oroonoko, his military merit, his gold and slave resources bear witness to a struggle for hegemonic masculinity in African societies of the period if one follows the character development closely. That Oroonoko belongs to the highest ranks of his society is literally inscribed in his face: the sides of his temples feature the cutaneous carvings of animals, such as "a little Bird" (92). Yet birth alone does not secure his social status. Oroonoko's constant efforts to reinforce his prestige are apparent from his long-standing preoccupation with war and slave trade in the Coromantien narrative, which resonates with the figure of the "big men" and chiefdoms in African history. His struggle for prestige continues even in the conflicted terms of slavery in the Surinamese part of the story. While in the British colony, it is Oroonoko who re-establishes, for instance, after a period of violent confrontation, peaceful relations between the indigenous inhabitants that allow him and the English "open, and free Trade with 'em" (103). This configuration resonates with West African culture. The Asante emerged

5 "Asante." *Encyclopedia Britannica*, 26 January 2021. ‹https://www.britannica.com/topic/Asante›. See also Ivor Wilks who traces the history of the Asante, one of the most powerful peoples of Ghana, from the fifteenth century onwards (Wilks 1993).

from the Akan states at the close of seventeenth century (Wilks 1993). The ethnic group is reported to have the "popular proverb [...] If you have not a master, a beast will catch you" (Patterson 1982: 27). The early Asante were a tribal community in which boundaries of social order were porous enough to allow for, and even to fuel, the competition for prestige (Wilks 1993: 95-98; Patterson 1982: 83). This competition extended to any so-called "*abirempon* (big men)", who endeavoured to establish themselves as dominant hegemonic males by engaging in the Atlantic slave trade and using slave labour to clear land and found villages (Miescher 2019: 40). The intradiegetic designations "Prince" and "General" for Oroonoko echo the "*abirempon*".

According to Patterson, the power structures among the colonial Ashanti are typically "personalistic", which means that power structures are direct and open and that the principle of kinship played a crucial role in them (Patterson 1982: 19). Patterson describes the personalistic power idiom as a network of interdependences, which exists irrespective of any Western notions of freedom: "the most unslavelike person was the one in whom a small number of claims, powers, and privileges were spread over a large number of persons; the slave, on the other hand, was someone in whom a large number of claims, privileges and powers were concentrated in a single person [the master]" (27). Within this framework, the only way for a slave to achieve privileges and powers was through the master.

This interdependence goes some way to account for the reversal of fortune that turns the enslaver into the enslaved and for the relation between Oroonoko and his former slaves in Surinam as well. The first response of the enslaved Africans at Parham Hill plantation when they recognize their former slaveholder in Oroonoko is grief. When Oroonoko assures them "he was no better" than "their Fellow-Slave", they deem this piece of news worthwhile "Mourning and condoling" (*Oroonoko*, 1995: 89). The enslavement of their master entails the dissolution of the little access to privileges and power they once had (through him). In traditional African societies, Patterson notes, the difference between enslaver and slave was "difficult for an outsider" to ascertain and came down to the "honorlessness of the slaves" (1982: 83). Oroonoko resists such honourlessness; that is, he insists on his honour despite his enslavement. Holding on to his former status as master, he is able to immediately command respect from his former and other fellow slaves when he decides to rebel. Oroonoko's act of rebellion entails the resumption of his former role as master by representing himself as their access to high social status, a state that the narrator calls "free", once they all escape and return to "his kingdom"

(106). Accordingly, Oroonoko then takes charge of the collective flight from the plantation, which constitutes the act of rebellion. Oroonoko's powerful speech reinforces his status as the hero of narrative and invites readers to side with the black rebels.

The representation of the majority of slaves (except for Oroonoko, Tuscan and Imoinda) has been understood as a justification of plantation slavery, dehumanisation and racialisation of Africans. Richard Frohock notes that "Behn's narrative implies that the vast majority of enslaved Coramantiens are naturally suited to their position in the colonial economy" (Frohock 1996: 442). The figure of the African enslaved enslaver complicates this view. Put simply, the narrative configuration shows the power of plantation slavery to trump and dismantle the power of all existing social relations between husband and wife, parents and children, but also (milder) forms of slavery of African societies with slaves.

Crucial to the configuration of the anonymous crowd of Africans on the plantation is their final acceptance of the British masters as their only option to remain alive irrespective of any other former claims, privileges, or power they once had. This resignation manifests itself in the African slaves' participation in Oroonoko's beating. Inasmuch as Oroonoko is defeated in his rebellious struggle for mastery, his former slaves lose his protection (as a master) again and, in turn, become complicit in his public humiliation. The configuration of the failed revolt – the defeat, Bynam's betrayal of the written contract of surrender, and Oroonoko's extremely brutal public flogging – operates as the materialisation of Western plantation slavery in the story. Oroonoko's furious condemnation of the slaves' cowardice – "he was asham'd of endeavoring to make those Free, who were by Nature *Slaves*" (*Oroonoko*, 1995: 109) – sets an end to his aspirations to act as the conduit to privileges for his former slaves and expresses his particular outrage about the cowardice of his countrymen. Moreover, the configuration of the Deputy Governor's betrayal – the disregard of the written terms of surrender – and the total humiliation of the whipping marks the turn from Oroonoko's wish to regain his full honour towards the ardent desire for revenge on Bynam and his accomplices.

The third and final reversal features in the execution scene at the end of the novella: unwitnessed martyrdom. The analogy of Oroonoko's quartering with the decapitation of Charles I disregards a crucial difference in Behn's configuration. The scene of Oroonoko's slaughter takes place in the absence of the prime witness, the homodiegetic narrator. This absence is crucial for the distinction between the representations of martyrdom and testimony according to Aleida Assmann. 'Martyrdom' is derived from Greek '*martys*' and "refers to the witness in the religious sense" (Assmann 2006: 268). The lexemes "*martyr* and *martyrdom* maintain an important link with the highly symbolic act of witnessing, as developed in the three monotheistic religions and immediately related to persecution and violent death" (ibid.). Martyrs in Judaism, Christianity and Islam undergo violent death and, in doing so, triumph over their persecutors. For the violent public death to attain the symbolic meaning of martyrdom, the martyr "depends on someone to witness the suffering, to identify him or her as a martyr (rather than a justly persecuted rebel), and to codify the story for future generations" (ibid.). Such witness and codification exist for Charles I (to attain the symbolic meaning of martyrdom), but the author-narrator's absence from the scene of execution bars the figuration of Oroonoko from it.

However, the narratorial absence corroborates the configuration of the final scene as a testimony in the tradition of ancient Greek tragedy and Shakespearean drama, according to which the messenger conveys the news of the catastrophe from which he has escaped. To quote the dying Hamlet, in act 5, scene 2, when he asks Horatio to be his witness: "Absent thee ... in this harsh world draw thy breath in pain, to tell my story" (qtd. in Assmann 2006: 267-268). The function of the witness is to describe "what cannot be brought onto the stage, in the name of those who are no longer able to speak for themselves" (Assmann 2006: 268). Likewise, the author-narrator is removed from the scene of horror while the last sentence of her testimonial configuration omits the main subject's name: "to make his Glorious Name to survive to all ages; with that of the Brave, the Beautiful and the Constant *Imoinda*" (*Oroonoko*, 1995: 119).

The testimonial register of the final scene is consistent with the notion of slavery as social death. Inasmuch as slavery brings about the "secular excommunication" of the enslaved (Patterson 1982: 5), the latter and in particular the enslaved African man is excluded from the powerful symbolism of martyrdom in Western representation. There is no possibility for triumph in the configuration of Oroonoko's death. Faith is not at stake in this scene, nor collective identity, nor solidarity or compassion (see Griffin 2019). Instead, the scene graphically configures torture with the exception of the pipe as a token of remaining masculine dignity. The scene, first published in London in 1688, influentially configures the iconography of the brutalized male black body, which has been remediated and fetishized in multiple media up to the present day (as such in the case of the video recordings of the murder of George Floyd by a U.S. policeman on 25th May 2020). At the same time, the narrative by virtue of its written composition and thanks to the literary acumen of its author represents readers up to the current day with the troubling discordances that challenge Western understandings of the relation of master and slave.

Having said this, the ending does not determine the significance of the entire narrative. The contradictions in Oroonoko's actions embedded in the storyworld resist the complete infrahuman codification of the final paragraphs (Gilroy 2000: 22). Crucially, the peripeteia of the plot lend Behn's hero the singularity that distinguishes this figure in literary history, transcends the operations of the then nascent racialized typologies as well as those of the moral exemplar and elevates him to the level of an exceptional human being: "*this Great Man*" (*Oroonoko*, 1995: 56). The incomparability inherent in the actions of the enslaved African warrior-prince thus corroborates the foundational role of Aphra Behn's *Oroonoko* in the emergence of the novel as a literary genre.

Bibliography

Akala. *Natives: Race and Class in the Ruins of Empire*. London: Tworoadsbooks, 2019.

Alkon, Paul. "Recent Studies in the Restoration and Eighteenth Century." *Studies in English Literature, 1500-1900* 29.3 (1989): 579-620.

Andrade, Susan Z. "White Skin, Black Masks: Colonialism and the Sexual Politics of *Oroonoko*." *Cultural Critique* 27 (1994): 189-214.

Anker, Elizabeth S. and Rita Felski, eds. *Critique and Postcritique*. Durham: Duke University Press, 2017.

Aravamudan, Srinivas. *Tropicopolitans: Colonialism and Agency, 1688-1804*. Durham: Duke University Press, 1999.

Aravamudan, Srinivas. "What Kind of Story Is This?" *Approaches to Teaching Behn's* Oroonoko. Ed. Cynthia Richards and Mary Ann O'Donnell. New York: MLA, 2014. 27-33.

Assmann, Aleida. "History, Memory, and the Genre of Testimony." *Poetics Today* 27.2 (2006): 261-273.

Athey, Stephanie and Daniel Cooper Alarcón. "*Oroonoko's* Gendered Economies of Honor/Horror: Reframing Colonial Discourse Studies in the Americas." *American Literature* 65.3 (1993): 415-443.

Auerbach, Erich. *Mimesis: Dargestellte Wirklichkeit in der abendländischen Literatur*. Bern: Francke, 1946.

Azim, Firdous. *The Colonial Rise of the Novel*. London: Routledge, 1993.
Behn, Aphra. *The Works of Aphra Behn. The Fair Jilt and Other Short Stories*. Ed. Todd, Janet. Vol. 3. 7 Vols. Columbus: Ohio State University, 1995.
Berlin, Ira. *Many Thousands Gone: The First Two Centuries of Slavery in North America*. Cambridge: Belknap Press of Harvard University Press, 1998.
Bläser, Stefanie. *Erzählte Zeit – Erzähltes Selbst: Zu Paul Ricoeurs Begriff der narrativen Identität*. Berlin: Pro Universitate Verlag, 2015.
Bode, Christoph. *Der Roman*. Tübingen: UTB Verlag, 2005.
Botelho, Keith M. "Credibility and Truth in *Oroonoko*." *Approaches to Teaching Behn's* Oroonoko. Ed. Cynthia Richards and Mary Ann O'Donnell. New York: MLA, 2014. 34-38.
Britland, Karen. "Aphra Behn's First Marriage?" *The Seventeenth Century* (2019): 1-21.
Brown, Laura. *Ends of Empire: Women and Ideology in Early Eighteenth-Century English Literature*. Ithaca: Cornell University Press, 1993.
Brown, Laura. "Romancing the Empire: *Oroonoko* and the Trade in Slaves." *The New Eighteenth Century: Theory, Politics, English Language*. Ed. Martha C. Nussbaum and Laura Brown. New York: Methuen, 1987. 41-61.
Cheah, Pheng. "Grounds of Comparison." *Diacriticis* 29.4 (1999): 1-18.
Chibka, Robert L. "'Oh! Do Not Fear a Woman's Invention': Truth, Falsehood, and Fiction in Aphra Behn's *Oroonoko*." *Texas Studies in Literature and Language* 30.4 (1988): 510-37.
Craton, Michael. *Searching for the Invisible Man: Slaves and Plantation Life in Jamaica*. Cambridge: Harvard University Press, 1978.
Doyle, Laura. *Freedom's Empire: Race and the Rise of the Novel in Atlantic Modernity, 1640-1940*. Durham: Duke University Press, 2008.
Epple, Angelika and Walter Erhart. "Practices of Comparing: A New Research Agenda between Typological and Historical Approaches." *Practices of Comparing: Towards a New Understanding of a Fundamental Human Practice*. Ed. Angelika Epple, Walter Erhart, and Johannes Grave. Bielefeld: Bielefeld University Press, 2020. 11-38.
Felski, Rita. "Good Vibrations." *American Literary History* 32.2 (2020): 405-415.
Felski, Rita. *The Limits of Critique*. Chicago: University of Chicago Press, 2015.
Felski, Rita. *Uses of Literature*. Oxford: Blackwell, 2008.
Ferguson, Margaret. "Juggling the Categories of Race, Class and Gender: Aphra Behn's *Oroonoko*." *Women's Studies* 19.2 (1991): 159-181.
Ferguson, Margaret. "News from the New World: Miscegenous Romance in Aphra Behn's *Oroonoko* and *The Widow Ranter*." *The Production of English Re-*

naissance Culture. Ed. David Lee Miller, Sharon O'Dair, and Harold Weber. Ithaca: Cornell University Press, 1994. 151-189.

Ferguson, Moira. "*Oroonoko*: Birth of a Paradigm." *New Literary History* 23.2 (1992): 339-359.

Frohock, Richard. "Violence and Awe: The Foundations of Government in Aphra Behn's New World Settings." *Eighteenth-Century Fiction* 8.4 (1996): 437-452.

Gadamer, Hans-Georg. *Truth and Method. Wahrheit und Methode*. Trans. Joel Weinsheimer and Donald G. Marshall. 2nd ed. London: Continuum, 1989.

Gilroy, Paul. *Against Race: Imagining Political Culture Beyond the Color Line*. Cambridge: Belknap Press of Harvard University Press, 2000.

Gilroy, Paul. *The Black Atlantic: Modernity and Double Consciousness*. London: Verso, 1993.

Goreau, Angeline. *Reconstructing Aphra: A Social Biography of Aphra Behn*. New York: Dial Press, 1980.

Greenblatt, Stephen. "Culture." *Critical Terms for Literary Study*. Ed. Frank Lentricchia and Thomas Mclaughlin. 2nd ed. Chicago: Chicago University Press, 1995. 225-232.

Griffin, Megan. "Dismembering the Sovereign in Aphra Behn's *Oroonoko*." *ELH* 86.1 (2019): 107-133.

Guffey, George. "Aphra Behn's *Oroonoko*: Occasion and Accomplishment." *Two English Novelists*. Ed. George Guffey and Andrew Wright. Berkeley: University of California Press, 1975. 2-41.

Hughes, Derek. "Blackness in Gobineau and Behn: *Oroonoko* and Racial Pseudo-Science." *Women's Writing* 19.2 (2012): 204-221.

Hughes, Derek. "Race, Gender, and Scholarly Practice: Aphra Behn's *Oroonoko*." *Essays in Criticism* 52.1 (2002): 1-22.

Hughes, Derek. *Versions of Blackness: Key Texts on Slavery from the Seventeenth Century*. Cambridge: Cambridge University Press, 2007.

Landy, Joshua. "In Praise of Depth: Or, How I Stopped Worrying and Learned to Love the Hidden." *New Literary History* 1.51 (2020). 145-176.

Lipking, Joanna. "'Others,' Slaves, and Colonists in *Oroonoko*." *The Cambridge Companion to Aphra Behn*. Ed. Derek Hughes and Janet Todd. Cambridge: Cambridge University Press, 2004. 166-187.

Miescher, Stephan F. "Masculinities." *A Companion to African History*. Ed. William H. Worger, Charles H. Ambler, and Nwando Achebe. Hoboken: Jon Wiley, 2019. 35-58.

Miller, John. "The Glorious Revolution: 'Contract' and 'Abdication' Reconsidered." *The Historical Journal* 25.3 (1982): 541-555.

Mintz, Sidney W. *Sweetness and Power: The Place of Sugar in Modern History*. New York: Penguin, 1986.

Morrissey, Lee. "Transplanting English Plantations in Aphra Behn's *Oroonoko*." *Global South* 10.2 (2016): 11-26.

Newton, John. *Thoughts Upon the African Slave Trade. By John Newton, Rector of St. Mary Woolnoth*. London: Printed for J. Buckland, in Pater-Noster-Row; J. Johnson, in St. Paul's Church-Yard; and J. Phillips, in George-Yard, [1788].

Nicolazzo, Sal. "Another 1987, or Whiteness and Eighteenth-Century Studies." *Eighteenth-Century Fiction* 33.2 (2020): 233-248.

OED. *Oxford English Dictionary*. Oxford University Press, 2021. Accessed online, 26 June 2021. ‹http://www.oed. com/›.

Osgood, Josiah. "Caesar and the Pirates: Or How to Make (and Break) an Ancient Life." *Greece & Rome* 57.2 (2010): 319-336.

Pacheco, Anita. "Royalism and Honor in Aphra Behn's *Oroonoko*." *Studies in English Literature, 1500-1900* 34.3 (1994): 491-506.

Page, Melvin E. and Penny M. Sonnenburg. *Colonialism: An International, Social, Cultural, and Political Encyclopedia*. Santa Barbara: ABC-CLIO, 2003.

Patterson, Orlando. *Slavery and Social Death: A Comparative Study*. Cambridge: Harvard University Press, 1982.

Patterson, Orlando. *The Sociology of Slavery: An Analysis of the Origins, Development and Structure of Negro Slave Society in Jamaica*. London: MacGibbon & Kee, 1967.

Polk, Khary. "Reviving *Oroonoko*." *The Journal of Negro History* 85.3 (2000): 154-161.

Postma, Johannes. *The Atlantic Slave Trade*. Gainesville: University Press of Florida, 2003.

Ricoeur, Paul. *Vom Text zur Person: Hermeneutische Aufsätze (1970-1999)*. Trans. Peter Welsen. Ed. Peter Welsen. Hamburg: Felix Meiner Verlag, 2005.

Ricoeur, Paul. *Time and Narrative. Temps et récit*. Trans. Kathleen Mclaughlin and David Pellauer. Vol. 1. 3 Vols. Chicago: University of Chicago Press, 1984.

Ricoeur, Paul. *Time and Narrative. Temps et récit*. Trans. Kathleen Mclaughlin and David Pellauer. Vol. 3. 3 Vols. Chicago: University of Chicago Press, 1988.

Ricoeur, Paul. *Time and Narrative. Temps et récit*. Trans. Kathleen Blamey and David Pellauer. 3 Vols. Chicago: University of Chicago Press, 1984, 1985, 1988.

Robbins, Bruce. "Chomsky's Golden Rule: Comparison and Cosmopolitanism." *Comparison: Theories, Approaches, Uses*. Ed. Rita Felski and Susan Stanford Friedman. Baltimore: Johns Hopkins University Press, 2013. 191-209.

Sass, Hartmut von. "Incomparability: A Tentative Guide for the Perplexed." *Practices of Comparing: Towards a New Understanding of a Fundamental Human Practice*. Ed. Angelika Epple, Walter Erhart, and Johannes Grave. Bielefeld: Bielefeld University Press, 2020. 87-109.

Schabert, Ina. *Englische Literaturgeschichte: Eine neue Darstellung aus der Sicht der Geschlechterforschung*. Stuttgart: Kröner, 1997.

Schneider, Ralf. "The Cognitive Theory of Character Reception: An Updated Proposal." *Anglistik* 24 (2013): 117-134.

Sedgwick, Eve Kosofsky. "Paranoid Reading and Repetitive Reading." *Touching Feeling: Affect, Pedagogy, Performativity*. Ed. Eve Kosofsky Sedgwick et. al. Durham: Duke University Press, 2002. 123-151.

Spengemann, William C. "The Earliest American Novel: Aphra Behn's *Oroonoko*." *Nineteenth-Century Fiction* 38.4 (1984): 384-414.

Sussman, Charlotte. "The Other Problem with Women: Reproduction and Slave Culture in Aphra Behn's 'Oroonoko'." *Rereading Aphra Behn: History, Theory, and Criticism*. Ed. Heidi Hunter. Charlottesville: University of Virginia Press, 1993. 212-233.

Watt, Ian. *The Rise of the Novel: Studies in Defoe, Richardson and Fielding*. London: Chatto & Windus, 1957.

Wilks, Ivor. *Forests of Gold: Essays on the Akan and the Kingdom of Asante*. Athens: Ohio University Press, 1993.

Articulating Differences: Practices of Comparing in British Travel Writing of the Long Eighteenth Century

Nadine Böhm-Schnitker

1. Introduction

The time frame from the Glorious Revolution to Romanticism – the time frame of the long eighteenth century – is crucially defined by an increasing dominance of comparative practices that are fundamentally "entrenched in networks of circulation of bodies, artefacts, discourses and ideas", as we argue in the introduction to this edited collection (16). In that context, the modern novel emerges as a symptomatic genre that provides ample opportunities for comparisons on all literary levels, first and foremost certainly on the level of the characters in a system of contrasts and correspondences together with the level of narrative transmission (see the contribution by Hartner/Schneider).[1] Comparisons are understood as the outcomes of comparative *practices* and, as such, they are "interwoven with the interests and perspectives of the ones who compare" (Epple/Erhart 2020: 16). They do not only occur intraculturally – for example with reference to modes of behaviour in different social classes or with regard to different genders – but also interculturally, predominantly with reference to other cultures and ethnicities. The texts under consideration here – Aphra Behn's *Oroonoko* (1688) and Daniel Defoe's *The Life and Strange Surprizing Adventures of Robinson Crusoe, of York, Mariner* (1719) – vicariously and imaginatively negotiate such comparative practices and they reflect on the fundamental interdependence of self and other in the emergence of the modern Western individual by a generic hybridity that combines (auto)biograph-

1 On different types of comparing in narrative fiction, see also the contribution by Anne Lappert in this volume.

ical with travel writing: the emerging novelistic 'individual' or 'self' is thus crucially articulated with the 'other' encountered abroad. A generic hybrid, Behn's novella represents a mixture between a memoir of the author herself, a biography of its main character Oroonoko, a novel, an Oriental romance, a heroic tragedy, and a New World travel story (see Gallagher 2000: 13). Defoe's *Robinson Crusoe* is equally defined by overlapping genre conventions, as this fictional autobiography draws on both travel writing and the spiritual autobiography.

The genre of the novel develops at a time when British colonial expansion is in the midst of a "shift from a subsistence-based to profit-oriented colonial economy dependent on African slaves" (Wheeler 1995: 825). However, the work force required for plantations, e.g. sugar plantations, was rather diverse between the seventeenth and the eighteenth centuries, and thus both the actual interethnic encounters of the emerging Empire as well as the genres negotiating such encounters draw on quite diverse "racialized differences competing for dominance", including "religion, national origin, ownership of property, or skin color" (Wheeler 1995: 839); thus, "emergent racialized categories of difference are indeed produced" in order to legitimate and undergird social stratifications between 'masters', 'servants' and 'slaves', but they "are not stable in either the literary or social text" (852). Indeed, skin colour seems to take on a new significance after 1680 (see 839), and hence I employ it as a particular focus point in this article on practices of comparing in British travel writing of the long eighteenth century.

In a social context, comparative practices can be considered paramount cultural practices that are employed for social stratification in the contact zones of colonial encounters. In the literary field, comparative practices crucially impact on the construction and authority of narrators, the construction and constellation of characters, the very notion of 'character' as well as the construction of space. It is my aim in this chapter to explore the cultural relevance of comparative practices in the emerging novel genre as a literary negotiation of British colonial expansion that is articulated with the emergence of the 'individual' as marked by categories of difference such as race, class and gender. For that end, I will focus on the interconnection between the literary construction of and interaction between characters and spaces as mediated by different kinds of narrators. I will show that the literary 'individual' emerges defined by a close articulation of economic/capitalist, political/colonial and social discourses that shapes and determines the viability of subjects in the long eighteenth century. Comparative practices are the means by which this subject gains its contours.

The strong generic impact of travel writing on the development of the novel in the long eighteenth century is reason enough to underline the relevance of "spatialization" in the genre (Herman 2002: 263), in the sense that narratives are "systems of verbal or visual prompts anchored in mental models that have a particular spatial structure. More exactly, narratives represent the world being told about as one having a specific spatial structure" (264). Travel writing enacts such a narrative construction of space and ties it closely to the characters that experience these spaces. It is the character narrators defined by 'whiteness' that guide readers into new and unseen spaces in which intercultural encounters occur. Spatial structures also impact on the possible interactions between the traveller with the people inhabiting the spaces encountered. Hence, my approach to comparative practices is defined by a double-focus on characters and spaces and their construction in the transnational contexts of travel writing. The "unparalleled popularity" (Batten 1978: 1) of travel writing in the eighteenth century is rooted in *practices* of comparing that comprise close observation and description of the environments and people encountered as well as collecting, sorting, classifying, contextualizing and naming (see Epple/Erhart 2015: 10). Drawing on postcolonial studies, I will focus on the co-emergence of 'individuals' and 'environments' in the intimate intertextualities between travel writing and the novel in the long eighteenth century (see Reckwitz 2003: 283).

The increase in publications on the intercultural encounter with the ethnic other in the British empire coincides with a transition of power forms: In a Foucauldian paradigm, the long eighteenth century is associated with a turn to biopower and, tied to that, the emergence of racism in the context of a biological understanding of 'races' that impacts on the way in which intercultural encounters become envisaged (see Foucault 1990: 137-143). While biopolitics represent a form of power intent on managing, securing and prolonging life (see 137-138), racism is the concomitant ideology and technology to safeguard the function of killing within such a power form (see Lemke 2003: 161) that develops more fully during the second half of the nineteenth century (see Foucault 1990: 149). As Thomas Lemke elucidates, racism serves to generate a norm; the norms producing a 'normal' body rely on practices of comparing to ascertain deviations from established norms, to evaluate differences and to structure interventions (see 162). Practices of comparing serve as the praxeological articulation of an emerging biopolitics with racism during the long eighteenth century, and this applies both to the construction of an Anglo-Saxon 'whiteness' as a norm and an African 'blackness' as a deviation from the established norm that only emerges through comparative practices that also need to tackle a complicated colour spectrum between these emerging 'poles'; hence, I will concentrate particularly on practices of comparing with the *comparata* being characters and the *tertium comparationis* being skin colour, social status, habitus, modes of behaviour and ways of thinking as markers of an emerging concept of 'race', while the agents performing the comparison are either narrators or characters. As Angelika Epple has shown, 'race' as a category of difference pertaining to human beings can be understood as an effect or outcome of comparative practices: "Comparing simultaneously creates similarities and differences in respect to a *tertium* (such as race). Overcoming racial discrimination in everyday life would mean overcoming discourses on racial comparisons" (2020: 323). An analysis and critique of racism thus needs to tackle comparative practices in particular. In Behn and Defoe, skin colour begins to be singled out as a central determiner of racial difference that allows for the classification and social stratification of bodies; this distinction turns into the central focus for racialized practices of comparing in the respective texts and it is these that deserve further scrutiny. My guiding hypothesis is that 'skin colour' as an analytical focus point may serve as a turnstile that interconnects questions of the expansion of Empire in its ideological, economic and spatial scope and helps to make 'self' and 'other' visible in interethnic encounters, in which 'self' and 'other' co-emerge as discursive products of travel writing.

Within the context of British Empire-building, "comparing as a globalized practice was perceived as practice of modern dominance, a tool of power, which perpetuates related relations of hegemony and subordination, center and periphery, sameness and difference" (Rocha Teixeira 2019: 6) and as a marker of modernity more generally (see Foucault 1974): "the encounters, conflicts, and entanglements of different cultures and the evolution of a comparative scholarly methodology were just two sides of one coin: the making of so-called 'Western' modernity" (Epple/Erhart 2020: 25). Hence, comparisons serve as discursive practices that construct the binaries they purport to describe. In transcultural encounters, however, comparisons are made reciprocally and may provide a means of resistance (see Rocha Teixeira 2019: 7). While taxonomies certainly represent the result of comparative practices as power/knowledge, they do not remain uncontested. Their cultural plausibility hinges on perspective, and hence narrative perspective is an important focus for the analysis of the (fictional) (auto)biographies chosen here. Postcolonial studies have significantly shaped the way in which Behn's and Defoe's narratives have been read. They raised awareness that, in travel writing, travellers "never look on places anew or completely independently but perceive them instead through an accretion of others' accounts" (Youngs 2013: 9). The whole undertaking of travel writing consequently represents a complex effort of cultural hermeneutics in the connection of intercultural encounters, a reflection on perception and its intermedial coding, as well as its translation into cultural forms. It is perhaps not surprising that travel writers set their tales in heterotopic spaces – colonies, islands, ships – and present the described interactions between characters as a kind of experiment that diminishes the tales' direct social impact.[2] Furthermore, the picaresque structure of the stories allows for the description of only loosely connected scenes that need not describe a continuous sphere of the real but that only present selections of possibilities. The comparative practices employed, however, clearly "contribute to shaping, ordering, and changing the world" (Kramer/Rohland 2021: 3), and have a crucial impact on the development of racism (see e.g. Wheeler 1995: 822-823; 852).

2. Aphra Behn, *Oroonoko* (1688)

Aphra Behn's 1688 novella *Oroonoko* became paradigmatic both for its importance for the development of the novel – there is an intertextual impact on Daniel Defoe's *Robinson Crusoe* (1719), for instance – despite the fact that it is interspersed with what we would now consider racist descriptions of its main character. The novella's ideological ambivalence is reflected on several literary levels, among them prominently the level of genre and the level of the narrative situation that is characterized by a clear difference between the narrating and the experiencing I of the novella's author-narrator.

Oroonoko provides an early example of the close connection of comparative practices, the embodiment of social positionalities and an emergent racism in a biopolitical context. Its cultural legacy reveals the wider repercussions of

2 A heterotopia serves as "a kind of effectively enacted utopia in which the real sites, all the other real sites that can be found within the culture, are simultaneously represented, contested, and inverted" (Foucault 1986: 24).

Behn's articulation of the literary value of prose fiction, gendered author positions and racialized notions of slavery. Being considered "the first English narrative with an African hero" (Gallagher 2000: ix-x), *Oroonoko* represents a novelty in terms of its production, its subject matter and its narrative strategy. The story centres on the fate of the African prince and later king Oroonoko as well as of his wife Imoinda. In close succession, both are abducted from Coramantien, an English trading port situated in today's Ghana, and taken to the English colony of Surinam in the mid-1660s that Behn claims to have visited herself in 1664.[3] Depicting the triangular trade between Britain, Africa and the West Indies, the author-narrator throws into relief the different memory traces that the characters take with them to the colony. In this setting, transcultural memories come to intersect; they "migrate from one continent to another with individuals. [...] As migrants carry their heritage, memories and traumas with them, these are transferred and brought into new social constellations and political contexts" (Assmann/Conrad 2010: 2). Behn's *Oroonoko* constructs transcultural memories of slavery as defined by multiple categories of difference and, more specifically, multiple intersections of race, class, and gender. With that, comparative practices become paramount for the different kinds of encounters set in the fictional space of Surinam. Furthermore, *Oroonoko* is fraught with questions of authorization and negotiations of power that are frequently played out on bodies. The novella performs the containment of a slave rebellion or revolution, ending with the representation of Oroonoko's dismembered body re-united by 'a female Pen' for commercial reproduction.

The colonial space in Surinam serves as a paradigmatic heterotopia (see Foucault 1986: 27) that allows for both a collision and a rearrangement of forms of knowledge and transcultural memories, thus provoking a plethora of comparative practices that define the narrative stance significantly: The author-narrator compares the Carib Indians of Surinam with the Coramantiens, and each group with the British settlers as well as 'common' slaves; she compares her own position in the colony with other representatives of power and with her former situation; she compares the power hierarchies in Surinam with those in Britain; she compares her gendered position with other options of narrating and compares her narrating with her experiencing self etc.

3 "During the trade war that broke out in 1665 [...] Behn traveled to the Low Countries on a spying mission for King Charles II" (Greenblatt 2013: 1005). Surinam, or Willoughbyland, was an English colony from 1650 to 1667.

Oroonoko, in turn, compares different kinds of behaviour, e.g. his own code of honour, with the other social groups represented in the novella; he compares himself with 'common' slaves and draws conclusions for his future social position. These comparisons are very visibly embodied, which is shown by the care the novella takes to describe characters' bodies, particularly Oroonoko's, and especially his gory end; the narrator's position is equally embodied as an overt, female author-narrator who, on the level of the real author, represents the first British woman to earn her living by her pen.

The complex articulation of the act of writing as a gendered practice with new constructions of memory is already stressed in the novella's paratext. In 'The Epistle Dedicatory', the author-narrator states that the following narrative is "a short Chronicle of those Lives that possibly wou'd be forgotten by other Historians, or lye neglected there, however deserving an immortal Fame" (5). In her recovery of lives that remain excluded from dominant historiographic discourse, Behn draws attention to a gendering in historiography by way of an implicit comparison: while male historiographers would most probably have overlooked her subject entirely, she as a female historiographer does record the biography of a black slave. This comparison between male and female historiographers with a view to their subject choice is geared towards an economic consideration: only as a novelty can the text be turned into a commodity – *Oroonoko* is a text that needs to be 'sold', it is an object of exchange between the writer, her patron and a wider public readership. Novelty is constructed by telling the tales of peoples deemed hardly representable as main characters in literature and by emphasising the exotism of both the characters and their different settings: "If there be any thing that seems Romantick, I beseech your Lordship to consider, these Countries do, in all things, so far differ from ours, that they produce unconceivable Wonders; at least, they appear so to us, because New and Strange" (7). In the paratext, the author-narrator defines both her narrative as well as her role as a narrator by a way of thinking in terms of identity and difference; the novella can thus be understood as the result of diverse comparative practices.

She opens her narrative with a central distinction between the native inhabitants of Surinam and peoples that, in contrast to these, can be turned into slaves.[4] While the Surinamese are governed by a hegemony based on consent, slaves can be dominated by force according to her account:

4 However, there is a central contradiction in the author-narrator's account when she mentions "Our Indian Slaves, that Row'd us" (*Oroonoko*, 1997: 51), which illustrates the

> So that they being, on all Occasions, very useful to us, we find it absolutely necessary to caress 'em as Friends, and not to treat 'em as Slaves; nor dare we do other, their Numbers so far exceeding ours in that *Continent*. Those then whom we make use of to work in our Plantations of Sugar, are *Negro's*, *Black*-Slaves altogether. (*Oroonoko*, 1997: 11)

Correspondingly, the native Indians are widely idealized in the novella, while the slaves, stemming mainly from Coramantien, are subject to a more complicated representational regime. Oroonoko being one of them, he needs to be singled out in different terms but skin colour, and the central category of difference here is class. As a king, Oroonoko embodies the title-giving oxymoron of the "Royal Slave" and thus represents an oddity in the general class of slaves, clearly marked by their skin colour and their presumed subservience in the text. This classification of peoples becomes most obvious at the moment when Oroonoko, himself a slave trader, is betrayed by his trading partners and sold into slavery. Once part of the trans-Atlantic slave trade, he becomes subject to a different system of classification because his skin colour turns him into a tradable commodity as soon as he leaves Coramantien and with it the social context in which he is distinguished as a king; the Middle Passage over the Atlantic marks his entry into a heterotopia in which the laws of the land are suspended. Or, as Catherine Gallagher has put it:

> the fact that the colonists were making up racialized slavery as they went along in the seventeenth century and that it was a local institution at the heart of an intercontinental enterprise led to marked discrepancies in the way Africans were perceived in the different 'worlds' of the trade. (2000: 9)

The author-narrator throws into relief the practice of racialization via skin colour when she, as a character in her own right, meets Oroonoko in Surinam and reveals who can be turned into a slave and who cannot. For example, Oroonoko's tutor, a French-man and a Christian, who belongs to Oroonoko's entourage when he is abducted, is the only one who remains a free man in Surinam, purportedly because he is a Christian (see *Oroonoko*, 1997: 40), a creed Oroonoko refuses to adopt. While, first and foremost, the marker here seems to be religion, it is also centrally skin colour: Oroonoko's French tutor is the only white member of his entourage; 'freedom' and 'whiteness' thus

---

instabilities of such categories are between the 1660s and 1680s and how contradictory the discourse on these differences can be correspondingly.

become conflated and associated. Oroonoko's perceived difference, however, needs to be adapted and assimilated to European (beauty) standards in order that his enslavement can be understood as a problem at all in the context of the novel's Eurocentric ideology:

> He was pretty tall, but of a Shape the most exact that can be fancy'd: The most famous Statuary cou'd not form the Figure of a Man more admirably turn'd from Head to Foot. His Face was not of that brown, rusty Black which most of that Nation are, but a perfect Ebony, or polish'd Jett. His Eyes were the most awful that cou'd be seen, and very piercing; the White of 'em being like Snow, as were his Teeth. His Nose was rising and *Roman*, instead of *African* and flat. (13)

In this racist idealization, Oroonoko's 'Africanness' is recognizable only with regard to his blackness, but a blackness that distinguishes him from 'typical' Africans who are defined by a "brown, rusty black" (13). The text indeed betrays a clear subdivision of the human continuum into those that can and those that cannot be enslaved. As part of this process of narrative assimilation, Oroonoko is made intelligible by reference to two different forms of art: in the quotation, his beauty is likened to a *statue* of blackness, and, in the novella more generally, he is portrayed as the protagonist of the *heroic tragedy*. As a beauty ideal, he becomes a textual commodity that the author-narrator herself can turn to profit; commodified beauty yields exchange value. Towards the end of the novella, however, his idealized body disintegrates entirely. Outside of the novella's established artful and artificial norms, Oroonoko becomes unintelligible, a disintegrated body (see Butler 2004: 30). Behn's novella reveals that Oroonoko is only intelligible by way of his assimilation to European conventions, and otherwise quite outside of the boundaries of 'the human' as constructed by these comparative practices.

As Oroonoko dies, the contours of the author-narrator, the heroine of the *auto*biography, come to be delineated all the more clearly. While the initial comparative practice articulated in the paratext distinguishes the female historiographer from her male colleagues by way of her subject choice – the biography of a black character hitherto allegedly unwritten – the main body of the text employs comparative practices that finally lead to the substitution of the biography with the autobiography; they help to fashion the female writer as authoritative author persona claiming cultural distinction in the face of the utter destruction of her subjects:

> They cut *Caesar* in Quarters, and sent them to several of the chief *Plantations*: [...]. Thus Dy'd this Great Man; worthy of a better Fate, and a more sublime Wit than mine to write his Praise; yet, I hope, the Reputation of my Pen is considerable enough to make his Glorious Name to survive to all Ages; with that of the Brave, the Beautiful, and the Constant *Imoinda*. (*Oroonoko*, 1997: 65)

What remains after the death of the subjects of Behn's biography, is her *auto*biographical self, the self that emerges as a consequence of her travels to Surinam. She returns with a story to sell and a self to promote. She represents herself as a female writer who is able – like Shakespeare in his own day – to grant literary eternity to her characters.

The construction of the author-narrator's individuality not only coincides with the destruction of her racialized protagonists but also with her masterly representation of space. Apart from her implicit comparison of herself both with Oroonoko and Imoinda, Behn also assumes a dominant role by way of spatialization. The author-narrator is the one to create the spatial structure of Surinam and to present a particular hierarchy of spaces that is also reflected in the mapping of the territory. Apart from mapping the territory (all texts analyzed here also include maps), the author-narrator describes spaces so as to set a scene for encounters and figural dramas. One short paragraph introduces the setting of the main action in the novella for Oroonoko: "The Scene of the last part of his Adventures lies in a Colony in *America*, called *Surinam*, in the *West-Indies*" (8), where the inhabitants live "so like our first Parents before the Fall" (9). The native inhabitants of Surinam are thus compared to the biblical Adam and Eve before sin came into the world. Surinam is portrayed as an Edenic space, a space in which actual experiences and historical events are still suspended in a mythical realm. This Eden is then constructed as the uninscribed foil for the events to come in the colonial space, in which slaves from "*Coramantien*, a Country of *Blacks* so called" (11), arrive to work in the plantations. That the cultural encounters staged in this setting contribute to the emergence of the white, western individual becomes conspicuous in a scene staged particularly for the native inhabitants of Surinam. Together with Oroonoko, the author-narrator and several other persons decide to travel to an "*Indian* Town" (47) and concoct a surprise visit as

> we, who resolv'd to surprize 'em, by making 'em see something they never had seen, (that is, White People) resolv'd only my self, my Brother, and Woman shou'd go [...]. By degrees they grew more bold, and from gazing

> upon us round, they touch'd us; laying their Hands upon all the Features of our Faces, feeling our Breasts and Arms, taking up one Petticoat, then wondering to see another; [...] In fine, we suffer'd 'em to survey us as they pleas'd, and we thought they would never have done admiring us. (48)

While it is the native inhabitants here who seem to appropriate the power of an observing gaze and prove transgressive in their haptic exploration of their others, the tables are soon turned. After making numerous enquiries about these strangers with a fisherman who mediates between the Surinamese and the "White People" – they ask "If we had Sense, and Wit? If we cou'd talk of affairs of Life, and War, as they could do?" (49) – the fisherman soon ascertains comparability (see 49). The author-narrator, however, concludes that the Surinamese prove so ignorant and gullible that "it were not too difficult to establish any unknown or extravagant Religion among them; and to impose any Notions or Fictions upon 'em" (49). This scene nicely illustrates the fact that comparisons are practices in particular historical and social contexts imbued with power hierarchies. '*Doing* comparisons' (see Epple/Erhart 2020: 20) depends on social status and the author-narrator, while granting the Surinamese some agency in this situation, soon reveals that the "White People" wield epistemological power to which the native inhabitants do not have access in Behn's narrative. Nevertheless, the encounter, quite literally, renders the contours of the author-narrator and her entourage visible; thus, comparative practices throw into relief the connection of whiteness and (epistemic) power embodied in the author-narrator once more. The reader learns that the skin the Surinamese touch is white, they learn what the author-narrator wears and the skills she has. Her 'self' is shaped in this encounter by the touch of the Indians, and it is a self whose characterization is directed as in a play by the author-narrator herself. She is the one to allocate roles and to highlight particular discoveries over others in a scene she herself has set.

The orchestration of arriving and leaving, presenting and hiding, permitting and forbidding is dependent on the author-narrator's strategies of spatialization. The individual and the surrounding environment are equiprimordial in *Oroonoko*. When the author-narrator learns about gold in the Amazonas, the river is described as being "almost as broad as the River of Thames" (51); this 'almost but not quite' similarity between the respective rivers illustrates how comparative practices subject Surinam to an English mapping. Historically, however, this power over space and gold is lost as the colony is ceded to the Dutch, a process that is frequently aligned with the Glorious Revolution that ends the Stuart dynasty in favour of King William of Orange (see Monika Class' article in this volume). As a staunch supporter of the Stuarts, Behn can only cling to the patronage by her Jacobite dedicatee Lord Maitland in 1688. The literal abduction of Oroonoko from Coramantien is transposed into a logical abduction that suggests that economically successful authorship by female writers is possible, albeit at the price of the utter commodification of the racialized other. *Oroonoko* as a text paving the way for the emergence of the novel thus closely aligns female middle-class authorship with whiteness and singles out skin colour as a crucial if not yet dominant racial signifier.

3. Daniel Defoe, *Robinson Crusoe* (1719)

Daniel Defoe's *Robinson Crusoe* "occupies a crucial place in literary history's account of the emergence of the modern English novel and for that matter of the beginning of the modern European novel" (Richetti 2018: xiii). Postcolonial theorists such as Edward Said "have looked especially at cultural forms as the novel", because he considers it "immensely important in the formation of imperial attitudes, references, and experiences" and, like Richetti, singles out *Robinson Crusoe* as the "prototypical modern realistic novel" that, symptomatically, deals with "a European who creates a fiefdom for himself on a distant, non-European island" (1994: 9-10). Said further considers Robinson's founding "a new world, which he rules and reclaims for England" as closely intertwined with the novel genre (Said 1994: 74). There are two issues at stake in these evaluations: Firstly, there is an odd slippage between England and Europe which is indicative of the co-emergence of a notion of 'whiteness' that is not clearly defined by nationality and the novel; secondly, the novel is established as the medium and central receptacle for articulations of aesthetic, economic and political discourses that allow for such an English/European modern identity to develop in contradistinction to 'the new world'. With comparisons as central cognitive practices defining modernity, the following analysis is an attempt at unravelling these interdependences that are constitutive of the 'modern' subject of the eighteenth century. Both the emergence of the modern novel and the emergence of the 'English/European' 'modern' subject envisioned as an 'individual' are rooted in comparative practices that intersect and ossify over time as myths of this origination.

"*Robinson Kreutznaer*" or later "*Crusoe*" (*Robinson Crusoe*, 2007: 5), the novel's hero and autodiegetic narrator, is of German descent, which might be the reason to construct the 'modern' subject as white or *European* rather than more specifically *English*. Robinson Crusoe, crucially, indicates the Anglo-Saxon roots of the Englishness presented in the novel. As Laura Doyle has convincingly established, this proves part and parcel of the contemporary articulation of discourses on Anglo-Saxonism, racism and freedom; besides, it indicates a "key shift in English self-fashioning, a turn away from a classical and Briton lineage and toward an Anglo-Saxon, Germanic one, a genealogy hereafter creating the nativist freedom legacy at the core of Whig ideology" (2007: 198). More generally, she traces "modern race ideologies to the Atlantic economy" and shows

> that in England a prior formation of racial thinking – predating its full-scale slave trade and linking race to a freedom legacy – has given rise to its plot, its purchase, and its force in (at least) the English-language Atlantic world. That is, in early seventeenth-century England, under conditions of civil war and an emergent capitalist economy, the coupling of race and freedom issued in the notion that true history entails the progress of a race toward religious, economic, and political freedom. [...] Ultimately, the notion of freedom as a racially inherited desire provided the mythic teleology of the English-speaking Atlantic world, one that still propels the speeches of its leaders. (Doyle 2007: 195-196)

Doyle describes a symptomatic connection between race, economics, politics and religion that also serves as the foundation of a view of history as directed from the desire for freedom to its eventual realization inherent in this mythic Anglo-Saxon genealogy which is bolstered further by legal discourses (see Doyle 2007: 198-199).

'The' novel offers a highly hybrid and variable genre for the further negotiation of this interconnection. As a commodity in its own right, the novel contributes to turning "the racialized rhetoric of liberty [into] a transatlantic phenomenon, embedding it deep in the structures of English-language narrative" (Doyle 2007: 200). The very language of the novel fundamentally hinges on its close ties with Britain's colonial expansion as an articulation of economics, politics, religion, and history as markers of British identity as 'white'. Anglo-Saxon whiteness is thrown into further relief in trans-Atlantic encounters as mediated in and by travel writing that *Robinson Crusoe* relies on as a generic precursor. Eve Tavor Bannet has highlighted the close interconnection between Britain's colonial itineraries and Robinson's route of travel:

> Giving Robinson's voyage such geographical specificity on what was British shipping's standard circum-Atlantic route to and from the Americas, enabled epitomes to make *Robinson Crusoe* a story about the perils that Robinson faced as a mariner in a dangerous multinational Atlantic world, dominated by Barbary pirates, Africans, and Caribs, as well as by the Spaniards and Portuguese. (2018: 130)

It is Robinson's encounters and indirect comparisons with these nationalities and ethnicities constituted as the others of Anglo-Saxon whiteness that further define the character. Robinson Crusoe represents the literary embodiment of the articulation of Whig economics, politics, Puritanism and a rhetoric of freedom as the norm of the subject of the emerging realism of the eighteenth-century novel. Defoe's novel draws its plot motivation from Britain's trans-Atlantic ties in its search for 'new' worlds and workforce in triangular trade connections as depicted in *Oroonoko* and makes Robinson emerge as an individualized *homo economicus* (Watt 2000 [1957]: 63) who is clearly marked as white and male. This emergence is made possible, among other things, by a racialized spatial politics with its concomitant comparative practices as well as by a closeting of homosocial desire by way of its transference onto the island as a heterotopic space.

In a first step, the very opening of the novel may serve to illustrate the emphasis on Robinson's German roots and his close connection to trade:

> I Was born in the Year 1632, in the City of *York*, of a good Family, tho' not of that Country, my Father being a Foreigner of *Bremen*, who settled first at *Hull*: He got a good Estate by Merchandise, and leaving off his Trade, lived afterward at *York*, from whence he had married my Mother, whose Relations were named *Robinson*, a very good Family in that Country, and from whom I was called *Robinson Kreutznaer*. (*Robinson Crusoe*, 2007: 5)

While this opening decidedly introduces Robinson as an *individual* – by way of starting with the first personal pronoun 'I' and the indication of his family genealogy together with his father's migratory background and social stratification – the paratext underlines the *exemplary* function of this individual for the reader in order to justify as well as perform a concentration on the middle classes in literature. In the "Preface", the fictional editor argues that "*If ever the Story of any private Man's Adventures in the World were worth making Publick, and were acceptable when Publish'd, the Editor of this Account thinks this will be so*" (*Robinson Crusoe*, 2007: n.p.). His simultaneous function as both individual and exemplum reveals the novelistic reliance on comparative practices – individual life stories need to be compared with a view to their 'tellability' (Baroni 2014), and since their tellability depends on a deviation from established norms, it is justified by way of defining sensational adventures as didactic *exempla* that invite readers to compare their own life stories with the *exemplum*.

Quite in line with the tradition of the spiritual autobiography, Robinson goes on to recount his sinful tendency to disobey his father who recommends, in a direct and explicit comparison of different classes,

> the upper Station of *Low Life*, which he had found by long Experience was the best State in the World, the most suited to human Happiness, not exposed to the Miseries and Hardships, the Labour and Sufferings of the mechanick Part of Mankind, and not embarrass'd with the Pride, Luxury, Ambition and Envy of the upper Part of Mankind.[5] (*Robinson Crusoe*, 2007: 6)

This paternal norm, however, lacks tellability in the novel, whereas Robinson's deviation from this norm becomes constitutive of the genre's plot lines – comparative practices are thus integral to the emergence of the novel more generally in that an interest in character depends on comparative practices on the side of authors, narrators and readers with regard to the difference between individual fictional characters and established social norms. While the novel's plot conforms to one of its generic precursors, the spiritual biography, in that it leads Robinson from his sinful life and disregard for both father and God through repentance to 'salvation', it is the time of repentance on the island that becomes the core interest for the narrative in *Robinson Crusoe*. It is exactly the deviation from the – religiously sanctioned – norm that generates 'interest' in both the senses of the motivation for reading and economic turnover. While one of the eighteenth-century ideals for a good life is moderation, the novel genre's *raison d'être* depends on the outcome of readers' evaluations of the deviations from the norm that generate interest. On the intratextual level, Robinson's disregard for established norms allows him to generate interest in an economic sense, too, since his journeys turn him into a successful businessman whose time on the island translates into money (see Spivak 1990: 6): Robinson owns a plantation in Brazil that generates profit for him even without his presence.

5 On social comparisons between classes in Defoe's novel and beyond, see the contribution by Hartner/Schneider in this volume.

Defoe's story is set "on the Coast of America, near the Mouth of the Great River OROONOQUE" (Defoe 2007: title page, n.p.) – the river that divides Guyana from Surinam – and thus in the vicinity of Behn's Surinam. While the setting at the river alludes to the name of Behn's protagonist, the two early novels are interconnected by intertextual ties with *Robinson Crusoe* consolidating the generic reliance on travel writing combined with the (auto)biography. Another central intertextual convergence lies in the descriptions of the respective narrators' others, and these descriptions are fraught with insecurities regarding the way in which the respective 'object' is to be narrated; it is this insecurity in the process of narration that reveals the crucial role of comparative practices as a basis of both modernity and the modern novel. As a generic conglomerate, the novel makes the white 'individual' emerge by way of comparative practices intended to reveal the similarities and differences between 'self' and its 'other'. 'Capturing' the other – either as slaves or as objects of narration – proves an endeavour fundamentally dependent on comparative practices. Both *Oroonoko* and *Robinson Crusoe* show that it is decidedly *practices* that are geared to render the resulting descriptions of the respective others in any way reliable, trustworthy and stable in a narrative. The narrative strategies employed for 'producing' the other in discourse are frequently characterized by repetitions intended to fix meanings; however, such iterative narrative practices may inject insecurities in the versions presented whenever they entail variations and contradictions. Symptomatically, in the process of reception and in the multiple adaptations and appropriations of *Robinson Crusoe* (see Richetti 2018: 15), these insecurities were frequently harmonized. As Rivka Swenson has shown, "Crusoe's errors and self-contradictions are the signal evidence of his own foregrounded composition-and-revision methodology (omitting, expanding, transposing, consolidating, making-things-up)" (2018: 20). There is a decided rift in what he narrates in his journal as a contemporary record of the experiencing I and how he represents the entries retrospectively (see Swenson 2018: 20-21); what is more, the limited supply in ink and paper on the island renders it questionable how extensive the journal actually is and (see *Robinson Crusoe*, 2007: 56; 89), consequently, how reliable Crusoe's narrative can be on the basis of this 'journal'. "In the journal, two voices overlap awkwardly" and construct a narrative mismatch of different versions of "two Crusoes" (Swenson 2018: 21), so that ultimately, the novel tells the story of "a writer who overtly manipulates his story and audience, shaping by hindsight, reading the present into the past, omitting and compressing toward an end, forging a chain of narrative reciprocity" (25). Clearly, it is the concatenation of events that is crucial and the question of whether these narrative concatenations add up or create inconsistencies. The novel thus invites practices of comparing both on the intratextual and on the intertextual level, and it is such networks of cross-references and strategies of narrative suture that prove fundamental for the discursive construction of eighteenth-century modernity.

While Behn installs an I-as-witness as narrator that moves increasingly into the centre of attention as her actual object, Oroonoko, slips from view, Defoe's novel is narrated by an I-as-protagonist, further characterized by a large difference between narrating and experiencing I, or what Rivka Swenson calls the "hindsight-version" of the narrator (Swenson 2018: 20). The ways in which Oroonoko and Friday are described bear multiple similarities that may also account for the fact that Friday is frequently considered to be a black character in readings or adaptations and appropriations of the novel (see Wheeler 1995: 823). The conflation between otherness and blackness rests on the conception of Friday as a slave, a conception, however, that frequently slips from 'slave' to 'servant' to 'man' in the novel and consequently proves highly slippery, reflecting "a larger cultural uncertainty about the significance of racial difference in the early eighteenth century" and its concomitant social stratification (Wheeler 1995: 821-822). For Defoe's Robinson Crusoe, I argue that comparative practices abound because they prove central for the hermeneutic process of encountering and understanding the island, its possible inhabitants and himself. Robinson implicitly compares the island to places he is familiar with and subjects it to comparable conceptual mappings. When he surveys the island from an elevated point of view, thus exerting the visual power of the male gaze over the landscape, he comments:

> I descended a little on the Side of that delicious Valley, surveying it with a secret Kind of Pleasure, (tho' mixt with my other afflicting Thoughts) to think that all this was my own, that I was King and Lord of all this Country indefeasibly and had a Right of Possession; and if I could convey it, I might have it in Inheritance, as completely as any Lord of a Mannor in *England*. (*Robinson Crusoe*, 2007: 85)

His cognitive grasp of the island is coded by political notions of sovereignty and economic as well as legal notions of possession and inheritance as established in *England*, which serves as a conceptual blend (see Fauconnier/Turner 2002) to hermeneutically appropriate the island. The male gaze that awards him a "*secret* Kind of Pleasure" surveying the landscape (Defoe 2007: 85, my emphasis) additionally entails the pleasure of voyeuristic desire and eroticizes Robinson's relation to the landscape (see Turley 2003: 3). Such eroticization is transferred onto his 'subjects' in his kingdom and becomes most visible when he observes his "Man *Friday*" (Defoe 2007: 175). The island and its people are thus tied together metonymically, shedding light upon one another by proxy; spatialization and characterization closely intersect. Such conceptual blends in the narrative serve as central comparative practices that allow insights into the ways in which Robinson Crusoe subjects the island and all its inhabitants to his cognitive mastery, which, as the 'sovereign' of the island, pre-empts himself from the process. While, in Robinson's narrative discourse, the comparative practice of blending presents a form of constructing different semantic fields as congruent, a focus on the metonymical practices of concatenation, of creating the "Collection of Wonders" (217) that constitutes the narrative, is a way to understand both Robinson's narration and himself. In the following, I am going to focus on the interrelation between Robinson Crusoe and Friday as well as Robinson and the island as central aspects for the complex articulation of the emergence of the modern individual under "the ideology of industrial capitalism" (Watt 2000: 67), the emergence of racism as part of a colonial discourse and the emergence of the novel genre.

While the "primacy of individual economic advantage has tended to diminish the importance of personal as well as group relationships, and especially those based on sex" (Watt 2000: 67), it is homosocial desire that eroticizes the relationships on the island. Similarly, with Friday, Crusoe "enjoys an idyll without benefit of a woman – a revolutionary departure from the traditional expectations aroused by desert islands from the *Odyssey* to the *New Yorker*" (Watt 68). After Watt, several critics have added a focus on sexual orientation to Robinson's readings as "*homo economicus, homo faber*, religious figure, [...] a masculine adventurer, an imperialist [... or] as an individual" (Downes 2010). Peter Hulme has established a reading of *Robinson Crusoe* as a "colonial romance" (1986: 208), situating "the true romance [...] between Crusoe and Friday", a relation charged with "erotic delight" on Crusoe's side (212). Hans Turley emphasizes Robinson's "homosocial relationship with Friday" and argues that his "[w]andering seems to become the repressive mechanism for his unarticulated desires, his undetermined identity" (Turley 2003: 5); hence, Robinson's travels as a form of colonial expansion appear correlated to his homoerotic desire that is partly fulfilled in interethnic encounters (see Poole 2014: 169). Melissa K. Downes maintains that the novel is defined by "a sexually coded imperialism" (2) that relies on "ordering principles and boundaries" whose transgression "would be highly threatening, particularly since such divisions are, themselves, unstable narratives" (3), thus underlining the importance of the disavowal of this desire for the viability of the emerging modern subject. In the wider context of queer theory, one cannot but agree with Eve Kosofsky Sedgwick, who argues that "the structuring of same-sex bonds can't, in any historical situation marked by inequality and contest *between* genders, fail to be a site of intensive regulation that intersects virtually every issue of power and gender"; drawing on Michel Foucault, she highlights that "modern Western culture has placed what it calls sexuality in a more and more distinctly privileged relation to our most prized constructs of individual identity, truth, and knowledge" (1993: 245). Hence, the modern individual that is represented in the realist novel – i.e., the novel that makes the enmeshment of individual identity, truth and knowledge co-emerge – is a construction based on the intersection of sexualities and imperialism; in *Robinson Crusoe*, this fundamental amalgamation is played out in the encounters between the colonizer Robinson, the island and his 'other', Friday.

Stereotyping is one of the strategies Robinson employs to render his picaresque narrative cohesive with regard to his rendition of 'character'. This focus on an 'other' as well as the suppression of the erotic dimension of this relation help to diverge attention from the wider colonial project of exploitation and to direct attention at the comparative practices required to decide whether the 'other' poses a threat or not. Stereotyping serves to render plausible the slippage between the terms designating Friday's status as either 'slave', or 'servant' or 'man' (see Wheeler 1995) since some descriptions need to be "anxiously repeated" to stabilize the respective subject positions (Bhabha 2008: 95). Crucially, as Homi Bhabha argues, colonial discourse is "structurally similar to realism" with regard to its representational strategies of representing the colonial other as "at once an 'other' and yet entirely knowable and visible" (101). Furthermore, stereotyping is akin to fetishism in that

> The fetish or stereotype gives access to an 'identity' which is predicated as much on mastery and pleasure as it is on anxiety and defence, for it is a form of multiple and contradictory belief in its recognition of difference and disavowal of it. This conflict of pleasure/unpleasure, mastery/defence, knowledge/disavowal, absence/presence, has a fundamental significance for colonial discourse. For the scene of fetishism is also the scene of the reactivation and repetition of primal fantasy – the subject's desire for a pure origin that

> is always threatened by division, for the subject must be gendered to be engendered, to be spoken. (Bhabha 2008: 107)

It is through stereotyping Friday that Robinson can get access to his own (modern, realist, white etc.) identity. Stereotyping strongly relies on comparative practices,[6] cognitive strategies that correspond to subconscious processes of desiring haunted by racism. Robinson's whiteness and masculinity only emerge as such after dominating and subjecting Friday (see Poole 2014: 170). To that effect, Friday must be held in place by practices of stereotyping (Bhabha 2008: esp. 94-95, 101-102) and it is this comparative practice that highlights the many intersections that define the 'modern' individual in the novel.

3.1 Racialized Spatial Politics in *Robinson Crusoe*

Making the island his own, Robinson follows an established script of colonization, declaring the island as uninhabited and wild, and thus as subjectable. Robinson fashions himself as 'master' in several ways, as a spatial master of the island, and as a master of his 'subjects', be they human or animal: "it was a merry Reflection which I frequently made, How like a King I look'd. First of all, the whole Country was my own meer Property; so that I had an undoubted Right of Dominion. *2dly*, My People were perfectly subjected: I was absolute Lord and Law-giver; they all owed their Lives to me" (*Robinson Crusoe*, 2007: 203). The life on the heterotopia of the island is thus characterized by economic anachronisms – Robinson as a capitalist entrepreneur and colonizer still combines several different functions in his own person quite contrary to

6 With regard to stereotyping, I take a detour from Epple's and Erhart's evaluation of Bhabha's approach, while I otherwise follow their definition of comparative practices. Epple and Erhart argue that postcolonial approaches often "repeated the dichotomies of 'colonial powers' and the 'colonial other' within their studies. This repetition has to do with the postcolonial interest in analyzing 'othering,' as Homi K. Bhabha would have it"; thus, these approaches place an emphasis on "the construction of the Other through comparison" rather than on "the very practices of comparing" (2020: 17). In my view, the process of stereotyping as a crucial strategy of othering is decidedly a comparative *practice* as it needs to be performed in any encounter with the other (who can challenge those practices by employing mimicry, for instance, which is a performative *practice* in its own right, see Bhabha 2008: 122-123). Stereotyping, in Bhabha's sense, is processual and hence requires constant iterations of comparative practices.

established divisions of labour (see Schmidt 2012: 193) – and, at least for contemporary readers, by political anachronisms since the absolutist reign along the lines of the Stuart dynasty Robinson imagines for himself has been abolished after the Glorious Revolution in 1688, which, however, only occurs after Robinson is rescued in the 1686 of the story world. For contemporary readers, the story world prompts and invites comparisons between their own political and economic structures and Robinson's with a view to the question in which contexts an individual can thrive and prove sovereign.[7]

The *terra incognita* of the island that Robinson explores is not restricted to the surface of the island, it is also and decidedly the spaces below ground that serve Robinson's "colonial project" (MacDonnell 2020: 2) at a time when "subsurface resource extraction began to play a principal role in catalyzing Britain's transition to industrial capitalism" (5). While Robinson marks the island by way of its spatial demarcation, cultivation and labour (see 10) as his own, it is the space below ground that serves as the ideal space of subjection, as Kevin MacDonnell argues:

> The subsurface environments in Defoe's fiction fulfill and, in some cases, restore the Edenic fantasy of unoccupied colonial space in a way that topographical surfaces could not. The ideal conditions for colonial occupation in the eighteenth century would have looked a lot like the subsurface environments Defoe constructs: malleable, abundant, and unpopulated. Alongside the seemingly inexhaustible supply of resources and commodities Defoe locates beneath the surface, he also uncovers core features of the national and racial character of British identity. (2020:18)

It is Robinson's cave in particular that represents a central space that negotiates not only the topological value of 'above' and 'below' the surface, but also the social and sexual significance of the cave apart from its economic one (see Poole 2014: 169-170). Generally, the cave is a space whose access Robinson carefully regulates, particularly when Friday appears on the island. The close

7 With such an interplay of space and time in the novelistic setting, the island can be further described as a chronotope, defined by Mikhail Bakhtin as "the intrinsic connectedness of temporal and spatial relationships that are artistically expressed in literature", so that time "thickens, takes on flesh, becomes artistically visible; likewise, space becomes charged and responsive to the movements of time, plot and history" (1981: 84). Importantly, this has effects on the representation of characters (see 85). Thus, the Robinsonade reflects on the emergence of the eighteenth-century individual as a product of several intertwining discourses.

connection between the presence of others and the protection of the cave already becomes clear when Robinson spots another human being's footprint "on the Shore, which was very plain to be seen in the Sand" (Defoe 2007: 130). This find sets off a bout of paranoia in Robinson: "like a Man perfectly confus'd and out of my self, I came Home to my Fortification, not feeling, as we say, the Ground I went on, but terrify'd to the last Degree, looking behind me at every two or three Steps, mistaking every Bush and Tree, and fancying every Stump at a Distance to be a Man" (130). It is after this event that he professedly calls his cave "my Castle" where he sought refuge "like one pursued" (131). Even when he dares to leave his 'Castle', he it is not without a feeling of being followed and "haunted with an evil Conscience" (134). The trace of another, the very index of presence, suffices to make him secure his cave as a fortress – a symptom that may be diagnosed as a case of "homosexual panic" (Sedgwick 1985: 91) *avant la lettre*. The trace of the other is finally 'fleshed out' by Friday, whose life Robinson saves and whom he consequently turns into his servant. The island is a space defined by Robinson's homoerotic desire (see Poole 2014: 170) that is clearly set off from the spaces of 'civilization' to which he returns after his sojourn on the island: only a few sparse sentences describe that he marries and has three children in England after his return, but he quickly leaves them for further adventures after his wife dies (*Robinson Crusoe*, 2007: 256). Crossing theses spaces by travelling, Robinson interconnects them for triangular trade and his desire for travelling similarly triangulates his homosocial desire.[8]

---

8 A further indication of homosocial desire is Robinson's moustache. On his slave-trading voyage to "*Guiney*", he falls into the hands of a Turkish pirate, who ordered Robinson "to lye in the Cabbin to look after the Ship" (Defoe 2007: 18); the duties of the household slave Robinson thus seem to entail sexual services (see Turley 2003: 7-8). After this homoerotic experience, he trims his beard in a Turkish style up to his "eleventh Year of [his] Residence" on the island and beyond (Defoe 2007: 123): "as I had both Scissars and Razors sufficient, I had cut it pretty short, except what grew on my upper Lip, which I had trimm'd into a large Pair of *Mahometan* Whiskers, such as I had seen worn by some *Turks*, who I saw at *Sallee*" and "they were of a Length and Shape monstrous enough, and such as in *England* would have pass'd for frightful" (127). Considering that "The savage and the Christian are the most important racialized categories between Europeans and others that help produce and maintain a sense of European superiority" (Wheeler 1995: 828), it is noteworthy that Robinson retains a style with much cultural effort that must remain associated with a Turkish pirate who enslaved him in several senses. Clearly, intercultural comparative practices would distinguish Robinson from

Interestingly, after coming across the footprint, Robinson already dreams of encountering a "Savage" (Defoe 2007: 167) and, in his dream, this savage is admitted to his cave: "he kneel'd down to me, seeming to pray me to assist him; upon which I shew'd my Ladder, made him go up, and carry'd him into my Cave, and he became my Servant" (167-168). The actual man that Robinson calls Friday only arrives more than one year after this dream, and then the regulations of access fall differently: "I carry'd him not to my Castle, but quite away to my Cave, on the farther Part of the Island; so I did not let my Dream come to pass in that Part, viz. That he came into my Grove for Shelter" (Defoe 2007: 173). While in the dreamscape, Robinson is 'free' to admit Friday to his Castle, and with it to the central symbol of a phallic fortress of identity, he cannot do so in the reality of the story world. The regulations of access are different in the dream and in the 'real', which first and foremost highlights that something needs to be regulated here, or, alternatively, that something needs to be narrated differently as wished for in the 'dream' – granting Friday access to the private places of the island that is metonymically connected to Robinson's body. With this juxtaposition of the dream and the real, the novel invites intratextual comparative practices that allow conclusions by way of the very contiguity of the respective scenes.

When Robinson describes Friday as he lies asleep in the cave after his rescue, he clearly fetishizes Friday's body in that he comments on body parts individually, again by a sort of listing. As Melissa Downes has shown, "The similarities of Crusoe's blazon of Friday to his other continual narrative listings of his possessions, both land and objects, show this relationship between self, possession, and the erotic. […] Indeed, within early eighteenth-century mercantilism the erotic is tied to dominating and possessing both humans (wives, mistresses, and slaves) as erotic possessions and to possessing land and material objects" (2010: 8). Focusing on comparative practices, this passage adds further aspects to this eroticized stock-taking. *Robinson Crusoe* reiterates Oroonoko's description in many respects, and thus the novel relies on intertextual comparative practices that help to reiterate and solidify a stereotype of the colonial 'other' that creates a lasting myth. The following description can thus be seen to be "part of a framework of comparative practices that have been established through repetition and routines, cultural habits, and historical patterns" (Epple/Erhart 2020: 18):

---

gentlemen in England, where he would appear to be 'frightful' and would be subject to othering in his very country of origin.

> He was a comely handsome Fellow, perfectly well made; with straight strong Limbs, not too large; *tall* and well-*shap'd*, and as I reckon, about twenty six Years of Age. He had a very good Countenance, not a fierce and surly Aspect; but seem'd to have something very manly in his Face, and yet he had all the Sweetness and Softness of an *European* in his Countenance too, especially when he smil'd. His Hair was long and black, not curl'd like Wool; his Forehead very high, and large, and a great Vivacity and sparkling Sharpness in his Eyes. The Colour of his Skin was not quite black, but very tawny; and yet not of an ugly yellow nauseous tawny, as the *Brasilians*, and *Virginians*, and other Natives of *America* are; but of a bright kind of a dun olive Colour, that had in it something very agreeable; tho' not very easy to describe. (Defoe 2007: 173; my emphases)

Based on this indirect form of an intertextual comparison, Friday and Oroonoko share that they are "tall" and of a good "Shape" (see *Oroonoko*, 1997: 13), have straight black hair (although due to the "Aids of Art" in Oroonoko's case, *Oroonoko*, 1997: 14) and "very piercing" (13) or sharp eyes, diverge in skin colour from their peers and have some similarity to Europeans (see 13). Even though Friday is a Carib Indian and not of African descent, the narrator deems it necessary to point out that his hair is not "curl'd like wool" (*Robinson Crusoe*, 2007: 173), a mention which, despite its negation, together with the similarity to Oroonoko's description, might account for the fact that Friday is frequently portrayed as an African in Robinsonades. What is more, his description hinges on precisely such comparative practices that make him emerge and solidify as Robinson's 'other', which goes to show that "[c]omparing is a 'relationing' activity that goes way beyond stating mere differences" (Epple/Erhart 2020: 17). The contours of both Robinson and Friday are being constructed by "doing comparisons" (20). Robinson places Friday on a racialized continuum spawned between 'Africanness' and 'Europeanness'; Friday's difference from 'Africans' goes hand in glove with similarities to Europeans that are clearly gendered: While there is something "very manly" in Friday's face, he shares with Robinson some European features, defined by a rather feminine "Sweetness and Softness" (*Robinson Crusoe*, 2007: 173).

Despite racial and sexual ambiguities, comparative practices help to establish the novel's modern subject as 'white' with the Anglo-Saxon European as the norm. This norm is further defined by an inclination to freedom rooted in this racialized origin, a freedom for example in the realm of religion (see *Robinson Crusoe*, 2007: 203), options of capital expansion or in the freedom of movement ingrained in the colonial enterprise. However, what remains foreclosed in this construction is its dependence on the exploitation of its 'others', be that humans or islands. It is the deep level of the novel, the exploitation of what is below the surface level of the earth, in other words, it is what happens in the cave that forms the 'subtext' of both the novel and its 'modern' individual. Comparative practices of the 'below' and the 'above' of the wider context of *Robinson Crusoe* undo the closeting of the exploitative and extractive foundations of the novelistic construction of the modern, white individual.

4. Conclusion

In this chapter, I have shown that comparative practices prove crucial in the emergence of the novel genre in the long eighteenth century. Relying, as it does, on generic precursors such as travel writing and the (spiritual) (auto)biography, the novel closely ties the construction of the modern individual to its colonial others, whose construction, in turn, depends on comparative practices that become solidified by processes of cultural iteration. The modern individual is clearly defined by the racialized marker of whiteness that is rooted in an Anglo-Saxon genealogy of 'Englishness', further associated with industrial capitalism, colonialism, (religious) freedom and heteronormativity. Literary authorship is a function of this conglomerate of intersecting discourses and defined by its own strategies of narrative mastery.

In *Oroonoko*, Aphra Behn's author-narrator emerges at her most overt in the interethnic encounters set in the heterotopic space of the colony. She is literally thrown into relief when she is touched, observed and described by Surinamese Indians as an experiencing I in the colonial encounter, and she is fully established as a white female author with a story to live by after the demise of her biographical subjects. Commercially profitable female authorship is enabled through the author-narrator's commodification of her subjects, and through her emergence as white in the process of establishing skin colour as a central signifier of social privilege in the novel. This authorization of the white, female writer hinges on stereotyping both the Surinamese and the Coramantiens. This discursive practice is closely articulated with strategies of spatialization that subject interethnic encounters to a colonial mapping and *mise-en-scène*, calibrated by the generic hybridity. The mixture of travel writing and the (auto)biography equally characterizes Daniel Defoe's *Robinson Crusoe* as the paradigmatic modern novel; implicit intertextual comparative practices help to congeal generic conventions over time, which shape collective processes of meaning making and may even impact on the interpretation and appropriation of extraliterary experiences (see Gymnich/Neumann 2007: 40; 46) as the plethora Robinsonades, both literary and real, illustrates. Hence, the way in which the novelistic subject is constructed can be shown to have a wider impact on general cultural subject constructions. *Robinson Crusoe* is a central text in defining English identity as 'white' in the sense of the Anglo-Saxon genealogy of its main character that is closely tied to capitalist structures of mercantilism and processes of colonial expansion. By the same token, the viability of modern subjects as presented in the novel hinges on the foreclosure of homosocial desire, a desire transposed onto travelling, exploring and expanding the narrow confines of "the upper Station of *Low Life*" (*Robinson Crusoe*, 2007: 6). The exploitation of resources and human beings comes to be legitimized through discourses of freedom and (God-granted?) success tied to this subject; the articulation of colonialism, capitalism, Puritanism, racism and heteronormativity requires some further disentangling in order to resist its detrimental effects for people(s) and environments alike.

The white, middle-class individuals of the modern novel that normalize these subject positions for their corresponding readership, are discursive effects of comparative practices as central strategies of modernity that define and delimit the viability of subjects as well as the options of interaction with their others and their (spatial) contexts. The performative power and particular functionalizations of comparative practices thus clearly require further critical unravelling, as they have been shown to be foundational for forms of exploitation that continue to riddle our present.

Bibliography

Assmann, Aleida/Sebastian Conrad. "Introduction". *Memory in a Global Age: Discourses. Practices and Trajectories*. Ed. Sebastian Conrad. New York: Palgrave, 2010, 1-16.

Bakhtin, Mikhail. "Forms and Time of the Chronotope in the Novel." *The Dialogic Imagination*. Ed. Michael Holquist. Austin: University of Texas Press, 1981. 84-258.

Baroni, Raphaël. "Tellability." *The Living Handbook of Narratology*. Last modified April 2014. Accessed online, 02 August 2021. ‹https://www.lhn.uni-hamburg.de/node/30.html›.

Batten, Jr., Charles L. *Pleasurable Instruction: Form and Convention in Eighteenth-Century Travel Literature*. Berkeley: California University Press, 1978.

Behn, Aphra. *Oroonoko: An Authoritative Text, Historical Backgrounds, Criticism*. Ed. Joanna Lipking. New York: Norton, 1997 [1688].

Bekers, Elisabeth. "Creative Challenges to Captivity: Slave Authorship in Black British Neo-Slave Narratives." *Life Writing* 15.1 (2018): 23-42.

Bhabha, Homi. *The Location of Culture*. London and New York: Routledge, 2008.

Butler, Judith. *Precarious Life: The Powers of Mourning and Violence*. London: Verso, 2004.

Das, Nandini and Tim Youngs (eds.). *The Cambridge History of Travel Writing*. Cambridge: Cambridge University Press, 2019.

Defoe, Daniel. *Robinson Crusoe*. Edited with an Introduction by Thomas Keymer. Oxford: Oxford University Press, 2007 [1719].

Downes, Melissa K. "Erotic Bo(u)nds: Domination, Possession, Enclosure and the Self in Daniel Defoe's *Robinson Crusoe*." *The Erotic in Context*. Ed. M. Soraya García-Sánchez, Cara Judea Alhadeff, and Joel Kuennen. Oxford: Inter-Disciplinary Press, 2010. 171-182.

Doyle, Laura. "Reconstructing Race and Freedom in Atlantic Modernity: Daniel Defoe's *Robinson Crusoe* and Olaudah Equiano's *Interesting Narrative*." *Atlantic Studies* 4.2 (2007): 195-224.

Eckstein, Lars. *Re-Membering the Black Atlantic: On the Poetics and Politics of Literary Memory*. Amsterdam: Rodopi, 2006.

Epple, Angelika. "Inventing White Beauty and Fighting Black Slavery: How Blumenbach, Humboldt, and Arango y Parreño Contributed to Cuban Race Comparisons in the Long Nineteenth Century." *Practices of Comparing: Towards a New Understanding of a Fundamental Human Practice*. Ed. Angelika Epple, Walter Erhart, and Johannes Grave. Bielefeld: Bielefeld University Press, 2020. 295-328.

Epple, Angelika and Walter Erhart. "Die Welt beobachten – Praktiken des Vergleichens." *Die Welt beobachten: Praktiken des Vergleichens*. Ed. Angelika Epple and Walter Erhart. Frankfurt: Campus, 2015. 7-31.

Fauconnier, Gilles and Mark Turner. *The Way We Think: Conceptual Blending and the Mind's Hidden Complexities*. New York: Basic Books, 2002.

Felski, Rita. *The Limits of Critique*. Chicago: Chicago University Press, 2015.

Felski, Rita and Susan Stanford Friedman. "Introduction." *Comparison: Theories, Approaches, Uses*. Ed. Rita Felski and Susan Stanford Friedman. Baltimore: Johns Hopkins University Press, 2013. 1-12.

Foucault, Michel. "Of Other Spaces: Utopias and Heterotopias." Transl. Jay Miskowiec. *Diacritics: A Review of Contemporary Criticism* 16.1 (1986): 22-27.

Foucault, Michel. *The Order of Things*. New York: Pantheon Books, 1971.

Foucault, Michel. *The History of Sexuality: An Introduction*. Vol. 1. London: Penguin, 1990.

Gallagher, Catherine, ed. *Aphra Behn: Oroonoko; or, the Royal Slave*. Boston: Bedford/St. Martin's, 2000.

Gautier, Gary. "Slavery and the Fashioning of Race in *Oroonoko, Robinson Crusoe* and Equiano's *Life*." *The Eighteenth Century* 42.2 (2001): 161-179.

Greenblatt, Stephen, ed. *The Norton Anthology of English Literature: The Major Authors*. 9th ed. New York: Norton, 2013.

Gymnich, Marion and Birgit Neumann. "Vorschläge für eine Relationierung verschiedener Aspekte und Dimensionierungen des Gattungskonzepts: Der Kompaktbegriff Gattung". *Gattungstheorie und Gattungsgeschichte*. Ed. Marion Gymnich, Birgit Neumann and Ansgar Nünning. Trier: wvt, 2007, 31-52.

Hartner, Marcus. "Placing Prospero's Island: (Post)Colonial Practices of Comparing in the Academic Reception of Shakespeare's *The Tempest*." *FIAR* 12.1 (2019): 73-85.

Herman, David. *Story Logic: Problems and Possibilities of Narrative*. Lincoln: University of Nebraska Press, 2002.

Hulme, Peter, ed. *The Cambridge Companion to Travel Writing*. Cambridge: Cambridge University Press, 2002.

Hulme, Peter, ed. *Colonial Encounters: Europe and the Native Caribbean, 1492-1797*. London: Methuen, 1986.

James, Erin. *The Storyworld Accord: Econarratology and Postcolonial Narratives*. Lincoln: University of Nebraska Press, 2015.

Lemke, Thomas. "Rechtssubjekt oder Biomasse? Reflectionen zum Verhältnis von Rassismus und Exklusion." *Biopolitik und Rassismus*. Ed. Martin Stingelin. Frankfurt a. M.: Suhrkamp, 2003. 160-183.

MacDonnell, Kevin. "Beneath Defoe's Island: Imperial Geopolitics and the Inorganic Economy in *Robinson Crusoe*." *Philological Quarterly* 99.1 (2020): 1-24.

Murphy, Robinson. "Black Friday, Queer Atlantic." *Research in African Literatures* 49.2 (2018): 182-198.

Pettinger, Alasdair and Tim Youngs, eds. *The Routledge Research Companion to Travel Writing*. London: Routledge, 2020.

Poole, Ralph J. "Tourniers Anal/yse von Defoes *Robinson Crusoe.*" *Gefährliche Maskulinitäten: Männlichkeit und Subversion am Rande der Kulturen*. Bielefeld: transcript, 2014. 163-202.

Reckwitz, Andreas. "Grundelemente einer Theorie sozialer Praktiken: Eine sozialtheoretische Perspektive." *Zeitschrift für Soziologie* 32.4 (2003): 282-301.

Richetti, John, ed. *The Cambridge Companion to "Robinson Crusoe."* Cambridge: Cambridge University Press, 2018.

Rocha Teixeira, Susana. "Introduction: Doing and Undoing Comparisons in the Americas from the Colonial Times to the Present." *Forum for Inter-American Research* 12.1 (Jun. 2019): 6-11.

Rohland, Eleonora and Kirsten Kramer. "Introduction: On 'Doing Comparison' – Practices of Comparing." *Contact, Conquest and Colonization: How Practices of Comparing Shaped Empires and Colonialism around the World*. New York [et al]: Routledge, 2021. 1-16.

Said, Edward. *Culture and Imperialism*. London: Vintage, 1994.

Schmidt, Johann N. "Von der Restauration bis zur Vorromantik." *Englische Literaturgeschichte*. 5th ed. Ed. Hans Ulrich Seeber. Stuttgart and Weimar, 2012.

Sedwick, Eve. *Between Men: English Literature and Male Homosocial Desire*. New York: Columbia University Press, 1985.

Sedwick, Eve. "Axiomatic." *The Cultural Studies Reader*. Ed. Simon During. London: Routledge, 1993. 243-268.

Spivak, Gayatri. "Theory in the Margin: Coetzee's Foe Reading Defoe's 'Crusoe/Roxana'." *English in Africa* 17.2 (1990): 1-23.

Swenson, Rivka. "*Robinson Crusoe* and the Form of the New Novel." *The Cambridge Companion to "Robinson Crusoe."* Ed. John Richetti. Cambridge: Cambridge University Press, 2018. 16-31.

Tavor Bannet, Eve. "*Robinson Crusoe* and Travel Writing: The Transatlantic World." *The Cambridge Companion to "Robinson Crusoe."* Ed. John Richetti. Cambridge: Cambridge University Press, 2018. 128-141.

Thompson, Carl, ed. *The Routledge Companion to Travel Writing*. London and New York: Routledge, 2016.

Thompson, Carl. *Travel Writing*. London: Routledge, 2011.

Turley, Hans. "The Sublimation of Desire to Apocalyptic Passion in Defoe's Crusoe Trilogy." *Imperial Desire: Dissident Sexualities and Colonial Literature*. Eds. Philip Holden and Richard J. Ruppel. London: University of Minnesota Press, 2003. 3-20.

Watt, Ian. *The Rise of the Novel: Studies in Defoe, Richardson and Fielding*. London: Pimlico, 2000 [1957].

Wheeler, Roxann. "'My Savage,' 'My Man': Racial Multiplicity in *Robinson Crusoe*." *ELH* 62.4 (1995): 821-861.

Youngs, Tim, ed. *The Cambridge Introduction to Travel Writing*. Cambridge: Cambridge University Press, 2013.

Oceans of Non-Relation: Affect and Narcissistic Imperialism in Sea Poetry by James Thomson, Charlotte Brontë, and Hannah More

Caroline Koegler

1. Introduction

A commonplace perception situates the British empire as an "empire of the seas" (Armitage 2004: 100). The ocean, surrounding the British Isles on all sides, encouraged as much as necessitated Britain's expertise at shipping and seamanship on its path to imperialism. Often seen as accelerating with the defeat of the Spanish Armada in 1588, British imperialism rose to prominence in the mid-eighteenth century after the Seven Years War against France that ensued in 1756, with Britain seeking to expand its power and territory in North America. Peace was restored through the Treaty of Paris in 1763, which gave Britain Canada, Grenada, and the Floridas, and significantly reduced French as well as Spanish influence on the North American continent. A good twenty-five years before, in 1740, James Thomson anticipates Britain's unfolding imperialist dominance in his infamous nationalist poem "Rule, Britannia!"[1] As a military and political entity, empire is still a "more wishful prospect than reality" (Nyquist 2018: 74) when Thomson's text amalgamates ideological undercurrents of empire that have long been in the making. The brutal quenching of Bacon's Rebellion in 1675 and the introduction of slave codes[2] in the Americas, for example, both have already been indicative of a gradual popu-

1 In the following, I am citing James Thomson (1740).

2 From the end of the seventeenth century, communities "from Barbados to Maryland" introduced "comprehensive slave codes" (the bulk before c.1730), consolidating the position of planters and establishing their absolute rule over the lives of enslaved people (Synder 2015: 82).

larisation of imperial expansionism and, particularly, racialisation.[3] Within this lineage, "Rule, Britannia!" is part of a larger historical moment in which the ideology of empire is transferred into "normative self-conception" (see Armitage 2004: 172). Each stanza, ending on emphatic pronunciations of denial and disavowal ("Britons never will be slaves"), cements the impression of a superior and supremacist Britain whilst simultaneously revealing a victimological strategy that conjures Britain's need of protecting itself against the injury and shame associated with the position of the enslaved. It predicts not only Britain's soon-to-be increasing political and military influence in the Atlantic world, but also facilitates performative entrainment of exceptionalism and, as this chapter argues, narcissistic non-relation, effected through language, form, and affect.

For the purpose of this chapter, "Rule, Britannia!" is understood as a powerful manifestation of an imperial politics of emotion, fostering exceptionalist self-perception at a crucial moment in the history of the British empire. Positioning enslaved others as a source of negative feeling and engaging in their (attempted) abjection, the poem disavows Britain's historic role in mass enslavement. It also performs an imperialist entitlement to signification that includes emotional attribution and the management of *relation*, tailoring 'relating' in ways that undermine the idea of other people's subjecthood and entitlement (to well-being, self-determination, recognition etc.). In charting imperial Atlantic negotiations of affective avowal and disavowal across a span of c.100 years, I will explore, in the following, how "Rule, Britannia!" engages in selective non-relational strategies (objectification, abjection), and how it and two other poems – Charlotte Brontë's "The Letter" (1846) and Hannah More's "The Sorrows of Yamba" (1999 [1795]) – negotiate this process via oceanic imagery. All poems prominently feature the sea: as a controlled subject as well as background to and mobilizer of Britain's rapidly expanding empire (Thomson); as a lamentable obstacle separating two lovers in an age of accelerating colonialism (Brontë); and as a counter-discursive sphere that can be used to challenge the morality of colonialism and the slave trade, indeed

3 Francois Bernier's A *New Division of Earth By the Different Species or Races Which Inhabit It* (1684), Carl Linnaeus' differentiation of different 'races' in *Systema Naturae* (1735), and Georges Louis LeClerc, Comte de Buffon's thirty-six volume *Histoire Naturelle* (1749-1788) are just some examples for works that are precursors of scientific racism, linking differences in physiognomy to different 'races' and hierarchizing them according to deviation from the 'white prototype' (see, e.g., Seth 2018: 176).

the very grandiose self-perception laid out in Thomson's poem (More). I am interested in how and where these texts position the sea to function both as a conveyer of imperial ideology and contact zone between metaphoricity and (wilful) materiality, even against their own imperialist grain, i.e., how they convey oceans as "a deeply historical location whose transformative power is not merely psychological or metaphorical [...] but material and very real" (Klein/Mackenthun 2004: 2); and how they cloud the morality of the imperial project by demonstrating, particularly, imperialism's affective deficiencies.

These affective deficiencies emerge most forcefully in the non-relation exhibited in the texts toward kidnapped and enslaved Africans transported to the Americas and their deaths in the waves. As meticulously argued by Terri Synder in *The Power to Die* (2015), for centuries, the waves bear the bodies of people who choose suicide over enslavement. In conditions of stark disempowerment, on the Atlantic, "Africans' suicides gave enslaved people a fleeting, if fatal, leverage, and the spectres of their self-inflicted deaths haunted the Atlantic trade" (41). Attempts by Europeans to prevent this are frustrated, as emerges from their "chronicle[s] [of] the actions of enslaved cargoes who killed themselves by leaping overboard, strangulation, or refusing to eat" (41). The waves also carry those bodies cast overboard by whites[4] seeking to discourage self-killings; they are fed to the sharks to underscore a lack of ceremonial burial (40). Yet people are also drowned by captains for economic advantage, as suggested by one of the most memorable court cases in British history, the Zong Trial in 1783. As such, if 'rule the waves; / Britons never will be slaves' is Thomson's motto, then this act of abjection not only heavily downplays efforts of resistance, often collective, on the part of the enslaved, it also reveals the sinister nature of "Rule, Britannia!", encapsulated in the materiality of those Atlantic waves that carry the dead bodies upon which Britain sails to prosperity – the "commerce" with which, as Thomson euphorically suggests in the poem, Britain's cities shall "shine".

In the present chapter, I discuss this nexus of oceanic materiality and affective non-relation under the heading of *oceans of non-relation* – a concep-

4 As already suggested in the previous footnote, 'race' is still a nascent epistemological category at the time in which some of the texts here discussed are published. While I occasionally use 'white' and 'black' as signifiers of different positionalities, this usage is tentative á la Seth, acknowledging that physiognomy is increasingly categorized and valorized according to its degree of deviation from the 'white prototype' (see, e.g., Seth 2018:176).

tual convergence partially inspired by Judith Butler's concept of 'grievability' and by research on comparing and imperial narcissism. Butler defines grievable life as life that "can be valued, and valued through time" (2015: 198); life that "conform[s] to certain conceptions of what life is, in order to become recognizable" (2016: 7). The poems exhibit the imperial power of determining the very coordinates of 'life,' of life worth living and life worth mourning, in paradigmatic form. I use 'non-relation' to denote all those directions into which recognisability – we might also say Adam Smith's more contemporaneous "fellow-feeling" (1759: 14) – does not expand as a result of such 'coordination,' which is a type of coordination that normalizes the notion of a lack of subjecthood and agency in the other. How is this achieved? This chapter suggests this is done through establishing an epistemological-affective process that combines attribution, comparing, and narcissistic disavowal. According to Antoine Berman, comparing has a translatory function that seeks "to open up in writing a certain *relation* with the Other, to fertilize what is one's Own through the mediation of what is Foreign" (1992: 57). However, such relating is also "diametrically opposed to [...] that species of *narcissism* by which every society wants to be a pure and unadulterated Whole" (Berman 1992: 4; my emphasis). Narcissism remains an underconceptualized term in Berman's study on German Romanticism, just as 'comparability' and 'incomparability' perform only an auxiliary role in his focus on 'translation.' In conjoining narcissism with the thematic complex of comparing, however, and also by stressing the frictions between "ethnocentric translations" and those that facilitate "an opening, a dialogue, a cross-breeding, a decentering" and "'a putting in touch with'" (ibid.), Berman lands us squarely in the epistemological-affective machinations of Euro-imperialism. Stained by ulterior motives, in the context of imperialism, comparing easily follows carefully engineered paths that protect privilege and power. In this context indeed, "comparisons are never neutral: they are inevitably tendentious, didactic, competitive, and prescriptive" because "[t]he epistemology of comparison is willed into existence by a certain will to power/knowledge" (Radhakrishnan 2013:16). It is because of comparing's intimacy with power-knowledge that the former might also forestall, rather than foster, *relation*, and it can do so in ways that potentially surprise in their flexibility of deploying comparability tropes. As Stanford Friedman also signals with her concept of "in/commensurability":

> On the one hand, comparison compels recognition of commensurability – likeness – but on the other hand, comparison acknowledges incommensura-

> bility – difference. [...] Comparison puts incommensurability and commensurability into dynamic interplay reflected in the slash that separates and connects: in/commensurability. (40)

Such 'in/commensurability,' where tying in with the power of signification, exhibits a privileged flexibility, i.e., can deploy comparability and incomparability to accommodate different, at times opposing ends.[5] For example, incomparability can be used to denote exceptionalism, as much as comparability can be used to reinforce comparative superiority and stronger claims to entitlement. As such, in/comparability can be situationally tailored to imperialist goals – a process that also relies on a strategic usage of people ('foreign' people, enslaved people) whom it can incorporate and "compel in a variety of ways to reflect back to the imperialist a grandiose self-image" (Simmons 2007: 1). This brings us back to the concept of non-relation. As Diane Simmons writes in *The Narcissism of Empire*, a narcissistic deployment of (signifying) power objectifies others and turns them into objects of use. Unable to perceive of others as partners or subjects with agency, feelings, motivations or motives independent of the wishes of the narcissist, narcissism describes a subject position "Enchanted by an 'other' who is nothing but his own reflection" signalling an "incapab[ility] of relating to a real other" (Spivak 1993: 32, see Drichel 330). In her own work on "The Disaster of Imperial Narcissism", Simone Drichel also highlights Leela Gandhi's observation of colonialism's "crisis of nonrelation" (2018: 184) and the "antirelational basis of imperialism" (185). While this suggests immense power on the part of the colonizer, it is important that non-relationality, or even antirelationality, still depend on the other's existence; still depend on in/comparability as a mechanism of harnessing others to nurture a grandiose self-image. Hence the spectacle, one could argue, of a perpetual, even frantic rehearsal of comparative superiority and comparative claim in Thomson's poem, alongside claims to essential incomparability encapsulated in the idea of godly intervention or the totalising abjection of enslaved peoples (which erases any agency or resistance on their parts). Herein then ultimately also lies a degree of (white) fragility in the narcissistic foundations of Euro-imperial non-relation and in/comparability.[6] As repeat-

---

5 I have discussed this type of privileged flexibility elsewhere: in relation to colonial discourse's strategic de-/re-/ and post-humanisations of racialized others (Koegler 2020).

6 Bakary Diaby has provided a broader discussion of 'white fragility' in relation to Romanticism, utilising DiAngelo's explanation of "a state in which even a minimum amount of racial stress becomes intolerable, triggering a range of defensive moves"

edly emphasized by research on narcissism, this includes erratic behaviour on the part of the narcissist when faced with attempts at defying their narcissistic power. Such defiance easily triggers a particularly destructive, narcissistic rage that can turn into desperation and depression when it cannot transform resistance into compliance, meaning that the process of objectification and mirroring breaks down. Triumphant or grandiose engagement in in/comparability can similarly collapse, an idea latent, for example, in Felski and Stanford Friedman's pondering if comparison might "decenter [and] unsettle standards of measure rather than reinforce them" (2013: 1), or even produce "a jolt to consciousness, initiating a destabilizing, even humbling, awareness of the limitedness and contingency of one's own perspective" (2). In the following, I analyze these productive tensions between in/comparability and non-relation, narcissism and vulnerability, ocean and affect, as well as metaphor, materiality, and resistance, by dedicating a sub-chapter to each poem. Towards the end, I will be interested in reaching beyond imperial narcissism as a meaning-making framework.

2. James Thomson's "Rule, Britannia!" (1740) and the Burden of Shame

James Thomson's exceptionalist-nationalist poem envisages Britain's "[rise] from out the azure main" as a form of Godly intervention. The angels' supposedly very own, emphatic declaration "'Rule Britannia, rule the waves; / Britons never will be slaves'" is repeated at the end of every single stanza and uncannily underscores the narcissistic necessity of perpetually re-inscribing incomparable superiority (also: beauty) and comparative liberty (Britons "never will be" 'like slaves'). Euphoria over Britannia's freedom here lies frightfully close to an endemic fear of power reversal: to be put in the position of 'slaves,' a status that Britain has itself created for so many people for the sake

(DiAngelo 2011: 54, see Diaby 118), including "weaponized emotion" (Diaby 118) such as white "anger" and "fear" (DiAngelo 2011: 54). According to Diaby, one of the "key aspects" for Romanticism is "the drive to keep whiteness meaningless" (123). It also "'holds racism in place' by keeping whiteness invisible and marking moments of its *visibility* as an upsetting to the natural(ized) order" (4). As a result, the very possibility of or attempt at breaking out of such a relationship is a minefield where white pain marks any impending levelling of hierarchies or resistance as a shameful violation of the 'natural' order of things.

of expansion and enrichment, is the shameful prospect 'Britannia' is confident to avoid – as long as she rules. With this juxtaposition, Thomson follows a conventional line of worlding that uses signifying power to attach shame to the position of 'the slave' (see Nyquist 2018: 69), indeed semantically collapses one into the other. This ostensibly effects detachment and distantiation from the experience of enslavement, however, the frequent, rhythmic repetitions of denial and also the proliferating, multi-referential semantics of enslavement that are used in the poem ultimately indicate that Thomson is on slippery ground, the control over signification nearly escaping him. As spelled out by Mary Nyquist, "'Rule Britannia' (1740) memorably evokes (1) personal, (2) internal political, and (3) external political slavery as a nearly magical, indissoluble trinity" (2018: 74); and further: "the refrain thus sings of determination to safeguard Britannia's external, political freedom" as it "raises the possibility of personal, domestic slavery, that is, of each individual Briton being enslaved to an individual slave-holder" (74-75). Nyquist's nuanced observation hints at the overwhelming realness attributed by the poem to the proposition of Britons' potential, multi-dimensional enslavement, conjuring a degree of dread that is absent where Thomson envisages the (potential) enslavement of others. This unevenly spread dread and grievability (as per Butler's conceptualization) signals an affective eclecticism that is similarly revealed in Thomson's claim 'Britons never will be slaves'. The claim implies an exceptionalism that is, in fact, historically incorrect, given the history of Roman slavery in Britain or, more contemporary to Thomson, instances of North African slavery[7] that were still an occasional feature at the time. It also ignores white indentureship such as in the Chesapeake colony where servants conventionally refer to themselves as 'slaves', the terms 'slave' and 'servant' often being used "interchangeabl[y]" (Todd 2010: 3174/7148 [Kindle Locations]). Another caveat lies in gendered power; Thomson's insistence on "Britons" forever defying enslavement is incompatible with historically increasingly popular, proto-feminist positionings of women as 'slaves' in a hetero-patriarchal society. While white feminist appropriations of the materially and politically very different experience of enslavement might count as another textbook case of 'why not compare', i.e., signal a problematic entitlement or 'access' to empire and its subjects, these perceptions are nonetheless becoming virulent in Thomson's

---

7 The term "North African slavery" (formerly often 'Barbary slavery') refers to a particular form of abduction and enslavement of Britons in the North African region, in the early modern period. For details, see works by Colley, Davis, MacLean and Matar.

time with "Writers ranging from Mary Astell to Mary Wollenstonecraft [sic!] to Jane Austen […] insist[ing] with varying degrees of vehemence on the slave status of supposedly free women in Britain" (Swaminathan/Beach 2016: 10). Thomson's 'management' of the slavery trope thus not only reveals a gendered standpoint, but also carefully circumnavigates some of the blots on his advocated idea of Britain's singular liberty. At the same time, however, he does not – or: chooses not to; cannot – entirely shake off negative affect such as dread or fear where it pertains to a potential reversal of the status quo; to a potential (re-)enslavement of Britons. This, of course, ultimately indicates the fragility, even paranoia, of a not yet so firmly established and consolidated empire possibly seeking to harness such fragility through a particularly kind of aggressive rhetoric.

As this already implies, Thomson's selective conjuring of dread and fear, paired with an at times victimising discourse of self-protection ("determination to safeguard Britannia's external, political freedom", in Nyquist's words) is not only uncanny, but also enabling. As Sara Ahmed illuminates with her concept of a racialized 'fantasy of violation' (see 2015: 62-81), white nationalistic discourse often positions others as a source of fear or dread, thereby warranting and legitimating white self-defence (control, exclusion, etc. of the presumed 'threat'). This applies to "Rule, Britannia!" insofar as ascribing negative affect to the fearsomeness of others drives the pretend, moralistic endeavour of maritime imperialism and also legitimizes aggressive militarism. As fear is attached even to the subjugated bodies of the enslaved and/or their condition (a moment of distinct depersonalisation), negative emotion is attributed from the signifying position – an attribution that legitimates enslavement of others as a pseudo-preemptive move. Here is also the "psychic use" that Simmons suggests the subjected fulfil from the perspective of their narcissistic conquerors (2007: 1). In addition to couching abuse, aggression, and enslavement in moral righteousness, Simmons suggests that enslaver-enslaved relations "provided rich opportunities for expressing feeling of contempt, ridicule and revulsion, allowing the imperialist to displace onto others his own feelings of shame and self-contempt" (ibid.). In this instance, Nyquist's and Simmons' arguments overlap; while Nyquist accentuates the self-protective stance of Thomson's text (slavery as the shameful prospect against which Britons need to protect themselves through military and political agitation), Simmons can be read as implying another kind of self-protection: where enslaved peoples become receptacles for displaced colonial shame and fear, they become objects of use insofar as their distantiation facilitates a distancing from uncomfortable emotions, i.e., from emotions that might endanger white confidence or entitlement to rule. If the former position legitimates casting aggression as self-protection (also encapsulated in the lines "Still more majestic shalt thou rise, / More dreadful from each foreign stroke;"), the latter enables a cleansing of the imperial project of uncanny, bad feelings that might obstruct the moral smoothness with which Britain glides to power.

The moral-affective defence mechanisms installed by Thomson help normalise a stance that readily accepts the doom of others. Be they enslaved or stem from other European nations, Thomson seems to embrace a social Darwinist perspective *avant la lettre* that preferably considers a lack of well-being in others as collateral damage ("The nations, not so blest as thee, / Must, in their turns, to tyrants fall;"). At times steeped even in *Schadenfreude*, the losses experienced by other 'nations' seem to be predominantly conjured to offset Britain's exceptional prosperity and self-determination ("While [Britain] shalt flourish great and free, / The dread and envy of them all"). Thomson's assertions thus also resonate with what Philip Wüschner has described as a form of narcissistic shame that is severed from remorse and notions of social responsibility. Narcissistic shame represents "the inverted picture of narcissistic rage that does not really care for the ones who have been wronged but only grieves the loss of social recognition" (2017: 99, see Malreddy 2019: 314). Following Wüschner, Malreddy has similarly suggested that "shame is not only a contingent emotion, but also a necessary trigger for a proper understanding of guilt" (2019: 314). This is highly relevant also for deciphering Thomson's narcissistic poetics of imperialism, as he repeatedly foregrounds the glory of a Britain that deeply humiliates other European nations, who in turn 'envy' Britons their unbounded power/freedom. Thomson thus implies that it is the 'loss of social recognition' that subjected nations will primarily invest with negative emotions, rather than the pain and losses experienced by their peoples. What is played on here, in other words, is the idea of one narcissist subduing another.

A central streak in this narcissistic-imperialist hustling for supremacy – military, political, and moral – is ensuring a compartmentalisation, and finally, abjection, of "'the not'" (Ahmed 2015: 86). Affectively speaking, 'the not' – the shameful and fearsome idea of inferiority and suppression of the self – is tentatively secured through a stance of disgust at "'that which is below'" which "functions to maintain the power relations between above and below, *through which 'aboveness' and 'belowness' become properties of particular bodies, objects and spaces*" (89; original emphasis). Shame plays a central role here. Disgust tentatively overwrites shame or, more to the point, turns it into the burden of others, simultaneously consolidating colonial hierarchies. It is these affects' close proximity to one another – shame, fear, disgust (Simmons speaks of "contempt, ridicule and revulsion" as essential to narcissistic objectification) – that consequently further contextualizes Thomson's strong language in positioning "Britannia" over others. The same proximity also explains Thomson's oscillations between such different emotions as euphoria and dread, confidence and shame/fear/disgust, and as such between stark avowal and disavowal. Britannia's burgeoning 'rule', or so Thomas ultimately suggests, is dependent not only on military or even ideological prowess, but also on fostering *affective* supremacy – an enterprise that is as violent and demanding as it is precarious.

3. "Sent from England's Shore": Charlotte Brontë's "The Letter" (1846)

"The Letter" was published in 1846 and as such a good hundred years after "Rule, Britannia!" It appeared in an anonymous collection by the Brontë sisters one year before the sisters began to publish their first major novels. The poem of seven stanzas – which has not received much scholarly attention – in many ways appears as a condensed version of some of the dynamics negotiated in, particularly, *Jane Eyre* and Emily Brontë's *Wuthering Heights*, published only two years later. The similarities between the texts prominently include reference to Britain's continuing imperial entanglements overseas and the emotional burden of empire that white families carry as a result of colonialism. They both are energized by fears of reverse-colonisation at the affective level, Rochester and Jane being pitted as suffering from Bertha's excruciating presence and the Earnshaws and Lintons from Heathcliff, the retaliating, racialized orphan-incomer. As I argue elsewhere, the novels' set-ups are deeply steeped in imperial economies of emotion, in so far as they position racialized others as the "origin of bad feeling"[8] which ostensibly legitimates their subjection and exclusion (in Bertha's case, of course, after Rochester has already taken her fortune via marriage). Bertha and Heathcliff are also depicted as inducing dread insofar as they supposedly threaten white health, genealogies,

8 These are Ahmed's words (2015: 43) which are coincidentally synonymous with Nelly's (one of *Wuthering Height*'s narrators) own words (see Koegler 2021: 273, 283).

and property relations, whilst at points also proving dangerously alluring in tune with miscegenation fantasies that were prominent at the time. As such feeding classic imperial 'fantasies of violation', the thematically closely related texts position disavowed, colonial subjects in the position of the aggressor (see Koegler 2020, 2021) and manufacture a need for white self-preservation that pushes back against racialized others. Once this push-back is complete and the racialized other is removed, reconciliation, relief, happiness, and the prospect of white procreation are restored.

Whilst Charlotte Brontë's "The Letter" does not personify the danger of reverse-colonialism via a Bertha or Heathcliff figure, it nonetheless already follows the bulk of affective strategies realized in more detail in *Jane Eyre* and *Wuthering Heights*. Like the novels, "The Letter" dramatizes negative impacts of Britain's overseas imperial entanglements on the British domestic scene. It is here encapsulated in a married couple's separation in the name of advancing the imperial endeavour. While the young wife pines for her husband, artificially confined to a desk in the bloom of her youth and bent over her letter, he, "loved though stern", is "detain[ed]" by "[r]emote colonial wilds" – an information revealed at the climactic end of the poem. Differently put, the poem couches the imperial endeavour as a sacrificial, white burden whose spectacle of titillating harm is displayed upon the mind, body, and emotions of a young white woman. As my language here suggests, the poem also already contains some of the erotic innuendos more overtly insinuated in the novels.

"The Letter" gives off an impression of haste and breathlessness. Readers hit the ground running: "What is she writing? Watch her now, / How fast her fingers move! / How eagerly her youthful brow / Is bent in thought above!" Question followed by request, followed by two exclamations – the alternating rhyme hurries readers along the lines and mirrors the 'hastiness' of the writer. Astonishment at the zeal and eagerness of this young woman is clearly registered; she is writing fast, her posture mirroring the intensity of her focus; she does not take heed of anything else. The remaining lines of the first stanza emphasize this very sentiment: her hair is obstructing her vision, she moves it carelessly aside. She does not notice as her "band of crystals" falls to the ground. Only as we reach the end of the stanza is it briefly implied that this unlikely stance bears romantic influences ("labour sweet"), and yet this is not fully explored until much later, the next three stanzas functioning as a retarding moment, heaping more mystery, even exasperation, upon the yet unanswered question: "To whom, then, doth she write?"

Before the crucial answer is provided, the unnaturalness of the young woman's occupation is repeatedly underscored by way of a Shakespearean comparison 'to a summer's day'. It is the "loveliest hour" of a "golden" day in June; nature is in full blossom, like herself, and yet, as the sun goes down, it has "not caught her eye". The speaker's performance of disbelief is still intensified as nature is endowed with human feeling, even flirtatiousness: "The cheerful lawn, and unclosed gate, / The white road, far away, / In vain for her light footsteps wait". Nature here functions not only as a mirror image (she, also, is 'in bloom') but also as a metaphorical lover, waiting for her teasing, "light footsteps". The tempting, "unclosed gate" might well be read as a fertility metaphor, the young woman's unnatural confinement and separation from her lover for now acting as a barrier against procreation. Not insignificantly for such a reading, the phallic "[t]all plants of bright and spicy bloom" that grow "[a]round the threshold" anticipate the introduction of *him* as "[a] stalwart form, a massive head, / A firm, determined face". Thoughts of his manly determination and rigidity, the very act of writing the letter, and wetting it with her plentiful tears – all this for now absorbs her attention, or: libidinal energies.

Stanzas four and five raise the tension further while the gaze – the speaker's, the woman's, the reader's – become still more important. Readers are overtly directed to look 'more closely', repeatedly encouraged to match her "eager will" with eager eyes: "Nay, watch her still more closely, ask / Her own eyes' serious light; / Where do they turn, as now her pen / Hangs o'er th'unfinished line? / Whence fell the tearful gleam that then / Did in their dark spheres shine?" The long postponed and still cryptic answer approaches at the end of stanza five after a further, incremental narrowing and focusing of the reader's gaze: "But look again; inured to shade / Your eyes now faintly trace / A stalwart form, a massive head, / A firm, determined face". The sixth stanza adds more detail, revealing some exotic "Black Spanish locks" and "sunburnt cheek", paired however with "A brow high, broad, and white" which unambiguously reveals his race. Similarly unmistakable is the morality of his endeavours, carved on his very brow: "every furrow seems to speak / Of mind and moral might". Still later, at the very end of the poem, this almost unearthly being ("Is this her god?") is revealed to be her comparatively profane "husband". He is her "heart of hearts", currently in "a strange and distant spot" and "Three seas and many a league of land" away. This vast distance the letter "must pass o'ver, / E're read by whom to whose loved hand / 'Tis sent from England's shore". The final lines provide the resolution, long awaited, and bring us full circle: "Remote colonial wilds detain / Her husband, loved though stern; / She, 'mid that smiling English scene, / Weeps for his wished return". Depravation, or so these last lines suggest, lies heavily on her. His absence is an imposition they both share and from which they both suffer. The climactic revelation of the addressee being her "husband" dramatizes her attachment and woundedness, signalled by her tears that she sheds isolated from her cheerful and blossoming surroundings.

In directly linking 'her' suffering-*cum*-libido and 'their' separation to the 'detaining', "Remote colonial wilds", the poem's exoticizing, even sexualising gaze projects agency and aggression onto the very colonial subjects that Britons seek out to sustain and accelerate the imperial cause. This, too, is a fantasy of violation as defined by Ahmed and version of 'the white man's burden', a burden that weighs down the shoulders of a young, beautiful female in the homestead as well as of the analogous "smiling English scene" which, or so is the implication, would deserve better than have its "open gate" ignorantly overlooked. However, carrying the burden of imperialism turns out to be a much more momentous task than failing the appreciation of a trivial summer's day, and even readers are conscripted into proving this truism: they are put into the position of having to scrutinize and finally understand the extent of her commitment – to him, to empire, to writing the letters that will reinforce their connection and relation. This is also enacted aesthetically: the poem's long and drawn-out circulations of the longed-for answers to burning questions – to whom is she writing? Whose is the face in the picture? – are the eroticized wilds through which *readers* have to wade in order to establish a sense of clarity.

These layers of comparative, sexualized load-bearing – the young woman, her husband, the reader – enlist Brontë's readers for the trans-Atlantic imperial endeavour, relating specific groups to one another (and not others) and encouraging select understanding and empathy – fellow-feeling – in very specific directions. As such, selective grievability plays an important role in the poem's affective universe. It is clearly located, first and foremost, in white people – her, him, even readers (who at Brontë's time would have been expected to be white). *They* clearly emerge as human-beings with personhood: intellect, understanding, feelings, needs. While the poem meticulously humanizes one group, another is not situated within the realm of the human. Subsumed under "colonial wilds" that "detain" her husband, colonial subjects are starkly de-individualized and dehumanized by comparison, pitted against the 'smiling English scene' and its graceful and energized, if suffering, inhabitant. Thus turned into objects of dread, "colonial wilds" are utilized to offset not only the sacrificial, noble, and enduring character of white colonists (who embrace exilic conditions for the sake of empire) but also England's much more delicate moral-*cum*-natural world that metaphorically shares in shouldering the draining burden that is empire.

Such usage, semantic and affective, of non/relation (for 'selective relation'), comparison, and metaphor reveals "[t]he Letter's" own investment in culturally normalized, imperial-narcissistic structures of affect. Only a select group will "be valued, and valued through time" (Butler 2015: 198) because they "conform to certain conceptions of what life is, in order to become recognizable" (Butler 2016: 7), even at the level of language ('colonial wilds' vs. an individualized couple). "The Letter", penned in white and unsubtly eroticized distress, is a documentation of colonial infrastructures – affective, logistical, technological – that will connect those who have sailed from England with their loved ones who remain at home, intricately interweaving empire's domestic, natural, and colonial geographies; entangling a married couple's own, emotional intimacy with Britannia's rule of seas, lands, and peoples; and drawing a strategic comparison between the conditions of confinement experienced by both genders. In this context, "sent from England's shore" denotes a liminal space ("shore") beyond which lies a great unknown, oceanic realm that 'the letter' has to cross *en route* to the other side, to reach his very hands. Not only do the waves carry away people like her husband, they also carry her words to that specific yet unspecific ("colonial wilds"), far-away destination. Considering this injection of estrangement and expansion into the affective, domestic realm of the poem, it is all the more significant that Brontë renders gratifying the truly multifaceted, 'white burden' of imperialism that continues to spur Britannia's rule far and wide and even in adverse conditions. While the epistolary correspondence is isolating and distressing to the young woman, it is also a "labour sweet" – a potentially eroticized as much as eroticizing act. This is exactly what is needed for sustaining empire. Valorising conquest and exploitation becomes more readily acceptable if deprivation can occasionally blur into (perceived) pleasure, tantalizingly linking aggression-coded-as-burden to positive, titillating affect. It is an affective-ideological feat here rendered almost to perfection.

4. Black Motherhood in the Anglo-Atlantic: Hannah More's "The Sorrows of Yamba" (1795)

Thomson's and Brontë's poems indicate the long *durée* of select relating under imperialism, just as they signal the continuing relevance of a critical whiteness studies approach in the context of long eighteenth century literature and the history of emotion. For the last poem that I will discuss, abolitionist writer Hannah More's "The Sorrows of Yamba" (1795), this applies in a similar way, my focus here also complementing recent research on Romanticism and abolitionism such as by Fran Botkin, Manu Samriti Chander, Bakary Diaby, Debbie Lee, Patricia A. Matthew, Helen Thomas, Paul Youngquist, and Joseph Rezek. These scholars have taken issue with the extent to which scholars of Romanticism have marginalized not only black and brown writers, but also topics like abolitionism and enslavement, i.e., topics that might threaten white morality and puncture the affective 'comfort zone' that has been erected around a rather homogenous group of white, and often male, Romantic writers[9]. Chander and Matthew understand canonization in this context as "a continual process of subjugation, a process that works by muting those voices that would call into question the superiority of authorized English literatures" (2018: 433) – and this ties in, of course, with the kinds of cultural 'superiority' and select grievability channelled in individual literary texts *á la* Thomson's "Rule, Britannia!" or Brontë's "The Letter". The affective mechanisms and politics reproduced in these texts no doubt tie in with the normalized disavowal of some writers and not others, as well as with rejections of themes that are out of line with imperial ideologies of racial supremacy. I am interested in the counter-discursive potentials of "The Sorrows of Yamba" in this context, as the poem not only centres on black experience but also formulates a direct, explicitly worded challenge of Thomson's "Rule, Britannia!"

Published in 1795, More's "The Sorrows of Yamba" focuses on an African mother and her account of the middle passage, depicting, according to Lee, "black single motherhood [a]s a state of utter desperation" (2013: 168): "the mother tosses her infant into the silvery ocean with this blessing" – and Lee quotes More:

9 See, for example, Youngquist's *Race, Romanticism, and the Atlantic* (2013) and Sandler's study *The Black Romantic Revolution. Abolitionist Poets at the End of Slavery* (2020).

Happy, happy, there she lies;
Thou shalt feel the lash no-more;
[...]
Thee, sweet infant, none shall sell,
Thou hast gain'd a wat'ry grave,
Clean escap'd the tyrant fell,
While thy mother lives a slave.

What More describes here resonates with Synder's discussion of child-killings in *The Power to Die*. Such killings are just one example of the extent to which enslavement threatened family and community attachments and yet, as both Synder and Lee point out, most accounts of such killings are passed down through white records,[10] at least until around the mid-nineteenth century when a new generation of African American abolitionists relate what is often first-hand experience of the Middle Passage (see Synder 2015: 16). More's rendition, too, is not an 'own-voice' account, and this might be why her idea of "the black mother's singleness, and along with it her despair and destruction", is essentially aligned with white, late eighteenth-century notions of "failed domesticity" (Lee 2013: 167) just as it is aligned with More's own evangelical beliefs that centre on the 'saving' of souls. The risk of this double alignment is, of course, that enslaved black women and their children are victimized and stripped of agency and resistance. In a previous work, "Slavery, A Poem" (1788), More has already written of "the dire victim torn from social life, / The shrieking babe, the agonizing wife! / She, wretch forlorn! is dragg'd by hostile hands" (1788: 8), etc. More thus "casts slaves into a mode of racial otherness not hitherto integral to female anti-slavery discourse" (Ferguson 1992: 7) and demonstrates the changing conventions in depicting enslaved persons in anti-slavery writings. While anti-slavery texts by white British female abolitionists have long depicted specific and named "slave-protagonists" who "variously resisted their situation" and in specific "geographical sites" (3), this changes around the time of the Parliamentary campaign in 1787 (in the context of which More writes her poem). It then becomes customary to turn enslaved persons into generic individuals largely "unproblematized, unvoiced, unthinking, and unnamed, victims at the mercy of unchristian British

10 Synder details this, listing "traders' letters, masters' diaries, travelers' accounts, and printed discussions of slavery across and beyond the Anglo-Atlantic" in the early modern period and later "legislative petitions and sporadic coroners' inquests" (2015: 16).

cut-throats" (4). The drawbacks of this change in conventional representation are particularly revealed when considering that, according to Lee, "[t]he verse authored by white men and women and blasted all over England tells a very different story from the documents floating on the edges of history in black women's words and, sometimes, in their own voices" (2013: 168). Lee reads an alternative archive of "Slave complaints, plantation journals, letters, engravings, and narratives" that show black mothers in a variety of scenarios:

> She is a fit caregiver, protecting her child's welfare over her own physical safety. She makes sure her children have a rich and stable community comprised of other black women and children that contrasts starkly with solitary middle- and upper middle-class English domesticity. She practices what all mothers, single or not, know to be true: 'it takes a village' to raise a child. (167)

In thus engaging with a new canon of documents, Lee draws out the "kinship bonds, family strength, and community action" between black 'lone' mothers that, or so she shows, did form as a distinct "counter-culture" and challenge to white patriarchal rule on the plantations (168). Against this background in particular, one could argue that More's choice of theme and generic black mother risks producing a black subject that "is granted only a diluted form of humanity grounded in pain and victimhood" (Festa 2010: 10). However, there is still more complexity: More's poem does not depict plantation life but the Middle Passage, where forging such communal bonds as envisaged by Lee would have been particularly difficult given that the people packed on the ships often neither knew each other nor spoke each other's languages. Even more importantly, even if More frames slave trade and enslavement in a way that is tailored to her white contemporaries, this also has the strategic component of lobbying those persons who hold political power. I would therefore suggest that More's 'tailoring' of Yamba's experience to stereotypical images of failed white motherhood (including infanticide) most poignantly reflects less her own preferential views of black motherhood than those normalized in her society – a society potentially unable to relate to the notion of powerfully bonding black mothers, and for all the wrong reasons. More thus no doubt reproduces but also manipulates her own society's normalized, affective politics of non-relation, one in which black mothers become intelligible as grievable only when and if their depiction follows the already disempowering script of failed, white motherhood (which More also, implicitly, criticizes with her depiction; see Ferguson 1992). Indeed, More plays on a practice of recognition that might reel in one image of victimized motherhood because it can compare to another, already familiar one. Whether intentionally or unintentionally, More's presentation of infanticide in the Anglo-Atlantic thus reveals a knowledgeable navigation of colonial-patriarchal narcissism that might extend its sympathy and might install political change only *if and where* this reflects morality and power back at the white (male) colonists – a classic white saviour trope. It is a strategy which, like so much of sentimentalist abolitionist writing, largely upholds the imperial-patriarchal emotional grid while aiming for changing the political and economic system: ending the trade in enslaved persons.

If More's victimising representation of black motherhood might then be understood as a covert (as well as limited) strategy of persuasion that is symptomatic of the normalized, colonial-patriarchal narcissism of her time and society, elsewhere, she tackles such narcissism much more overtly through direct references to Thomson's "Rule, Britannia!":

> Ye that boast "*Ye rule the waves,*"
> Bid no Slave-ship soil the sea;
> Ye that "*never will be slaves,*"
> Bid poor Afric's land be free.

Taking on an egalitarian sentiment, More here demands an equal standard for Britons and Africans where, as per Christian obligation, Britons must not inflict on others what they themselves are so eager and proud to avoid for their own people. Countering Thomson's monopolising as much as perverted notion of 'freedom' (which, apparently, includes the 'freedom' to enslave others), More undermines the normalization of commingled narcissism and essentialism in Thomson's poem. Indeed, with her request for a more egalitarian framework, More goes against imperialism's paradigmatic belief in white supremacy that also informs Brontë's conjuring of the dehumanized and yet threatening "colonial wilds". I am here also reminded of Synder's suggestion that Olaudah Equiano's *Interesting Narrative* "report[s] that he 'envied' the dead their 'freedom' and did not criticize the suicide attempts of captives aboard ships" (2015: 30). This reveals the extent to which imperial ideology not only normalizes white claims to a kind of freedom that harms and takes freedom away from others, but also transcodes 'freedom' itself: for an African person like Equiano (and Synder also lists other examples), freedom becomes coterminous with 'death', instigated by imperialism's claustrophobic power of subjection and signification. More's counter-discursive stance in relation to Thomson is also revealed here:

Naked on the plat-form lying,
Now we cross the tumbling wave!
Shrieking, sick'ning, fainting, dying,
Deed of shame for Britons brave!
At the savage captain's beck,
Now, like brutes, they make us prance;
Smack the cat about the deck,
And in scorn they bid us dance.

The third line ("Deed of shame for Britons brave!") picks up the sentiment of abject shame encapsulated in Thomson's semanticization of slavery; it is here inverted by More who positions Britons as shameful for subscribing to the ideology and enterprise of enslavement. Crucially, More insists on the fact that shame is not inherent in or essential to any particular positionality (i.e., the enslaved), but is instead defined by one's actions – here the actions of Britons who engage in mass-enslavement. Still more to the point, More insists that shame is not naturally or morally triggered by the fear of a "loss of social recognition" (Wüschner 2017: 99), as it is in Thomson's poem. Instead, shame is triggered – or: should be triggered – by the pain one inflicts on others. As such, and between and beyond the text's victimizing tendencies, More's poem also harbours an insistence on *relation* – a relation that respects the other as a subject toward whom it bears a responsibility and duty of both care and respect. She carves out just how effortlessly non-relation may slide into sadism and torture, encouraging readers to establish an emotional reaction that perceives of other mothers as fellow human-beings regardless of their physiognomy and/or ethnic background. It is, of course, the view and the discourse of someone speaking from a racially privileged as well as clearly gendered position (as am I). It must be clear, therefore, that the critique of white non-relation practiced here by More – while important in its own, historical context – remains a partial one; the deconstruction of white imperial narcissism is an in itself incomplete project, belonging in a much larger effort of establishing a greater diversity of voices, both current and historical.

5. Conclusion

The poems I have discussed in this chapter speak to (trans-)Atlantic imperialism from different times and different vantage points. Thomson and Brontë follow similar affective patterns whilst More's is a counter-discursive if partially flawed as well as privileged stance that challenges Thomson's normalization of narcissistic imperialism. All engage in/with the affective politics that I now have outlined several times: an investment in select grievability, linked to (white) European bodies; imperial-narcissistic non-relation that drains others of subjecthood and turns them into objects of use (victims included) in order to mirror or humour dominant (in whatever form) images of imperial-patriarchal self-conception; a tendency toward a flexible deployment of in/comparability that is symptomatic of signifying power and oscillates between denoting *relating* (to some groups and not others) and superiority, either comparative or essential. The trope of the ocean is employed differently by the poems, featuring as a trailblazing facilitator of imperialism as well as ruled subject in "Rule, Britannia!"; as a vast, troubling expanse that needs to be reached across in order to sustain affective relations between a married couple in "The Letter" (which is a sharp counterpoint to the customary, often systematic destruction of family bonds and attachments during the Middle Passage and on the plantations); and as a metaphoric-discursive as well as material counterpoint to triumphalist and normalized imperial non-relation, in "The Sorrows of Yamba". Differently put, the ocean itself is treated as an object of use in ways that appropriate it for the political, ideological, and affective efforts that sustain the plausibility, even morality, of the imperialist enterprise (Thomson, Brontë). In More's poem, the Atlantic becomes a crime scene of slave ships, abuse, death, and desperation, related from the perspective of the enslaved (which is not an 'own-voice'). More renders visible and readable the Atlantic as the figurative and material realm of narcissistic non-relation that it is – even if this is via a process of appropriation in which she, too, uses oceanic imagery for furthering her own political agenda (in which Christianity is a central one next to abolition). Considering the materials and the authors' standpoints, then, this has been a selection of poems that has offered only glimpses beyond the veneer of white oceanic imagery and instrumentalization, these glimpses coming in from the historical scholarship I have also brought to the scene. It is a compilation in which the biased as much as triumphalist colonial usage of sea metaphors ('rule' of 'the waves', etc.) and material-colonial usage of the ocean is starkly apparent; a context in which More's intervention is a pertinent one, as it reminds her majority-white readers of the existence of another side of history, however partially represented. As per sentimentalist abolitionist tradition, More demands affective recognition of the enslaved (albeit within rather limited frames), not only condemning the white atrocities committed in and around the Anglo-Atlantic, but also, and more specifically, heightening awareness of shame's proper roots in care and responsibility. In thus conveying African people's well-being as something that should morally be of interest to the British public, she fosters a critical perspective that is entirely, even pathologically, absent from "Rule, Britannia!" and "The Letter", even though it itself remains heavily gauged by imperial-patriarchal expectations.

In my discussion, I have sought to increase the visibility of normalized structures of imperial non-relation and objectification – practices of 'draining' others of subjecthood and agency and turning them into objects of use that reflect power, grandiosity, legitimacy, and so forth, back to the superior, white self. This turning of others into mirror images of preferred self-concepts is an important, if neglected, aspect of 'comparing' and its lack of neutrality. Strategic in/comparability, i.e., the privileged capacity to 'mete out' comparability according to specific goals and preferences, or in relation to some (presumed) facets of an inferiorized, scrutinized other, is, after all, a primary mechanism through which non-relation is negotiated. In historical scholarship, then, research on non-relation and practices of comparing have something to say to each other, revealing affective machinations of specific texts as well as of specific formal practices such as metaphorization ("the fundamental instrumentalism of metaphor"; Stanford Friedman 2013: 36), that are part and parcel of much larger imperial-ideological forms and functions some of which continue to be invisibil(ized) and/or taken for granted to this day. Scrutinising how entire spaces – or oceans – become repositories for white (and/or male) feelings, infused with happiness or excitement, dread or fear; and asking not only "why compare?" (Radhakrishnan) or "why not compare" (Stanford Friedman) but also who compares and to what effects/affects can contribute to forging a meaningful perspective on and/or practice of comparing in the context of the Euro-imperial past of the long eighteenth century, its normalized structures of affective non-relation, and some of these structures' continuing, *durée*. It is possible that Felski's and Stanford Friedman's tripartite approach of collision, reciprocal defamiliarization, and collage (2013: 4) could pose an incentive in this context. Collision's commitment to a multiplicity of voices and listening (inspired by Mary N. Layoun); reciprocal defamiliarization's investment in "displac[ing] the Self-Other binary and emphasiz[ing] unknowability" (inspired by Radhakrishnan); collage's refusal of "hierarchy and instrumentalism" and focus on "what texts share" (inspired by modernist Dadaism) (Stanford Friedman 2013: 41-42) – these conjoint methodologies can well encourage, as well as benefit from, a more sustained, critical engagement with the imperial-narcissistic cycles of affective self-aggrandizement and/or white fragility that continue to haunt both public and academic discourses.

Bibliography

Ahmed, Sarah. *The Cultural Politics of Emotion*. New York: Routledge, 2015.

Armitage, David. *The Ideological Origins of the British Empire*. Cambridge: Cambridge University Press, 2004.

Berman, Antoine. *The Experience of the Foreign: Culture and Translation in Romantic Germany*. Trans. S. Heyvaert. Albany: State Univ. of New York Press, 1992.

Brontë, Charlotte. "The Letter." *Poems*. Ed. Ellis Currer and Acton Bell. London: Smith, Elder and Co., 1846. 86-89.

Butler, Judith. *Notes Toward a Performative Theory of Assembly*. Cambridge: Harvard University Press, 2015.

Butler, Judith. *Frames of War: When is Life Grievable?* London: Verso, 2016.

Chander, Manu Samriti. *Brown Romantics. Poetry and Nationalism in the Global Nineteenth Century*. Lewisburg: Buknell University Press, 2017.

Chander, Manu Samriti and Patricia A. Matthew. "Abolitionist Interruptions: Romanticism, Slavery, and Genre." Special Issue of: *European Romantic Review* 29.4 (2018): 431-434.

Colley, Linda. *Captives*. New York: Pantheon Books, 2002.

Davis, Robert C. *Christian Slaves, Muslim Masters: White Slavery in the Mediterranean, the Barbary Coast, and Italy, 1500-1800*. New York: Palgrave, 2003.

Diaby, Bakary. "Feeling Black, Feeling Back. Fragility and Romanticism." *Symbiosis* 23.1 (2019): 117-138.

DiAngelo, Robin. "White Fragility." *International Journal of Critical Pedagogy* 3.3 (2011): 54-70.

Drichel, Simone. "The Disaster of Colonial Narcissism." *American Imago* 75.3 (2018): 329-364.

Felski, Rita and Susan Stanford Friedman. "Introduction." *Comparison. Theories, Approaches, Uses*. Eds. Rita Felski and Susan Stanford Friedman. Baltimore: Johns Hopkins University Press, 2013. 1-12.

Ferguson, Moira. "British Women Writers and an Emerging Abolitionist Discourse." *The Eighteenth Century* 33.1 (1992): 3-23.

Festa, Lynn. "Humanity without Feathers." *Humanity: An International Journal of Human Rights* 1.1 (2010): 3-27.

Gandhi, Leela. *Affective Communities: Anticolonial Thought, Fin-de-siècle Radicalism, and the Politics of Friendship*. Durham: Duke University Press, 2006.

Klein, Bernhard and Gesa Mackenthun. "Introduction." *Sea Changes*. Ed. Bernhard Klein and Gesa Mackenthun. London: Routledge, 2004.

Koegler, Caroline. "Posthumanism and Colonial Discourse: Nineteenth Century Literature and Twenty-First Century Critique." *Open Library of Humanities* 6.2 (2020).

Koegler, Caroline. "Follow the Hatred: The Production of Negative Feeling in Emily Brontë's *Wuthering Heights* (1847)." *NOVEL: A Forum on Fiction* 54.2 (2021): 270-286. [Forthcoming].

Lee, Debbi. "Black Single Mothers in Romantic History and Literature." *Race, Romanticism, and the Atlantic*. Ed. Paul Youngquist. Abingdon: Routledge, 2013. 161-177.

MacLean, Gerald. *The Rise of Oriental Travel: English Visitors to the Ottoman Empire, 1580-1720*. New York: Palgrave, 2004.

Malreddy, Pavan Kumar. "Imperialist Shame and Indigenous Guilt: George Orwell's writings on Burma." *European Journal of English Studies* 23.3 (2019): 311-325.

Matar, Nabil. *Turks, Moors, and Englishmen in the Age of Discovery*. New York: Columbia University Press, 1999.

Matar, Nabil. *Britain and Barbary: 1589-1689*. Gainesville: University Press of Florida, 2005.

More, Hannah and Eaglesfield Smith, "The Sorrows of Yamba; or, The Negro Woman's Lamentation." Repr. in *Slavery, Abolition, and Emancipation: Writings in the British Romantic Period*. 8 Vols. Ed. Peter J. Kitson and Debbie Lee. Vol. 4, *Verse*. Ed. Alan Richardson. London: Pickering and Chatto, 1999 [1795]. 224-231.

More, Hannah. *Slavery, A Poem*. London: T. Cadell, 1788.

Nyquist, Mary. "The Liberty of Naming," *Revisiting Slavery and Anti-Slavery. Towards a Critical Analysis*. Ed. Laura Brace and Julia O'Connell Davidson. Cham: Palgrave Macmillan, 2018. 65-96.

Radhakrishnan, R. "Why Compare?" *Comparison. Theories, Approaches, Uses.* Eds. Rita Felski and Susan Stanford Friedman. Baltimore: Johns Hopkins University Press, 2013. 15-33.

Reynolds, Larry J. "Slavery and the Civil War." *Nathaniel Hawthorne in Context.* Ed. Monika M. Elbert. Cambridge: Cambridge University Press, 2018. 57-67.

Sandler, Matt. *The Black Romantic Revolution. Abolitionist Poets at the End of Slavery.* London: Verso, 2020.

Seth, Suman. *Difference and Disease Medicine, Race, and the Eighteenth-Century British Empire*. Cambridge: Cambridge University Press, 2018.

Simmons, Diane. *The Narcissism of Empire. Loss, Rage and Revenge in Thomas De Quincey, Robert Louis Stevenson, Arthur Conan Coyle, Rudyard Kipling and Isak Dinesen*. Brighton: Sussex Academic Press. 2007.

Smith, Adam. *The Theory of Moral Sentiments*. Printed for A. Millar, in the Strand; And A. Kincaid and J. Bell in Edinburgh. London, 1759.

Spivak, Gayatri Chakravorty. "Echo." *New Literary History* 24.1 (1993): 17-43.

Stanford Friedman, Susan. "Why Not Compare?" *Comparison. Theories, Approaches, Uses*. Ed. Rita Felski and Susan Stanford Friedman. Baltimore: Johns Hopkins University Press, 2013. 34-45.

Swaminathan, Srividhya, and Adam R. Beach. "Invoking Slavery in the Eighteenth-Century British Imagination." *Invoking Slavery in the Eighteenth-Century British Imagination*. Ed. Srividhya Swaminathan and Adam R. Beach. Abingdon: Routledge, 2016. 1-19.

Synder, Terri L. *The Power to Die: Slavery and Suicide in British North America*. Chicago: University of Chicago Press, 2015.

Thomson, James. *Alfred: A Masque. Represented Before Their Royal Highnesses the Prince and Princess of Wales, at Cliffden, on the first of August, 1740*. London: Printed for A. Millar, 1740. 42-43.

Todd, Dennis. *Defoe's America*. Cambridge: Cambridge University Press, 2010.

Vitkus, Daniel J., ed. *Piracy, Slavery, and Redemption: Barbary Captivity Narratives from Early Modern England.* New York: Columbia University Press, 2001.

Wüschner, Philipp. "Shame, Guilt, and Punishment." *Foucault Studies* 23 (2017): 86-107.

Youngquist, Paul, ed. *Race, Romanticism, and the Atlantic.* Abingdon: Routledge, 2013.

Practices of Comparing in Eighteenth-Century Grammars of English

Göran Wolf

1. Introduction

The eighteenth century did not contribute comprehensive language-internal developments to the history of the English language (see Romaine 1998: 1, Görlach 2001: 8, or Hickey 2010: 2). Yet, the eighteenth century is a remarkable period in the history of English because it is embedded within a longer stretch of time at the beginning of which "English was still a minor language in Europe; by the end it had become one of the major languages of the world" (Bloomfield/Newmark 1963: 289). This transformation, however, is not the only language-external event that marks the period as crucial for the history of the English language. More developments took place and two important ones are vividly captured by the titles of chapters in the early editions of well-known text books: "The Appeal to Authority, 1650-1800" (Baugh 1959) and "The Problem of Correctness and Good Usage: 1600-1850" (Bloomfield/Newmark 1963). The place in which language usage, correctness and authority were negotiated with regard to the English language throughout the (long) eighteenth century were grammars of English. It is these grammars and also related works that constitute the source for what is presented here.

Grammars of English are a remarkable group of texts in the eighteenth century, since their rate of publication experienced a considerable increase (Michael 1970: 2; also see Alston 1965). They have been subjected to extensive research for decades and studies show that they are multi-faceted sources. As such, eighteenth-century grammars of English (and related works) can also contribute to a detailed understanding of eighteenth-century practices of comparing. Indeed, the works appear to exhibit instances of intra- and intercultural comparison. The cases of intracultural comparison seem to serve language description and language prescription, the cases of intercultural comparison seem to support language emancipation and arguments related to the self-assertion of the English language. In order to demonstrate this, the chapter on hand will proceed as follows. The next subchapter introduces, explains and illustrates a fundamental concept which helps to position the grammars within their immediate context, i.e., the history of grammaticography, as well as to relate the presented instances of comparison to the methodological repertoire found in the grammars. The third subchapter is the informative core of this paper. It gives a qualitative analysis of selected passages from both well-known and lesser-known titles of eighteenth-century grammaticography. Accordingly, noteworthy aspects are highlighted and summarized in this paper's conclusion.

2. Eighteenth-Century Grammars of English as 'Discourse Tradition'

Before I turn to the notion of 'discourse tradition' and its applicability with regard to (eighteenth-century) grammaticography, a brief note on the selection of sources and their context shall be permitted. In this contribution, I present findings that relate to the research carried out for my dissertation (Wolf 2011). For the latter I studied the grammars of 112 authors covering the period from 1600 to 1900. Obviously, the selection presented here is restricted to eighteenth-century authors.[1] The selection still includes a) widely known works, such as Robert Lowth's *A Short Introduction to English Grammar* (1762), Lindley Murray's *English Grammar* (1795), or Joseph Priestley's *The Rudiments of English Grammar* (1761), that, as will be indicated further below, have been the subject of very thorough scholarly examination, b) lesser-known pieces, such as James Buchanan's *The British Grammar* (1762), which have gained some attention in scholarship (see e.g. Emsley 1933), and c) almost unknown specimens that are named and listed in Alston's eminent bibliography (1965), but whose scholarly consideration does not go much beyond that.

1 The number of grammars and related works to which I point because of their practices of comparison is still smaller. This, however, does not translate into the statement that the presented cases of comparison are the only ones observable in the texts. The presented instances in which comparisons form substantial parts of the methodological and conceptual make-up of the selected texts are instances that have made a lasting impression on the present author whose main examination of the primary texts took place a decade ago.

Eighteenth-century grammars of the English language have been studied and described in full detail. The works themselves were without doubt normative and, therefore, their prescriptivism essential in the development of standard English (e.g. Beal 2004, Tieken-Boon van Ostade 2006 and Beal 2010). Their authors, motivations and approaches as well as their general context have also been subjected to close scrutiny (see Tieken-Boon van Ostade 2008). As far as research interest is concerned, a few grammarians certainly stand out, most notably Robert Lowth, Lindley Murray, and Joseph Priestley. The studies of their lives and works do also include investigations into the personal background of the works as well as their conceptual contexts (e.g. Fens-de Zeeuw 2011, Hodson 2006, Rivers/Wykes 2008, Straaijer 2011, Tieken-Boon van Ostade 1996, Tieken-Boon van Ostade 1997, Tieken-Boon van Ostade 2010 and Tieken-Boon van Ostade 2011).

One aspect that has been stipulating research and that is almost virtually present in all research up to the present is the interrelationship of the grammars themselves (e.g. Leonard 1929, Vorlat 1964, Robins 1986, Sundby/Bjørge/Haugland 1991, or Tieken-Boon van Ostade 2008). Whereas there are many characteristics that make us conceive of eighteenth-century grammars as a coherent group of texts, it is their mutual interference, or interdependence, that truly displays the grammarians as a group of interrelated authors. The notion of 'discourse community' appears to be applicable in this regard. That this is a successful undertaking has been shown by Richard Watts, who convincingly conceptualized grammarians as a group of authors who share common goals, expertise, and communicative means (see Watts 1995 and 2008). Still, if we wish to perceive those authors as a '*discourse* community', we might want to consider the *discourse* itself.[2]

In this discourse – it does not only take place in the grammatical treatises proper, but also quite frequently in their prefaces, dedications, and footnotes –, the members of the discourse community of grammarians exchange opinions and experiences. For example, they acknowledge each other *expressis verbis*. In the preface of *An Easy English Grammar*, Alexander Murray, for instance, places himself into that discourse:

> I must acknowledge, that it is not the want of English Grammars, that makes me trouble the Public with a new one. So far from this being the case, I have

2 Of course, all of the notions related to 'discourse' are ultimately informed by Michel Foucault's 1971 work.

> thirty different books on the subject lying about me [...]. Yet I am not singular in opinion, that something is still necessary, though perhaps, not so much with respect to the matter as the manner of forming the most useful school-book [...]. (Murray 1787: iii)

Considering this example of mutual referencing, it is clear that the discourse of eighteenth-century grammarians is a conscious one. If an author states in his work that his grammar cannot sufficiently replace preceding works and that such an accomplishment can only be achieved by authors such as Robert Lowth or Samuel Johnson (Bicknell 1790: xii), we deal with another exemplary manifestation of this discourse. Because of such observations, I have suggested that grammars be viewed as a 'discourse tradition' (Wolf 2011). Since this concept is still not widely known in English linguistics, the term and its application require further explanation. First suggested by Brigitte Schlieben-Lange (1983), the concept of 'discourse tradition' has been elaborated by Peter Koch (1997) and by Wulf Oesterreicher (1997). Essentially, the concept is an addition to Coseriu's threefold concept of language (see Coseriu 1988) in which the universal level is speech in the sense of 'ability to speak', the historical level is the individual language, and the individual level is the speech act (see Koch 1997: 44). 'Discourse tradition' is an addition, because Koch doubles the historical level, and 'discourse tradition' is the concept that is able to cross boundaries of individual languages. The latter is crucial if applied within the context of grammaticography. In that regard, it is also noteworthy that the concept of 'discourse tradition' draws upon an essential analogy: If there are 'rules' in languages, there are rules in discourse traditions, too (see Koch 1997: 45). These rules – and this is where the concept links up with Watts' 'discourse community' – are inherited, conserved and communicated by cultural communities such as professional, literary, or political groups (see Koch 1997: 49).

Some rules, or discourse conventions, of the specific discourse tradition of 'grammar-writing' are: 1) the didactic way of proceeding from smaller to larger linguistic units, i.e., from letters/sounds via syllables and individual words to sentences, 2) the frequent imitation of classroom dialogue by writing in question-and-answer mode, and 3) the rigid structure of topical chapters proceeding from definitions via discussions to exemplifications. Another very specific 'discourse rule' in (eighteenth-century) grammars of English is employing definitions to clarify the usage of technical terms or to introduce new, difficult, or arcane concepts. Containing numerous definitions, eighteenth-century grammars display a high degree of uniformity and Ian Michael has hinted at that phenomenon in his seminal work on grammatical categories (1970). He specifically drew attention to uniformity with regard to the very foundational definition of the term 'grammar' itself. He said that, if a definition is given – if not, grammarians took the definition as preconditional –, it is presented in form of the "conventional formula", which generally, i.e., across centuries until the dawn of philology, reads grammar as "the art of speaking and writing correctly" (Michael 1970: 189). To illustrate this point, an exemplary selection of eighteenth-century definitions is given here. The list is not exhaustive. The definitions are given without original, yet with added emphases:

1) Grammar is the Knowledge or Art of Expressing our Thoughts in Words join'd together in Sentences according to the Use, Form and *Propriety* of every Tongue either in Speaking or Writing. (Gildon/Brightland 1711: i)
2) Grammar is the Art of Speaking rightly. (Greenwood 1711: 34)
3) Grammar is an Art, which teacheth the way of writing and speaking truly and *properly*. (Maittaire 1712: 1)
4) Grammar is the Art of Speaking and Writing truly and *properly*. (Greenwood 1737: 2); English Grammar is the Art of speaking and writing English truly and *properly*. (ibid.: 3)
5) Question. What doth the English Grammar teach? Answer. To speak, or write English truly and *properly*. (*A New English Grammar* 1746: 1)
6) Grammar is the Art of Speaking and Writing truly and *properly*. (Gough 1760: 1)
7) Grammar is the art of using words *properly*. (Priestley 1761: 1)
8) Grammar is the Art of expressing the Relations of Words in Construction, with due Quantity in Speaking, and Orthography in Writing. Hence it is, that a Grammar of whatever Language, shews the Art of Speaking and Writing that Language well. What does the English Grammar teach? The English Grammar teaches to speak and write the English language rightly. (Buchanan 1762: 1f.)
9) Grammar is the Art of rightly expressing our thoughts by words. (Lowth 1762: 1)
10) Grammar is the art of writing or speaking any language correctly […]. English Grammar is the art of writing or speaking the English language *properly*. (Burn 1766: 19)

11) Grammar is the Art of speaking and writing *with Propriety*. (Hodgson 1770: 1)
12) A New Grammar of the English Language; or An Easy Introduction to the Art of Speaking and Writing English *with Propriety* and Correctness (Fenning 1771: front matter)
13) Grammar is the Art of speaking or writing any Language rightly; as Hebrew, Greek, Latin, English, &c. M. What is English Grammar? S. The Art of speaking or writing the English Tongue. (Metcalfe 1771: 1)
14) Grammar is the Art of Speaking, or Writing a Language *properly*. English Grammar is the Art of Speaking or Writing the English Language *properly*. (Raine 1771: 1)
15) Grammar is the art of speaking and writing correctly. Latin or English Grammar is the art of speaking and writing the Latin or the English language correctly. (Adam 1772: 1)
16) Grammar is the Art of expressing our Thoughts *with Propriety*, either in Speaking or Writing. (Ward 1777: 1)
17) Question. What is Grammar? Answer. The Art of rightly expressing our Thoughts by Words. (Corbet 1784: 9)
18) Grammar in general, may be denominated an art of speaking and writing *with propriety*. (A., M. 1785: 5)
19) Grammar is the art of speaking and writing any language *with propriety*. English Grammar teaches to speak and write the English Language *properly*. (Murray 1787: 1)
20) Grammar teaches the proper use of words, and enables us to communicate our thoughts with perspicuity. (Brittain 1788: Introduction [1])
21) Grammar, is the Art of speaking, and writing, any Language *properly*, and correctly. (Chown 1788: 5)
22) Grammar is that art which teaches due and *proper* arrangement, and also the choice of words, in order to express our thoughts by the mouth, or in writing. (Bicknell 1790: 1)
23) Grammar is the Science of using Words correctly. (Francis 1790: 11)
24) What is English Grammar? The art of speaking and writing the English language correctly, according to rules and general practice. (Webster 1790: 5)
25) Grammar, in general, teaches us the art of expressing our thoughts *with propriety*; therefore the English Grammar instructs us how to convey our thoughts *in proper English*. (Hornsey 1793: 13)

26) Grammar is the art of speaking or writing a language *properly*. (*A Short English Grammar* 1794: 1)
27) English Grammar is the art of speaking and writing the English language *with propriety*. (Murray 1795: 1)
28) The English Grammar is the Art of speaking and writing the English Language *with* Correctness and *Propriety*. (Postlethwaite 1795: 1)
29) English Grammar is the art of speaking or writing the English language *properly*. (Rhodes 1795: 7)
30) Grammar is the Art of speaking, or of writing, a Language *with propriety*, and the intent of Language is to communicate our thoughts to others. (Coar 1796: 1)
31) Grammar is the art of speaking and writing correctly. (Bullen 1797: 1)
32) Grammar is the art of speaking and writing *with propriety*. (Kitson 1798: 1)
33) Grammar is the art of speaking and writing a language *with propriety*. (Gardiner 1799: 1)
34) Grammar is the art of speaking and writing *with propriety*. (Eves 1800: 1)

With or without the added emphases, the list shows that in the eighteenth century the formula is almost always: 'grammar is the art of speaking and writing properly/with propriety'. Of course, 'properly' and 'with propriety' in the examples above relate to Michael's 'correctly'. Still, it is not the same proposition. Proper language use is not that language use which is correct because it corresponds to all available and grammatically correct patterns found in language. Proper language use is that language use which is proclaimed as correct because it is the language use of those who *behave properly*, i.e., in a manner that is approved and accepted by the social and educational elite. This specific reference to propriety is what signals prescriptiveness in the definitions; the preferred language use is charged with the ideology of propriety just described. That, however, is typical of eighteenth-century grammars and it is normal in a century in which empirical approaches to language(s) had not yet been established. The link between propriety and preferable language patterns against the background of uniform definitions is also relevant for what is delineated in the next subchapter.

3. Instances of Practices of Comparing

Before I foreground the selected practices of comparison as they can be witnessed in the grammars, I should like to comment very briefly on the notion of 'practices of comparing'. I do not subscribe to any but the fundamental meaning of the lexeme *comparison*: 'the action, or an act, of comparing, likening, or representing as similar' (see OED 2020).

Practices of comparing are fundamental in many grammars and there is one specific form that appears to be the base prescriptiveness, the predominant quality in most of them. This practice likens wished-for language usage to appropriate social behaviour as the definitions of the term *grammar* above showed. The most frequent concept named in the corresponding definitions is that of 'propriety/proper'. To repeat, it must be emphasized that this notion is social in meaning, not necessarily language-based. This is very apparent if we consider the definitions in a) and b) below, which, in addition to the formulaic definitions, were presented in rhyming couplets for entertaining and mnemonic reasons.

a) Grammar, by proper Rules laid down, does teach / The strict Proprieties of ev'ry Speech; / Instructs to speak, or read, with proper grace, / To write correct; and elegance to trace [...]. (Smetham 1774: 103)
b) Grammar, that useful, ornamental Art, / Does Rules to speak, & read, and write, impart. (Francis 1790: 45)

It is noteworthy that the concept of 'propriety' in both examples is likened to *grace*, *elegance* and *ornament*, i.e., terms belonging to the word field of 'attractiveness', 'refinement', and 'neatness'. Thus, conduct and appearance serve as general focus points when explaining the concept of 'proper language'.

In example c), the author starts off his treatise with a comparison that relates to the opposite of the wished-for, appropriate language usage:

c) For as an uncouth, ambiguous, imperfect Language, is a sure Sign of a slothful or low Genius in the People; a Language that is copious and clear, and easy, shews a good Understanding and Capacity, and hath many Advantages which are very valuable. (Wilson 1724: 4)

It can be taken for granted that this specific instance of comparison was implicitly given in most grammars. It can also be found in the editorial composition of works that are labelled as grammatical treatises. John Ash's 1786 edition of *Grammatical Institutes* contains an additional chapter called "Select Lessons, to instil just Sentiments of Virtue into Youth". They were meant to help develop, for example, "solid glory and real greatness", "true politeness", "justice" and "Christian fortitude" (Ash 1786: 165-169). This case, like other explicit statements, is indicative of the continuous association of correct language usage with propriety. All the more so, if it is borne in mind that it is precisely the following meaning of *proper* that surfaced at the beginning of the eighteenth century and dominated the word's semantics throughout this century: 'conforming to recognized social standards or etiquette; decent, decorous, respectable, seemly' (see OED 2020).

All eighteenth-century grammars follow a pedagogical agenda. Most, if not all, of them were meant to be used as textbooks for teachers of the subject, or the authors themselves were teachers who put together what they thought was essential for their own purposes. Whatever the concrete motivation and whatever the education goal, authors needed to be very descriptive when detailing problems, phenomena, etc. The longer passage in d) is taken from Thomas Smetham's *The Practical Grammar*:

d) Great differences have arisen among grammarians and teachers, concerning the proper manner of pronouncing the letter *a*. Many insist that it ought to be pronounced *broad*, according to <u>the Scotch manner of speaking; though contrary to the practice and opinion of the *best orators*, and most *elegant speakers*</u>; when, if they did but examine into the matter, they would find, that the broad sound of the vowel *a* is *the very thing which appears <u>so disagreeable to the ear of such as converse with the Scotch</u>*. The learned Doctor Johnson tells us, that *a* has three sounds; namely, *slender, open*, and *broad*. The *slender* is the true English sound; as in *face, mane*, &c. and in all words ending in *ation*; as *creation, multiplication*, &c. The *open* is the Italian *a*; as in *father, fancy, glass*, &c. The *broad* is the German *a*; in *wall, call*, &c. Those teachers who would instruct their pupils to pronounce the letter *a* according to the Scotch mode, which is <u>the disagreeable broad sound</u> borrowed from the Germans, should recollect that <u>they will insensibly bring them to that disagreeable, pedantic, and ridiculous manner of speaking</u>, commonly called the Scotch drawl; for, according

> to their customary manner of speaking, the word *cake* would be called *cauke; bake, bauke; candle, caundle; caper, cauper,* &c. when they might with equal propriety change the other English vowels into French and German vowels [...]. (Smetham 1774: 37-38)

Two points are illustrated. First, it shows how authors turn to comparative descriptions that involve references to other languages when describing contemporaneous phenomena observed in the speech of fellow English-speakers: their usage is described as an "open Italian" or "broad German" vowel. Second, the passage reveals that authors associate desired language behaviour with favourable qualities and undesired language behaviour with devaluations. This is seen in the underlined sequences (please note that italics are kept as in the original).

Whether wholly prescriptive or almost formally descriptive, whether pejoratively evaluating or naively assuming, all eighteenth-century grammars can be seen as means in the emancipation process of the vernacular language English *vis-à-vis* the universal language Latin. Raising the status of English, this process also involved debates questioning the applicability of grammatical description to languages such as English. The quantity and the quality of eighteenth-century grammars give evidence that this was no longer a question for the authors. Their almost unequivocal view that English could be captured by contemporaneous grammatical concepts and should also be taught accordingly often coincided with patriotic expressions:

e) It is *the glory of the English* to understand *their own language*: we cannot begin too early to lay a good foundation in this." (Rhodes 1795: vi; my emphasis)
f) I am not so insensible of the Advantages of the dead Languages, as to discourage the teaching of them at a proper Time; but this I am willing to maintain, that *the Study of our own, ought to precede* that of all others [...]. (Hodgson 1770: v-vi; my emphasis)

The opinion observable in e) and f) above was also present in grammars of the first half of the eighteenth century. In grammars of the early decades of the eighteenth century, however, authors had to address the applicability of grammatical concepts and categories to English. In order to support their argument that, of course, grammar can be applied to English, authors make use of expressions that represent the impossibility to apply grammar to a language as barbarity:

g) Youths are [...] hurried into Latin, before they are well able to read English: as if this last were so despicable, that it needed not, or so barbarous, that it could not be digested into a Grammatical Method. (Mattaire 1712: iii-iv)

Again, I should like to emphasize that throughout the second half of the eighteenth century authors no longer had to argue in favour of English *grammar*. Yet, they still needed to challenge priorities in education, presenting Latin, for example, as dead, useless, puzzling, or absurd:

h) [Let students] acquire a masterly and critical Knowledge of their own Language! which has been so amazingly sacrificed and neglected for a smattering in Latin and Greek, with which, after they have mispent so much precious Time, they are to hold no more Correspondence than with the Chinese! ... Notwithstanding I may appear to be animated with a more than ordinary, tho' I hope, becoming Zeal in the Cause of a proper English Education, and cannot give my Assent to the whole of a young Gentleman's Time being engrossed and sacrificed to a dead Verbality [...]. (Buchanan 1762: xvii)?
i) A practice still more ridiculous has universally prevailed, till very lately, in all our schools; that of straining the English Tongue, without any reason or necessity, to be subservient to the puzzling rules, exceptions, and intricacies, of the Latin Grammar; by which the mind is incumbered with innumerable unnecessary distinctions [...]. (Smetham 1774: iii)
j) The utility of an English education has induced many to write [...] the importance or significancy thereof, is now pretty well understood, and the absurdity of young pupils learning the Latin language, or any other, in preference to their own, has been so sufficiently pointed out as to render a repetition of that sort quite unnecessary. (Hornsey 1793: 3)

The support of the English language and the elevation of its status are not just carried by debasing statements about Latin. The latter are complemented by subjective comparisons leading to the equation of (natural) beauty with the English language. John Ash, for instance, would like young pupils to gain an "intimate Acquaintance with the Proprieties and Beauties of the English

Tongue" because it "would be [...] desirable and necessary [and] far preferable to a Smattering of the learned Languages" (Ash 1761: iii). It is noteworthy that the notion 'propriety' is coordinated with 'beauty'. These expressions are also quite central in the conclusion of Thomas Smetham's explanation of why, in his view, English is not only a vernacular applicable to grammar and capable of outstanding communication (see l) below). This explanation is preceded by an enumeration of stereotypical comparisons in k). There, various languages are presented according to alleged perceptions as follows:

k) The Hebrew hath been called the most emphatical language in the world; the Greek, the most lofty; the Latin, the most majestic; the Italian, the most soft; the Spanish, the most noble; and the French, the most polite. In the English are happily united the emphatical expression of the Hebrew, the sublimity of the Greek, the majesty of the Latin, the softness of the Italian, the nobleness of the Spanish, and the politeness of the French. Besides, it is not so confined as the Hebrew, so irregular as the Greek, so unequal as the Latin, so effeminate as the Italian, so precise as the Spanish, nor so volatile as the French. (Smetham 1774: vi)
l) In the English Tongue we may, with propriety, address God with the spirit of adoration, Monarchs with the spirit of freedom, Neighbours, with the warmth of friendship, and Beauty with the softness of persuasion. (Smetham 1774: vi-vii)

This stream of comparisons culminates in a statement that, again, ascribes unrivalled verbal expressibility to beauty and, thus, claims the superiority of English over all other languages worth mentioning:

m) The English Language owes its excellency to its being a composition of the most heterogeneous ingredients; a medley of innumerable other languages. The beauties of almost every tongue have been selected to grace ours; and, with few or none of the defects of any, to present us with the charms of all. (Smetham 1774: vii)

It is intriguing that, at the beginning of the eighteenth century, there are authors who also claim superiority for English, but try to deny the linguistic facts of English being heavily influenced and altered by language contact. Indeed, they strive for a 'pure' English that does not "want any foreign Help to express the nicest Sense out of its own Store" (Gildon/Brightland 1711: [iii]). They are in contrast to Smetham who appears to take delight in the hybridity of English leading to the language's superiority. Gildon and Brightland were clearly not of that opinion. They admit, yet disapprove that English "receiv'd innumerable Shoals of stranger words" and chauvinistically conclude that "to carry this Humour still on, is to Debase, not Advance, our Native and Masculine Tongue" (Gildon/Brightland 1711: [iii]). Whether they would have changed their views, had they been of Smetham's generation is a mute point. It needs to be added, however, that Smetham is not necessarily an isolated case. Yet, other authors appear to have taken a more objective perspective towards the described developments:

n) [M]any Norman words and phrases were by degrees blended with the Saxon, tho' it's general form and construction still remained the same. From the Conquest to the Reformation, our language continued to receive occasional supplies of foreign words. Our terms of dress we borrowed from the Italians; those of War and Cookery from the French; our commercial words were chiefly imported from Lombardy; and those of Navigation from Holland. In addition to these the learned have enriched it with many significant expressions drawn from the treasures of Greek and Latin literature, by which means our language has acquired such a degree of strength and copiousness, that it is able to express every subject with elegance and accuracy. (Bullen 1797: 138)

It also needs to be added that the presentation of English as an excellent, if not superior, language is no novelty of the second half of the eighteenth century. We already find authors at the beginning of the eighteenth century who maintain similar ideas and concepts:

o) Now since no Language in the World seems more capable of having all manner of Learning treasur'd up in it, than our English Tongue; why may we not [...] set up Grammar, Rhetoric, and Philosophy Schools in our Mother-Tongue, that Foreiners abroad may covet to learn our Language [...]. (Lane 1700: xviii)

The wording is less pompous and certainly much clearer in its expression. To A. Lane, eloquence is not only a desirable behaviour. It is a skill that is likened to naval and military skills:

p) Leaders and Commanders, both by Sea and Land, [...] who *by their Learning, Civility and Eloquence in their Mother-Tongue,* [would enlarge] their Dominions no less than by their Arms. (Lane 1700: xix; my emphasis).

So language becomes a valuable weapon, or at least a further means to enlarge the spheres of influence of a country that was to become a world power.

To end this subchapter, the following comment shall be permitted. It is surprising and, at the same time, it is not surprising that there is no mention of languages which existed side by side with English across Britain and Ireland. In the eighteenth century, all of them, i.e., Cornish, Gaelic, Irish, Manx and Welsh were still very much living languages. A lack of knowledge and awareness cannot be assumed. The treatises of MacCurtin (1728), Richards (1753), Walters (1771), Vallancey (1773) and Pryce (1790) show too clearly that there must have existed an awareness of and perhaps a genuine interest in the Celtic languages of Great Britain and Ireland. The publication of said works can certainly be seen as an honest acknowledgment of the fact that the archipelago was multilingual. Given that, it is not right to associate the progress of eighteenth-century English with relentless imperial expansion at the expense of Cornish, Gaelic, Irish, Manx and Welsh. Yet, it is right to assume that the progress of English went hand in hand with neglectful behaviour towards the neighbouring languages foreshadowing the nationalism that was to take root in England and elsewhere in the following century. It is also right to add that the development towards strong national(ist) sentiments had already started in the previous century: "[O]ur own Language is to bee esteemed a chief part of the honor of our Nation, which wee all ought to our utmost power, to advance." (Wharton 1655: [To the reader])

4. Conclusion

This contribution set out to study practices of comparing in eighteenth-century grammars of English. The examination of which has added to what is consensus among scholars of (eighteenth-century) English grammaticography: "Behind a superficial appearance of uniformity, imitativeness and dullness the English grammars in fact contain a most surprising diversity of outlook and of categories. This diversity is new and important evidence, but can be adequately displayed only by extensive quotation" (Michael 1970: 2).

Having looked at various examples of intra-cultural as well as intercultural comparison, it appears that they help to demonstrate what is meant to be taught, to describe what is desired language behaviour, to explain that English deserves its place in the educational canon, and to maintain that the excellency of the English language is the result of its meandering history.

With regard to two more instances in the primary material, it can be concluded with confidence that practices of comparing can be read as heralds of the discourse of linguistic nationalism and as harbingers of language philosophy: "By the aid of Language we study the ideas of others; we compare opinions with opinions; and improve upon the comparison. Our understanding is expanded, our passions refined, our vices corrected, and our virtues improved." (Smetham 1774: i) In very few cases of which Priestley certainly is an outstanding example, practices of comparing can also be read as precursors of descriptive linguistics:

> Grammar may be compared to a treatise of Natural Philosophy; the one consisting of observations on the various changes, combinations, and mutual affections of words; and the other of the parts of nature: and were the language of men as uniform as the works of nature, the grammar of language would be as indisputable in its principles as the grammar of nature: but since good authors have adopted different forms of speech, and in a case that admits of no standard but that of custom, one authority may be of as much weight as another; the analogy of language is the only thing to which we can have recourse, to adjust these differences; for language, to answer the intent of it, which is to express our thoughts with certainty in an intercourse with one another, must be fixed and consistent with itself. (Priestley 1761: vi)

Yet, this paper's scope was too limited to be able to state whether practices of comparing were motors of arriving at descriptive grammaticography. Nevertheless, they were undoubtedly an integral part of the methodological makeup of eighteenth-century grammars and must therefore be understood as a convention within the discourse tradition of grammar-writing.

Bibliography

Primary Sources[3]

A., M. *The Elementary Principles of English Grammar*. Bridport: S. Margrie, 1785.

Adam, Alexander. *The Principles of Latin and English Grammar*. Edinburgh: A. Kincaid and W. Creech, 1772.

A New English Grammar. London: no publisher, 1746.

Ash, John. *Grammatical Institutes*. 4th ed. London: E. & C. Dilly, 1761.

Ash, John. *Grammatical Institutes*. A new edition, revised, corrected, and enlarged. London: Charles Dilly, 1786.

A Short English Grammar. London: C. Dilly, 1794.

Bicknell, Alexander. *The Grammatical Wreath*. London: A. Bicknell, 1790.

Brightland, John. *A Grammar of the English Tongue*. London: Mr. Guy et al., 1712.

Brittain, Lewis. *Rudiments of English Grammar*. Louvain: L. J. Urban, 1788.

Buchanan, James. *The British Grammar*. London: A. Millar, 1762.

Buchanan, James. *An Essay towards Establishing a Standard for an Elegant and Uniform Pronunciaton of the English Language*. London: Edward & Charles Dilly, 1766.

Bullen, John. *Rudiments of English Grammar*. London: P. Gedge, 1797.

Burn, John. *A Practical Grammar of the English Language*. Glasgow: Archibald McLean, 1766.

Chown, William. *English Grammar Epitomised*. Northampton: T. Dicey, 1788.

Coar, Thomas. *A Grammar of the English Tongue*. London: James Phillips, 1796.

Corbet, John. *A Concise System of English Grammar*. Shrewsbury: T. Wood, 1784.

Devis, [Ellen]. *The Accidence*. London: J. Beegroft et al., 1775.

Dilworth, Thomas. *A New Guide to the English Tongue*. 37th ed. London: T. Moore, 1783.

Eves, [Mrs.]. *The Grammatical Play-Thing*. Birmingham: T.A. Pearson, 1800.

Farro, D. *The Royal Universal British Grammar and Vocabulary*. London: J. Hodges, 1754.

Fenning, Daniel. *A New Grammar of the English Language*. London: S. Crowder, 1771.

3 Unless otherwise stated, all primary texts have been available as facsimile pdf-files in the Eighteenth-Century Collections Online at ‹https://www.gale.com/intl/primary-sources/eighteenth-century-collections-online› between November 2019 and March 2020.

Francis, William. *A Concise Introduction to English Grammar*. Marlborough: E. Harold, 1790.
Gardiner, Jane. *The Young Ladies' English Grammar*. York: T. Wilson & R. Spence, 1799.
Gildon, Charles & John Brightland. *A Grammar of the English Tongue*. [Facsimile Reprint]. Menston: The Scolar Press, 1967 [1711].
Gough, James. *A Practical Grammar of the English Tongue*. 2nd ed. Dublin: I. Jackson, 1760.
Greenwood, James. *An Essay Towards a Practical English Grammar*. London: R. Tookey, 1711.
Greenwood, James. *The Royal English Grammar*. London: J. Nourse, 1737.
Hodgson, Isaac. *A Practical English Grammar*. London: B. Law, 1770.
Hornsey, John. *A Short English Grammar*. York: Wilson, Spence and Mawman, 1793.
Jones, Hugh. *An Accidence to the English Tongue*. London: John Clarke, 1724.
Kenrick, William. *A New Dictionary of the English Language*. London: John and Francis Rivington et al., 1773.
Kitson, Roger. *A Short Introduction to English Grammar*. Norwich: Stevenson & Matchett, 1798.
Lane, A. *A Key to the Art of Letters*. London: J. Churchill et al., 1700. Accessed via Early English Books Online, 26 March 2020. ‹http://eebo.chadwyck.com/home›.
Lougthon, William. *A Practical Grammar of the English Tongue*. London: Cæsar Ward & Richard Chandler, 1734.
Lowth, Robert. *A Short Introduction to English Grammar*. London: J. Hughs, 1762.
MacCurtin, H. *The Elements of the Irish Language*. Lovain: Martin van Overbeke, 1728.
Maittaire, Michael. *The English Grammar*. London: W. B. for H. Clements, 1712.
Metcalfe, Lister. *The Rudiments of the English Tongue*. 2nd ed. Newcastle: T. Saint, 1771.
Murray, Alexander. *An Easy English Grammar*. 2nd ed. London: B. Law, 1787.
Murray, Lindley. *English Grammar*. [Facsimile reprint] Ed. R.C. Alston. Menston: The Scolar Press, 1968 [1795].
Postlethwaite, Richard. *The Grammatical Art Improved*. London: J. Parsons, 1795.
Priestley, Joseph. *The Rudiments of English Grammar*. London: R. Griffiths, 1761.
Pryce, William. *Archæologia Cornu-Britannica; or, an Essay to Preserve the Ancient Cornish Language*. Sherborne: W. Cruttwell, 1790.
Raine, Matthew. *English Rudiments*. Darlington: John Sadler, 1771.

Rhodes, Benjamin. *A Concise English Grammar*. Birmingham: J. Belcher, 1795.
Richards, Thomas. *Introduction to the Ancient British, or Welsh Language*. Bristol: Felix Farley, 1753.
Sheridan, Thomas. *British Education*. Dublin: George Faulkner, 1761.
Smetham, Thomas. *The Practical Grammar*. London: J. Cooke, 1774.
Vallancey, Charles. *A Grammar of the Iberno-Celtic, or Irish Language*. Dublin: R. Marchbank, 1773.
Walters, John. *A Dissertation on the Welsh Language*. Cowbridge: J. R. and D. Thomas, 1771.
Ward, H. *A Short, but Clear System of English Grammar*. Whitehaven: [n.p.], 1777.
Webster, Noah. *Rudiments of English Grammar*. Hartford: Elisha Babcock, 1790.
Wharton, Jeremiah. *A New English Grammar*. London: W. Dugard, 1655.
Wilson, Thomas. *The many Advantages of a Good Language to Any Nation*. London: J. Knapton, etc., 1724.

Secondary Sources

Alston, R. C. *A Bibliography of the English Language from the Invention of Printing to the Year 1800*. Vol. 1: *English Grammars Written in English and English Grammars Written in Latin by Native Speakers*. Leeds: E. J. Arnold & Son, 1965.
Baugh, Albert C. *A History of the English Language*. 2nd ed. London: Routledge & Kegan Paul, 1959.
Beal, Joan C. *English in Modern Times 1700-1945*. London: Arnold, 2004.
Beal, Joan C. "Prescriptivism and the Suppression of Variation." *Eighteenth-Century English. Ideology and Change*. Ed. Raymond Hickey. Cambridge: Cambridge University Press, 2010. 21-37.
Bloomfield, Morton W. and Leonard Newmark. *A Linguistic Introduction to the History of English*. New York: Alfred A. Knopf, 1963.
Coseriu, Eugenio. "'Historische Sprache' und 'Dialekt'." *Energeia und Ergon. Sprachliche Variation – Sprachgeschichte – Sprachtypologie*. Vol. I: *Schriften von Eugenio Coseriu (1965-1987)*. Ed. Jörn Albrecht. Tübingen: Gunter Narr, 1988. 45-61.
Emsley, Bert. "James Buchanan and the Eighteenth-Century Regulation of English Usage." *Publications of the Modern Language Association* 48 (1933): 1154-1166.
Foucault, Michel. *L'ordre du discours. Leçon inaugurale au Collège de France prononcée le 2 décembre 1970*. Paris: Gallimard, 1971.

Fens-de Zeeuw, Lyda. *Lindley Murray (1745-1826), Quaker and Grammarian.* Utrecht: Landelijke Onderzoekschool Taalwetenschap, 2011.

Görlach, Manfred. *Eighteenth-Century English.* Heidelberg: Universitätsverlag C. Winter, 2001.

Hickey, Raymond. "Attitudes and Concerns in Eighteenth-Century English." *Eighteenth-Century English. Ideology and Change.* Ed. Raymond Hickey. Cambridge: Cambridge University Press, 2010. 1-20.

Hodson, Jane. "The Problem of Joseph Priestley's (1733-1804) Descriptivism." *Historiographia Linguistica* 33 (2006): 57-84.

Koch, Peter. "Diskurstraditionen: zu ihrem sprachtheoretischen Status und ihrer Dynamik." *Gattungen mittelalterlicher Schriftlichkeit.* Ed. Barbara Frank, Thomas Haye, and Doris Tophinke. Tübingen: Gunter Narr, 1997. 43-79.

Leonard, Sterling A. *The Doctrine of Correctness in English Usage 1700-1800.* Madison: University of Wisconsin, 1929.

McArthur, Tom. "On the Origin and Nature of Standard English." *World Englishes* 18 (1999): 161-169.

Michael, Ian. *English Grammatical Categories and the Tradition to 1800.* London: Cambridge University Press, 1970.

OED. *Oxford English Dictionary.* Oxford University Press, 2020. Accessed online, 26 March 2020. ‹http://www.oed. com/›.

Oesterreicher, Wulf. "Zur Fundierung von Diskurstraditionen." *Gattungen mittelalterlicher Schriftlichkeit.* Ed. Barbara Frank, Thomas Haye, and Doris Tophinke. Tübingen: Gunter Narr, 1997. 20-41.

Rivers, Isabel and David L. Wykes. *Joseph Priestley, Scientist, Philosopher, and Theologian.* Ed. Isabel Rivers and David L. Wykes. Oxford: Oxford University Press, 2008.

Robins, Robert H. "The Evolution of English Grammar Books since the Renaissance." *The English Reference Grammar. Language and Linguistics, Writers and Readers.* Ed. Gerhard Leitner. Tübingen: Max Niemeyer, 1986. 292-306.

Romaine, Suzanne. "Introduction." *The Cambridge History of the English Language.* Vol. IV: *1776-1997.* Ed. Suzanne Romaine. Cambridge: Cambridge University Press, 1998. 1-56.

Schlieben-Lange, Brigitte. *Traditionen des Sprechens. Elemente einer pragmatischen Sprachgeschichtsschreibung.* Stuttgart: Kohlhammer, 1983.

Stammerjohann, Harro. *Lexicon Grammaticorum. A Bio-Bibliographical Companion to the History of Linguistics.* 2nd ed., revised and enlarged. Ed. Harro Stammerjohann. Tübingen: Max Niemeyer, 2009.

Straaijer, Robin. *Joseph Priestley, Grammarian: Late Modern English Normativism and Usage in a Sociohistorical Context*. Utrecht: Landelijke Onderzoekschool Taalwetenschap, 2011.

Sundby, Bertil, Anne Kari Bjørge, and Kari E. Haugland. *A Dictionary of English Normative Grammar 1700-1800*. Amsterdam: John Benjamins, 1991.

Tieken-Boon van Ostade, Ingrid. *Two Hundred Years of Lindley Murray*. Ed. Ingrid Tieken-Boon van Ostade. Münster: Nodus Publikationen, 1996.

Tieken-Boon van Ostade, Ingrid. "Lowth's Corpus of Prescriptivism." *To Explain the Present. Studies in the Changing English Language in Honour of Matti Rissanen*. Ed. Terttu Nevalainen and Leena Kahlas-Tarkka. Helsinki: Société Néophilologique, 1997. 451-463.

Tieken-Boon van Ostade, Ingrid. "Eighteenth-Century Prescriptivism and the Norm of Correctness." *The Handbook of the History of English*. Ed. Ans van Kemenade and Bettelou Los. Malden: Blackwell, 2006. 539-588.

Tieken-Boon van Ostade, Ingrid. *Grammars, Grammarians and Grammar Writing in Eighteenth-Century England*. Ed. Ingrid Tieken-Boon van Ostade. Berlin: Mouton de Gruyter, 2008.

Tieken-Boon van Ostade, Ingrid. "Lowth as Icon of Prescriptivism." *Eighteenth-Century English. Ideology and Change*. Ed. Raymond Hickey. Cambridge: Cambridge University Press, 2010. 73-88.

Tieken-Boon van Ostade, Ingrid. *The Bishop's Grammar: Robert Lowth and the Rise of Prescriptivism*. Oxford: Oxford University Press, 2011.

Vorlat, Emma. *Progress in English Grammar 1585-1735. A Study of the Development of English Grammar and of the Interdependence among the Early English Grammarians*. 4 Vols. Luxembourg: Pfeiffer, 1964.

Watts, Richard J. "Justifying Grammars. A Socio-Pragmatic Foray into the Discourse Community of Early English Grammarians." *Historical Pragmatics. Pragmatic Developments in the History of English*. Ed. Andreas Jucker. Amsterdam: John Benjamins, 1995. 145-185.

Watts, Richard J. "Mythical strands in the ideology of prescriptivism." *The Development of Standard English 1300-1800. Theories, Descriptions, Conflicts*. Ed. Laura Wright. Cambridge: Cambridge University Press, 2000. 29-48.

Watts, Richard J. "Grammar Writers in Eighteenth-Century Britain: A Community of Practice or a Discourse Community?" *Grammars, Grammarians and Grammar-Writing in Eighteenth-Century England*. Ed. Ingrid Tieken-Boon van Ostade. Berlin: Mouton de Gruyter, 2008. 37-56.

Wolf, Göran. *Englische Grammatikschreibung 1600-1900 – Der Wandel einer Diskurstradition*. Frankfurt/Main: Peter Lang, 2011.

Authors and Editors

Nadine Böhm-Schnitker works as a stand-in professor of English Literature and Literary Theory at the University of Konstanz and serves as a 'Privatdozentin' for English Studies: Literature and Culture at Friedrich-Alexander-University Erlangen-Nürnberg.

Monika Class is Junior-Professor in English at Mainz University and Principal Investigator of "The Visceral Novel Reader," who has published in Anglophone literatures and cultures focusing on embodiment.

Marcus Hartner is lecturer in English literary and cultural studies at Bielefeld University. He served as principal investigator in a research project on the eighteenth-century novel within the collaborative research centre *Practices of Comparing* (SFB 1288).

Caroline Koegler is Assistant Professor of British Literary and Cultural Studies at the University of Münster, Germany, and principal investigator of "Literature and the Market," a research project that is part of Münster's collaborative research centre *Law and Literature* (SFB 1385).

Anne Lappert is an independent scholar. She holds an M.A. degree from Bielefeld University and worked as a researcher for the SFB1288 Practices of Comparing (B05).

Ralf Schneider is Professor and Chair of English Literature at RWTH Aachen University and founding director of the Aachen Center for Cognitive and Empirical Literary Studies (ACCELS).

Julia Wiedemann is assistant professor in English Literary Studies and co-ordinator of the European Studies programme at the Catholic University of Eichstaett-Ingolstadt.

Göran Wolf lectures in medieval English language and literature. His research interests include e.g. English grammaticography, dialect spelling, or Anglophilia in eighteenth-century Germany.

Cultural Studies

Gabriele Klein
Pina Bausch's Dance Theater
Company, Artistic Practices and Reception

2020, 440 p., pb., col. ill.
29,99 € (DE), 978-3-8376-5055-6
E-Book:
PDF: 29,99 € (DE), ISBN 978-3-8394-5055-0

Elisa Ganivet
Border Wall Aesthetics
Artworks in Border Spaces

2019, 250 p., hardcover, ill.
79,99 € (DE), 978-3-8376-4777-8
E-Book:
PDF: 79,99 € (DE), ISBN 978-3-8394-4777-2

Nina Käsehage (ed.)
Religious Fundamentalism
in the Age of Pandemic

April 2021, 278 p., pb., col. ill.
37,00 € (DE), 978-3-8376-5485-1
E-Book: available as free open access publication
PDF: ISBN 978-3-8394-5485-5

Cultural Studies

Ivana Pilic, Anne Wiederhold-Daryanavard (eds.)

Art Practices in the Migration Society

Transcultural Strategies in Action at Brunnenpassage in Vienna

March 2021, 244 p., pb.
29,00 € (DE), 978-3-8376-5620-6
E-Book:
PDF: 25,99 € (DE), ISBN 978-3-8394-5620-0

German A. Duarte, Justin Michael Battin (eds.)

Reading »Black Mirror«

Insights into Technology and the Post-Media Condition

January 2021, 334 p., pb.
32,00 € (DE), 978-3-8376-5232-1
E-Book:
PDF: 31,99 € (DE), ISBN 978-3-8394-5232-5

Krista Lynes, Tyler Morgenstern, Ian Alan Paul (eds.)

Moving Images

Mediating Migration as Crisis

2020, 320 p., pb., col. ill.
40,00 € (DE), 978-3-8376-4827-0
E-Book: available as free open access publication
PDF: ISBN 978-3-8394-4827-4

All print, e-book and open access versions of the titles in our list are available in our online shop www.transcript-publishing.com